THE CATHOLIC CHURCH
AND THE QUESTION
OF PALESTINE

THE CATHOLIC CHURCH AND THE QUESTION OF PALESTINE

Livia Rokach

Saqi Books

BX
1628
.R64
1987

Library of Congress Cataloging-in-Publication Data

Rokach, Livia.
   The Catholic Church and the question of Palestine.

   Bibliography: p.
   Includes index.
     1. Catholic Church—Relations (diplomatic)—
Israel. 2 Catholic Church and Zionism. 3. Israel—
Foreign relations—Catholic Church. 4. Jewish-Arab
relations—1917- . I. Title.
BX1628.R64 1987 327.45′634′05694 87-9885

British Library Cataloguing in Publication Data

Rokach, Livia
   The Catholic Church and the question of
   Palestine.
   1. Catholic Church and Zionism
   I. Title
   261.7   BX1396.6
ISBN 0-86356-128-4

First published 1987 by
Saqi Books, 26 Westbourne Grove, London W2 5RH
and 171 First Avenue, Atlantic Highlands, New Jersey 07716

© Saqi Books 1987

Printed in Great Britain by
Billing & Sons Ltd
Worcester

Contents

List of Popes from 1914 to the Present Day

Pope	Date of Election	Date of Death or Abdication
Benedict XV (Giacomo Della Chiesa)	3 September 1914	22 January 1922
Pius XI (Ambrogio Damiano)	6 February 1922	10 February 1939
Pius XII (Eugenio Maria Pacelli)	2 March 1939	9 October 1958
John XXIII (Angelo Giuseppe Roncalli)	28 October 1958	3 June 1963
Paul VI (Giovanni Battista Montini)	21 June 1963	6 August 1978
John Paul I (Albino Luciani)	26 August 1978	29 September 1978
John Paul II (Karol Wojtyla)	16 October 1978	

Abbreviations

CCCA	Christian Communities Committee of Algeria
CNEWA	Catholic Near East Welfare Association
EEC	European Economic Community
LNM	Lebanese National Movement
MECC	Middle East Council of Churches
NCNS	National Catholic News Service
PLO	Palestine Liberation Organization
UAR	United Arab Republic
UN	United Nations
UNESCO	United Nations Educational, Scientific and Cultural Organization
UNSCOP	United Nations Special Committee on Palestine
US	United States
USSR	Union of Soviet Socialist Republics
WJC	World Jewish Congress
WZO	World Zionist Organization
ZOA	Zionist Organization of America

1
The Catholic Church and pre-State Zionism

The first official comment on zionism by the Catholic Church appeared in *Civiltà Cattolica* in May 1897, on the eve of the first Zionist Congress which was held in August of that year in Basle, Switzerland:

> One thousand, eight hundred and twenty-seven years have passed since the prediction of Jesus of Nazareth was fulfilled, namely that Jerusalem would be destroyed... As for a rebuilt Jerusalem which might become the centre of a reconstituted state of Israel, we must add that this is contrary to the predictions of Christ himself who foretold that 'Jerusalem shall be trodden down of the Gentiles, until the time of the Gentiles be fulfilled' (Luke 21:24), that is... until the end of the world.[1]

Quite apart from the theological arguments employed, this article was a clear warning that zionism was on a collision course with the Catholic Church. Seven years later, this was confirmed in a letter from the head of the Church to Theodor Herzl, the founder of political zionism:

> We are unable to favour this movement [zionism]. We cannot prevent the Jews from going to Jerusalem — but we could never sanction it. As the head of the Church I cannot answer you otherwise. The Jews have not recognized Our Lord, therefore we cannot recognize the Jewish people, and so, if you come to Palestine and settle your people there, we will be ready with Churches and priests to baptize all of you.[2]

The promulgation of the Balfour Declaration on 2 November 1917 was preceded by intense diplomatic activity, involving contacts between the zionists and various countries and political bodies. The Vatican was approached by Nahum Sokolov, who had been appointed by the World Zionist Organization (WZO) to obtain the approval of the French and Italian governments.[3] He was received by Pope Benedict XV on 10 May 1917. According to Sokolov, the Pope gave him encouragement and moral support, and concluded the audience with the words, 'Yes, I believe that we should be good neighbours.'[4] Sokolov, however, either misunderstood or deliberately distorted the Pope's position. In a conversation with the Vatican secretary of state Cardinal Gasparri prior to the audience, the zionist leader had emphatically denied any plans for a Jewish state.[5] But as soon as suspicions in this sense were aired, Benedict XV made his position quite clear: 'no' to Jewish sovereignty in the Holy Land.

It can safely be assumed that no Vatican directives in the spirit inferred by Sokolov after his conversation with the Pope were issued to the Catholic hierarchy. Among the evidence supporting this view is a letter written to the Zionist Organization of America (ZOA) on 10 November 1918 — a full year after the Balfour Declaration — by Mons. Cardinal Gibbons. In the letter, which was in reply to a ZOA request for a statement in honour of the first anniversary of the declaration, reference is made to the Sokolov version of the meeting. Cardinal Gibbons' response implies that it was from this ZOA request that he had first learned 'of the approval accorded by His Holiness Benedict XV to the plan providing a homeland in Palestine for the members of the Jewish race'.[6]

The Church's interest in Palestine was, however, entirely self-centred. Thus the entry of British troops into Jerusalem under General Allenby on 10 December 1917 was hailed by the entire Catholic press as a triumph for Christianity, an act that restored lasting Christian rule in the Holy Land, a redemption of the Christian communities and Holy Places from Muslim rule. Within the perspective of the 'salvation' of the Holy Land from the 'clutches of the Turk', both Arab and Jewish ambitions appeared secondary. The assumption was that under these circumstances, the Jewish presence in the Holy Land would in any case remain subordinated to Christian control and Christian interests. Zionism was considered an impracticable project, doomed to failure on both economic and demographic grounds. From a theological point of view, the situation was described as at best embodying the realization of God's vengeance upon the Jews, at worst as the initial phase of a universal, divine scheme of reunification under the auspices of Christianity. Some newspaper editorials spoke of the 'Christian take-over' of Palestine in near-messianic terms. Assuring its readers that, 'whatever fate awaits the Holy Land of this we have a surety, never again will it depart from Christian control', the Catholic *New World* of Chicago wrote, for example, on 14 December 1917:

> The Jew will most certainly be welcome in the country of his forefathers. He will have a country of his own. He will be a citizen of it. But neither Jew nor Gentile shall ever more be able to make the place hallowed by the life and death of Christ a place of persecution for his followers.

Some Catholic organs were, however, more realistic in their prophecies. The *American Catholic Quarterly Review*, in its April 1918 issue, asserted, in an article significantly entitled 'Christ's Attitude towards the Politico-Religious Expectations of the Jews', that the Jewish messiah as imagined by Jewish nationalism, and intimately intertwined with religious beliefs, was to be a political figure who would brutally crush all opposing kingdoms:

> Revengeful as the Jewish character was, the complete destruction of their enemies was one of the great moments in the national expectations, and in the satisfaction of their vindictiveness many Jews saw part of the glory of their future happiness.

Once again, these words seem to contain an implicit warning.

In contrast with Sokolov's earlier version regarding the Vatican's supportive attitude towards the zionist idea, Pope Benedict XV explicitly expressed his fears regarding zionist activities at that time. Cardinal Bourne, the archbishop of Westminster, who undertook a tour of the Middle East from December 1918 to March 1919, was received by the Pope on the eve of his departure. He described the head of the Church as 'full of anxieties' over future events in the Holy Land. Upon his return, Bourne reported to the Pope that the zionists were indeed working to gain political control. At the same time the Latin patriarch of Jerusalem, Mons. Luigi

Barlassina, reported to the Vatican that 'atheism, communism and immorality were rampant among recent Jewish immigrants'.[7] On 10 March 1919 the Pope, in a consistorial allocution, expressed his concern over the situation in Palestine, stating that 'it would be a great grief to the Holy See if in Palestine the preponderant position were given to infidels'.[8] A month later, on 15 April 1919, Cardinal Gibbons, undoubtedly prodded by Rome, pleaded with the US president Woodrow Wilson to take measures to safeguard the Holy Places.

By 1920 the initial enthusiasm over the British Empire's 'Christian take-over' seemed to be fading in the Catholic press as well. Disappointment was voiced here and there at the failure of an agreement whereby France, as a Catholic power, would have been charged with a mandate over the Holy Land. But a note of anxiety over forthcoming developments in Palestine was clearly discernible in the wake of repeated protests by Catholics and other Christians living in the Middle East at both zionism and the British mandate. Concern reached a new peak when, in December 1920, Muslim-Christian Associations in Palestine (founded with the express purpose of bringing about a revocation of the Balfour Declaration) convened the Third Arab Congress in Haifa to demand that the British mandate be immediately replaced by a national Arab government in the country.[9] In the spring of 1921 the revolts fermenting in Palestine received wide coverage in the Catholic press. A letter from the archbishop of Galilee, Mons. Haggear, to *Les Missions Catholiques* was reproduced or quoted at length in the Church press in both Europe and the US. In his letter, Mons. Haggear observed that Palestine had become the site of religious and national rivalries. He added, 'Catholic missionary progress in the Holy Land has been hampered during the war by unusual difficulties, and now the situation is even worse'.[10]

It was not until the papal allocution of 14 June 1921, however, that the Church's unequivocal anti-zionist stance was officially reaffirmed. Inspired by the May revolt of the Palestinian Arabs, the Pope declared:

Not only has the situation in Palestine not improved, it has been made worse by the new civil arrangements which aim, if not in their authors' intentions, at least in practice, to oust Christianity from its previous position and put the Jews in its place. We therefore warmly exhort all Christians, including non-Catholic governments, to insist that the League of Nations examine the British mandate in Palestine.[11]

The Pope's peremptory request was widely supported by Catholic public opinion, especially in the United States. In July 1921 the National Catholic News Service (NCNS) released a report on the dismal situation in Palestine. The Brooklyn *Tablet*'s front-page headline ran, 'Christians are Menaced by Jews; the Zionist Movement Threatens to Gain Complete Control of Institutions in Palestine'. The NCNS report published alongside informed its readers that many Christians were leaving Palestine because they were 'tired of Jewish interference'. Periodicals such as the *Catholic World* and *Catholic Historical Review* also gave wide coverage to the Pope's allocution.

On 15 May 1922 the Vatican submitted to the League of Nations an official memorandum based on the Pope's allocution and sharply criticizing the objectives of a Jewish national homeland in Palestine. Signed by Cardinal Gasparri, the memorandum stated:

> The Holy See is not opposed to Jews in Palestine having civil rights equal to those possessed by other nationals and creeds. But it cannot agree to Jews being given a privileged and preponderant position *vis-à-vis* other sections of the population. [12]

There was also intense diplomatic activity, especially by the French, Italian and Brazilian governments, in an attempt to delay the League of Nations ratification of Britain's mandate until the Balfour Declaration had been reversed. The Vatican's objections were seen as one of the main reasons that the mandate had still not been ratified by June 1922. Finally, on the eve of the debate in the British parliament which was to re-examine the issue in the light of Britain's continuing difficulties in obtaining the mandate, Mons. Barlassina made a special trip to London to plead the case of Palestine's Arab population with British public opinion and the British authorities. As a result, the House of Lords adopted a resolution on 21 June 1922 declaring the terms of the mandate contrary to the wishes of Palestine's inhabitants. Shortly afterwards, in a shrewd tactical move, Winston Churchill, then colonial secretary, issued a White Paper which, although not constituting a revocation of the Balfour Declaration, aimed to convince the opponents of zionism that restrictions would be imposed on the political future of the Jewish inhabitants in Palestine.[13]

But the main battle over the future of Palestine was being waged in the United States, where the zionists were mounting a massive effort to counter pressures hostile to their objectives by means of a formal congressional resolution in support of the Balfour Declaration. The US Catholic hierarchy and public opinion in the US, however, were on the whole supportive of the Vatican's position. The diocesan press, directly guided by the hierarchy, published reports deploring zionist activities and dispatches from Rome expressing the views of the Holy See. The news of the House of Lords resolution was welcomed as a 'check on zionist ambitions' and seen as a result of the Vatican's protests to the League of Nations. The zionists were also criticized for their attempts to 'curtail' the Vatican's political power and to assume political power themselves, in a manner betraying 'their continued hatred of the Catholic Church'. Not one Catholic paper was sympathetic to the zionist campaign. However, there was also an evident concern to prevent the Catholic community's becoming isolated within the national context. In the US as a whole, a large part of the prevalently Protestant public opinion (and political power) was supportive of the zionists' efforts, and the zionist lobby's organizational efficiency had already outstripped those of all countergroups. Editorials were careful to distinguish between zionists, to whom the Catholics were opposed, and American Jews, with whom they had tolerably good relations. Criticism of zionist ambitions was always prefaced by statements deploring racial prejudice against the Jews. When explaining the Vatican's objections to the Balfour Declaration, the editor of *New World* claimed, for example, that the Pope was motivated by humanitarian concerns as both Muslims and Christian Arabs in Palestine were now being dispossessed. He also pointed out that American Jews were far from being in agreement with the zionist movement, which represented a minority trend, albeit an aggressive one.[14]

The zionist lobby nevertheless succeeded in bringing about a congressional resolution favourable to its aims. Approved by the House of Representatives on 30 June, following its promulgation by the Senate, the resolution, formally signed by President Harding in September, was couched in terms which might appear to be concessions to the Vatican's position and to domestic Catholic opinion. In reality, however, it consisted of a scarcely veiled reformulation of the Balfour Declaration itself:

> Resolved by the Senate and House of Representatives of the United States of America in Congress assembled, that the United States of America favours the establishment in Palestine of a national home for the Jewish people, it being clearly understood that nothing shall be done which may prejudice the civil and religious rights of Christians and all other non-Jewish communities in Palestine, and that the Holy Places and religious buildings and sites in Palestine shall be adequately protected. [15]

The congressional resolution, combined with Churchill's White Paper 'trick' (see pages 15-16) which even some Catholic circles interpreted as acceptance of the Vatican's objectives, was to be decisive for future events in Palestine. In fact, it was a defeat for the Catholic Church. A defeat that had to be swallowed in silence: with the mandate firmly in British hands as of 1923, it was only when the next Palestinian Arab revolt broke out in 1929 that the question of Palestine regained public attention on the Catholic scene. In the summer of 1929, zionist provocations in Jerusalem, especially at the sites of the Holy Places, reached a new peak. The Arab reaction, combined with Britain's inability to mediate, helped inflame the situation. A worldwide zionist campaign was launched to present the Jewish community in Palestine as innocent victims of Arab ferocity and thus obtain renewed support for zionist political aims. The *Osservatore Romano*, the official Vatican daily newspaper, deplored the violence and the rest of the Catholic press followed suit, noting that the Vatican had warned the British of the rising tension and had recommended 'certain changes in policy' in order to avert a bloody conflict. The trouble was clearly defined as stemming from economic injustice due to Jewish immigration. Mons. Barlassina was quoted as saying that both Christians and Muslims strongly opposed this continued immigration. He was also reported to be advising the Vatican on policy in view of the deepening crisis. [16]

With few exceptions, editorials and articles throughout the Catholic press explained the reasons for the hostility towards zionist policies. Dispatches from Jerusalem reported that the Jews were demanding supremacy, through the institution of 'a Jewish police force, a Jewish defence force, a Jewish administration'. The Balfour Declaration was repeatedly singled out as the root of the tragedy now being played out in Palestine. The current situation there was ascribed, quite correctly, not to mere outbursts of religious intolerance but to political grievances stemming from the declaration. In examining the events that had led up to the violent explosion of tension, the US Catholic periodical *Commonweal* made specific mention of a mass demonstration organized by the 'zionist fascists' — a reference to the rightwingers of Zabotinsky's Revisionist Party — in front of the house of the Mufti of Jerusalem.[17] Peremptorily dismissing charges of Arab intolerance, the editor of the *Tablet* wrote that, 'There was once religious warfare in the Holy Land. The paper said nothing about it. It was when Christ was crucified.'[18] In the autumn of 1929, as the British commission of inquiry was elaborating its findings, the US Catholic periodical *America* quoted at length from the Arab press (which described the tension resulting from zionist usurpation of the land) and noted the zionists' expansion of economic control in Palestine. The paper also wrote that, according to the Simpson Report, 'Jewish settlers have every advantage — capital, science and organization.'[19] Other Catholic publications followed this lead, questioning the validity of the Balfour Declaration and criticizing Jewish immigration to Palestine. The theological arguments according to which the Jews had no right to the Holy Land because of their crucifixion of Christ and their rejection of the New Covenant were also invoked to reaffirm opposition to zionist settlement and policies in Palestine.

In the 1930s Catholic opinion had its attention focused mainly on the Vatican's virulent anti-communist campaign. As the 'persecution of Catholics by communism and socialism' became the theme of the day, the Jews, zionism and the question of Palestine were also included in this perspective. Jews were generally identified with communism and hence regarded as enemies of the Church. In general, the Catholic press — particularly in the United States, where anti-communism was also used by the Catholic community to achieve a higher profile within the framework of a society previously dominated by Protestant exclusivism — felt that the 'plight' of Catholics in the Soviet Union, Republican Spain and socialist Mexico was more dramatic than that of the Jews under fascist and nazi regimes, but received less attention. Zionist demands for higher quotas of Jewish emigration to Palestine were seen as too successful in vying with Catholic demands for aid to Catholic emigrés from communist-dominated countries.

In July 1937 the British Peel Commission was charged with examining the situation in Palestine in the wake of the outbreak of the 1936 Great Arab (Palestinian) Revolt. A general strike had held for over a year and armed struggle was spreading all over the country. The commission recommended that the land be partitioned into separate Jewish and Arab states, with the Holy Places in Jerusalem and Bethlehem remaining under British mandatory control. The plan led to a storm of protest among Palestinian Arabs, both Muslim and Christian. In a memorandum to the British government on 6 August, the Holy See expressed its opposition to the partition of the Holy Land. In particular, it stated its concern over the geopolitical and other divisions that such a partition would inevitably cause among Christian communities, composed mainly of Arab Christians, living in Palestine. It also protested at the proposal that Holy Places such as Lake Tiberias and Nazareth should be included within the territory of the Jewish state. The memorandum left no doubt as to the Vatican's continuing opposition to the idea of zionist sovereignty in Palestine.[20] The Peel Commission's recommendations were later abandoned due to strong opposition and mounting world tension. In 1939 the British government issued a White Paper restricting Jewish immigration to Palestine and zionist land purchases therein. The White Paper was warmly welcomed by the great majority of Catholic public opinion. In the United States, in particular, anti-zionist feeling among the Catholic community was now running high. Church publications such as *Sign* and *Tablet*, among others, reaffirmed that 'Palestine is not and never will be a national home for the Jew.'[21]

With the outbreak of the Second World War, public interest in the question of Palestine subsided. The Vatican, however, remained vigilant. On 22 June 1943, in a memorandum to Myron C. Taylor, US delegate to the Vatican, Archbishop Amleto G. Cicognani, then apostolic delegate to the United States, restated the Vatican's position on Palestine in no uncertain terms. Cicognani, who had discussed the issue with Taylor a few days before, mentioned that the Vatican had recently taken action on behalf of Jewish children and youths interned in Slovakia, obtaining their release and permission for them to emigrate, as well as British permission for them to enter Palestine. But Cicognani also recalled Pope Benedict XV's repeated pledges to oppose the creation of a Jewish state in Palestine. Attached to his note was a copy of Cardinal Gasparri's memorandum to the League of Nations of 4 June 1922.

Cicognani's own memorandum to Taylor went on to state:

Catholics the world over are piously devoted to this country [Palestine], hallowed as it was by the presence of the Redeemer and esteemed as it is as the cradle of Christianity. If the greater part of Palestine is given to the Jewish people, this would be a severe blow to the religious attachment of Catholics to this land. To have the Jewish People in the majority is to interfere with the peaceful exercise of these rights in the Holy Land already vested in Catholics.

It is true that at one time Palestine was inhabited by the Jewish race, but there is no axiom in history to substantiate the necessity of a people returning to a country they left nineteen centuries before.

If a 'Jewish Home' is desired, it should not be too difficult to find a more fitting territory than Palestine. With an increase in the Jewish population there, grave new international problems would arise. Catholics all over the world would rise up. The Holy See would be saddened, and justly so, because a similar step could hardly be in harmony with the charitable assistance that the non-aryans have received and will continue to receive from the Vatican.[22]

This memorandum came almost exactly one year after the announcement in New York, in May 1942, of the Biltmore Program, whereby the zionist movement for the first time officially stated its support for the partition of Palestine with a view to the establishment of a Jewish state at the end of the war. The American Zionist Emergency Committee waged an intensive campaign to mobilize both Jewish and non-Jewish opinion behind the Biltmore Program. In 1944, as the scale of the Jewish holocaust became known, the US congress came under tremendous pressure, and ultimately passed the following resolution:

Resolved that the United States shall use its good offices and take appropriate measures to the end that the doors of Palestine shall be opened for free entry of Jews in that country, and that there shall be full opportunity for colonization so that the Jewish people may ultimately reconstitute Palestine as a free and democratic Jewish commonwealth.[23]

Once again, the positions of the Catholic Church and the US government on Palestine were diametrically opposed — in sharp contrast to their close alliance in other areas of foreign policy.

The end of the war brought the full horror of nazi atrocities to world attention. Catholic opinion, along with that of every other denomination, was shocked and appalled. Among Catholics, however, sympathy for the plight of Jewish survivors did not automatically take the form of support for zionist demands to permit unlimited emigration to Palestine of the masses of displaced persons. In fact, the Catholic response was determined not so much by concern for the Palestinian Arabs' fate as a result of such immigration, as by other considerations. Foremost among these was the preoccupation with Christian refugees from East European countries who did not want to return to their now 'communist-controlled' countries. Catholics, especially in the US, felt that the zionists were unjustly monopolizing world attention as regards the displaced persons, among whom there were not only Jews but also Christians. Furthermore, the zionists' presenting the two questions of refugees and Jewish statehood in Palestine as one 'package' issue was hampering Catholic demands for unrestricted immigration rights to the US for 'their' displaced persons. American Catholics felt that the popular perception of the refugee problem as solely a Jewish concern was being further distorted by the zionist clamour for immigration to Palestine. At the same time, the insistence on Palestine deprived the Catholics of massive Jewish support in the US for their own campaign to permit unlimited immigration of displaced persons to America.

This concern was reflected in a somewhat problematic manner in an editorial on 17 May 1946 in *Commonweal*:

> We fully recognize the desperate need of Europe's remaining Jews for a homeland in which they can be reasonably confident of living unmolested. We are likewise aware that the Jewish colonies in the Holy Land have in fact proved a great economic asset to their Arab neighbours. We are aware that the question has been used by Arab nationalists as a means to arouse passions which need never have been aroused. But we are likewise and equally suspicious of zionist nationalism and we cannot withhold our sympathy from the natives of Palestine who, however shortsightedly, seem to prefer to keep their country for their own use. Americans, of all people, can with the least grace criticize

others for attempts to restrict immigration. And hence, we cannot make up our minds, especially since we believe that the first duty of our own country is itself to provide a haven of refuge to the harbourless.[24]

Another reason behind Catholic opposition to zionist plans lay in the Church's militant anti-communist stance under Pope Pius XII. In this context, Catholic fears as to possible communist penetration of the Middle East were connected on the one hand to suspicions of left-wing prevalence among zionists in Palestine and on the other hand to the argument that Western acquiescence to zionist aspirations would lead the Arab world to ally itself with the Soviet Union. Finally, there were Catholics who, on theological grounds, believed firmly in the need to establish Christian control over the Holy Land. This idea was reaffirmed in 1945 by Mons. Abraham Assemani, the Jerusalem Latin Patriarchate's representative to the United States, in an article given unusually wide circulation in the Catholic press. Mons. Assemani warned that Christian rights in the Holy Land were being ignored and urged Christians to demand absolute sovereignty over the Holy Places as well as the establishment of an Allied Commission to safeguard Christian interests.[25]

As the zionist schemes became more explicit, Catholic concern took on a further dimension. When the Palestinian resolutions were debated in the US Congress in 1944, Mons. Thomas J. McMahon, national secretary of the prestigious American Catholic Near East Welfare Association (CNEWA), which had been created in 1926 by Pope Pius XI, warned of the danger to Christian communities throughout the Middle East should the West agree to the zionists' demands. Because of its direct and close links with the Vatican, the CNEWA was the foremost authority for the American Catholic hierarchy and public opinion on all matters related to Palestine. It can also be seen as having served as the mouthpiece of the Pope and the Vatican authorities in the United States on Middle East issues. McMahon's assertion that Arab nationalism had to be taken into account in order to ensure the safety of Christian minorities in Islamic countries may therefore be considered as an authoritative directive from the Vatican authorities to Western Catholicism. In an article given wide publicity in periodicals and the diocesan press throughout the United States, following congressional approval of the pro-zionist resolutions of 1944, Mons. McMahon further urged that Christians throughout the world demand with one voice that the 'homeland of Jesus be kept sacred and inviolable'. While Islam could not 'expel Jesus from Palestine', McMahon expressed the fear that a Jewish state would do just that. The solution he proposed was that of an internationalization of the whole of Palestine, with predominant Christian control.

When the United Nations Special Committee on Palestine (UNSCOP) convened in 1947 to decide on a solution to the question of Palestine, the CNEWA asked to appear at the hearings also as a representative of Palestinian Christians. In his letter to the United Nations, McMahon wrote:

> We are completely indifferent to the form of the regime which your esteemed committee may recommend, provided that the interests of Christendom, Catholic, Protestant and Orthodox, will be weighed and safeguarded in your final recommendations.[26]

McMahon explained this as a plea that the settlement decided upon 'should not be allowed to exile Jesus', and that custody of the Holy Land should be confided to Christianity.

Liberal Catholic opinion also seemed to oppose a zionist solution for Palestine. Among others, the prominent French theologian Jacques Maritain, well known for his public condemnation of anti-Jewish persecution, wrote in the Catholic press:

> It appears that the solution of a Jewish state in Palestine will inevitably be the next solution attempted by the angel of an ever sorrowful and frustrated history.[27]

During the months between 29 November 1947, when the UN General Assembly voted for partition, and 15 May 1948, when the state of Israel was actually proclaimed, Catholic opinion followed the fighting in the Holy Land with undoubted anguish. In Palestine the Christian Union, a group which comprised eleven Christian communities of all denominations, issued a dramatic appeal on 3 March 1948:

> The Christian Union wishes to declare in unequivocal terms that they denounce the partition plan, being of strong convictions that this plan involves a violation of the sacredness of the Holy

Land, which by its nature is indivisible... It is our firm conviction that peace will not be restored unless those bodies who undertake the determination of the future of Palestine remove the causes which have made a battlefield of the Holy Land.[28]

In dispatches circulated by the NCNS, Fr Anthony Bruya of the Franciscan Order in Jerusalem reported on the deteriorating situation in Palestine. His reports told of massacres such as Deir Yassin,[29] of the flight of many Christians from the Holy Land, of signs of an approaching full-scale war. They were carried by a large number of Catholic publications which also devoted editorials to the situation. C.G. Paulding, the Catholic editor of *Commonweal*, and untiring in his condemnation of all forms of anti-Jewish discrimination, wrote:

It is not a step towards anything save a future of misery when a certain number of Jewish fanatics forget all the Jews throughout the world and pretend to create in Palestine, by extreme violence, something they would call a nation, but which would be nothing but a self-administered ghetto. In Palestine they are not opening a new world to the Jews, they are closing to the Jews the world toward which we are working.[30]

Notwithstanding the pressing appeals from Christians in Palestine and the almost unanimous condemnation of zionist military operations by Catholic opinion, the Vatican made no explicit public statement following the November 1947 UN vote to partition Palestine. Only on 1 May 1948 did Pope Pius XII issue an encyclical epistle, entitled *Auspicia Quaedam*, devoted to problems of war and peace. The central part focused on Palestine:

At the present moment there is another matter which saddens and afflicts our heart very much. We mean the Holy Places of Palestine, which for a long time have been disturbed by sorrowful events, and which almost every day are devastated by new killings and ruin. Yet if there is one part of the world which should be particularly dear to every well-disposed and civilized mind, it should certainly be Palestine, whence the Light of Truth sprang for all humanity, where choirs of angels announced peace on earth to men of goodwill, and, finally, where Jesus Christ, suspended from the Tree of the Cross, brought salvation to all mankind and stretched out his arms as if to invite all nations into a fraternal embrace, consecrating the great precept of charity by shedding his own blood. We desire, therefore, Venerable Brethren, that prayers during May should especially have the purpose of asking the Holy Virgin that the condition of Palestine may be finally settled according to equity, and that there, too, peace and harmony may happily triumph.[31]

The next day a truce was declared in Palestine — it was to last no more than a few days. But by that time, the zionist forces had already completed the operations foreseen in the Dalet Plan.[32]

Whatever the Pope might have meant by the vague term, a settlement 'according to equity', it was too late to turn back the clock. Two weeks later, as the last British troops left for home, a 'Jewish state' was proclaimed in Palestine.

To Catholic opinion at large, the news came as a shock. Twenty years later, a German nun, speaking for Catholics living in Jerusalem at that time, recalled, 'I well remember our firm conviction that it [the Jewish state] would never come into being.'[33] And the Holy See? The event undoubtedly marked a defeat for the Vatican's declared policies in Palestine. But could the Catholic Church have had a greater impact on events, in a pro-Palestinian sense, in the historical context of the time? The question remains open. Two points, however, are worth mentioning. The first concerns the decisive role played by the Catholic governments of Latin America in favour of the UN partition resolution and the creation of the state of Israel. Notwithstanding its opposition to the zionist state, the Holy See was less effective in exerting pressure on these governments than the US was in persuading them to support the zionist scheme. Moreover any pressure exercised by the Vatican in this instance was a far cry from that brought to bear in other circumstances, for instance in cases where Catholics were excommunicated for support of 'marxist' movements or authorities. One example inevitably comes to mind in this context: the contrast between the Vatican's *de facto* acceptance of Latin American support of Israel, and its mobilization of Vietnamese Catholics called upon to boycott and fight the Nationalist communist government of Ho Chi Minh.

The second point relates to the fact that had the Vatican *publicly* taken a more vigorous, unequivocal stance against the fascist and nazi regimes, its credibility in opposing zionism might have been greatly enhanced in post-war years. It might also have been less exposed to instrumental accusations of 'anti-semitism', which were to undermine its just stand on Palestine.

2
The Catholic Church and 'Arab Palestine' before 1948

During the half-century preceding the partition of Palestine, the attitude of the Catholic Church towards zionism was, as we have seen, almost without exception negative. Its outlook on the Arab world, on emerging Arab nationalism and on the possibility that the Holy Land might come under Arab control, on the other hand, was marked by diffidence or, at best, ambiguity.

The fact that Christians, including Catholics, had played a major role in the foundation and promotion of the Arab nationalist movement was of minor importance for the Church. Indeed, Christian Arab nationalists were mostly of profound secular convictions. Their aim of achieving a secular, 'national' Arab society was mainly a reaction to centuries of oppressive Islamic rule under the Ottoman empire. They were convinced that a 'de-confessionalization' of the existing legislation was the only way to achieve equality between all citizens and all communities. In other words, it was a necessary step on the road towards the emancipation of Arab societies from their state of under-development in the modern world. Many of these early Arab nationalists had been educated in France and were, so to speak, the sons of the French revolution — an anathema to the Catholic Church which, on an institutional level, traditionally preferred to make alliances and agreements with other religious powers and institutions, thus allowing it to conserve its own property and privileges.

At the time, the Church was still pervaded by a Euro-centric 'Crusader mentality', which could hardly be expected to harmonize with the goals of Arab nationalism, whether of Christian or Muslim origin. This trend became particularly evident when British troops entered Jerusalem in December 1917. Catholic opinion in the West was made to focus almost exclusively on the alleged religious significance of the event, interpreted as the triumph of Christianity over Islam. Readers of the Catholic press were treated to visions of restored Christian rule in the Holy Land, now 'rescued' from the clutches of 'the awful Turk'. The Allied troops, as so-called Christian armies, were compared to the Crusaders in their successful undertaking to 'wrest this truly Christian inheritance from the dominion of the Muslim'. In an article entitled 'Crusaders in Khaki', *America* asserted that the reconquest of Jerusalem served to restore self-respect to Christians, who had felt humiliated and disgraced as long as the Holy Land was under Muslim rule. Now that Jerusalem was safely in Christian hands, the Holy Land would remain under lasting Christian rule:

> Over the mosque of Omar, the Crescent has been lowered before the Cross. A sigh of relief and gratitude has gone up from the nations that still worship Christ... They can sing their *Te Deum* for Bethlehem and Gethsemane, Calvary and the Holy Sepulchre are once more in Christian hands. Never again should the Turk be allowed to keep guard over the holiest spot in the world. No statescraft, no game of shifting world politics should ever be tolerated by which these hills... will pass out of the power of the Crusaders who have just entered the portals of the Sacred City.[1]

There was no reference to the fact that here was one empire about to succeed another, in the control of lands whose inhabitants were to be given no say in their destiny. The fatal complications that would ensue were similarly ignored.

These attitudes were gradually to change, however, with developments in the area. Although Catholic attention in 1920-21 was focused on opposition to the Balfour Declaration and zionist ambitions, some quarters also voiced objections to any accommodation with the Arabs over the future of Palestine. Between the ratification of the British mandate in 1923 and the eruption of violence in Jerusalem in the summer of 1929, Christian, and in particular Catholic, communities and institutions in Palestine experienced a period of growth and expansion. At the same time, the Arab Muslim-Christian Associations, founded with the express purpose of opposing the Balfour Declaration, were becoming more active and managing to get their voice heard in the media. These associations had already passed a resolution at the Third Arab Congress in Haifa in December 1920, demanding the revocation of the British mandate and the establishment of a national Arab government in Palestine. The associations could count on the support of the Latin patriarch of Jerusalem, Mons. Barlassina, who regularly reported to the Vatican on growing concern among the Arab population in view of the continued Jewish immigration and the expanding zionist organization.

It was an irony that, due to Western support for zionist ambitions, the replacement of the 'awful Turk' by 'Christian rule' had led to an 80 per cent increase in inter-communal violence in the Holy Land during the decade 1919-29. The threat that this now represented to the well-being of Christian groups and institutions forced the Catholic media to take a new interest in the overall situation of the Arabs. Reports on zionist 'usurpation of the land' were given wide coverage to explain the roots of the violence. A new interest was also shown in establishing contacts with Arab cultural and religious bodies. The NCNS circulated an article on the subject, quoting a teacher at the Pontifical Oriental Institute in Rome, who said, 'the positive features of Islam... could combat the evils of our age. Islam occupies an intermediate position between the doctrines of bourgeois capitalism and Bolshevist communism.'[2]

There was an underlying ambivalence, however. A typical example could be found in an editorial in the 5 November 1930 edition of *Commonweal*:

The peculiar need of the Jews for a geographical home, the peculiar historic and spiritual appropriateness of locating their home in Palestine, are beyond question... On the other hand, the resentment of the Palestinian Arabs at what they feel to be an alien invasion is as little to be conjured away. And when we consider the homogeneity of the whole Muslim body, and the 75,000,000 Indian Muhammadans who at any moment may take up actively the cause of their Arab co-religionists, we can understand Britain's present minimizing of their undertaking.

This was a curious way of posing the question. No less unfortunate was the way in which Catholic opposition to zionism took on the colours of the virulent anti-communist campaign, thus tending to equate pro-Arab attitudes with outright support for reactionary, and even fascist, regimes and trends. Phrases expressing the belief that 'one can expect more from the Muslim Arabs than from the atheistic Bolshevik Jews', disseminated by the Catholic press in its analysis of the international situation, hardly denoted an intelligent understanding of the developing conflict in the Middle East.

But other voices were to be heard, such as that of Amin Rihani, a Lebanese Christian who had emigrated to the United States and was an articulate commentator on events in Palestine, zionist plans and British intentions. His articles appeared regularly in American Catholic periodicals. George Antonius' famous book *The Arab Awakening* (first published in 1938) also had a considerable influence on Christian public opinion, particularly in France.

However, Antonius' thesis — that of an Arab Confederation (or more specifically a 'Greater Syria') including Palestine — was to meet strong resistance on the part of the Church. In fact, the Vatican's position on the subject was substantially in line with the tenor of a memorandum of 14 March 1944 to the US secretary of state Cordell Hall from Myron Taylor, the American delegate to the Holy See, although the memorandum contained no specific reference to the Church's position. It should be borne in mind that Taylor was also in complete agreement with the Holy See's opposition to the establishment of a Jewish state in Palestine:

> I have repeatedly expressed the opinion that no encouragement should be given to the 'establishment, after the war, of a pan-Arab Confederation'. I have serious doubts as to the opportuneness of encouraging a similar racial and religious bloc that would put in motion such external and internal controversies as would render vain any effort to control, influence or deal with the problems concerning the single parts of a similar confederation because of the effect that the forces combined in the latter will have on them... It seems to me that the whole plan to encourage a consolidation of the Arab world is full of dangers of many kinds.[3]

On the whole, however, and taking into account the Church's Euro-centric mentality at that time, the political stance adopted by Catholicism towards Arab demands in Palestine can be seen as more favourable than that shown towards other Third World liberation movements, especially those 'suspected' of progressive trends. The

Vatican made far greater efforts than any other Western body to prevent the zionist state from coming into being. Moreover, had it not been for the Vatican's adamant opposition, the Western powers (followed by those other states that have extended diplomatic recognition to the state of Israel) would probably have agreed to recognize Jerusalem as the Israeli capital as early as 1949-50. Furthermore, for the next four decades, i.e. up to the present day, the Vatican was to be the only Western state apart from Spain not to extend *de jure* recognition to Israel or to establish formal diplomatic relations with it. On the other hand, in the months following the UN partition resolution of 29 November 1947, the Holy See adopted an extremely cautious attitude, keeping a diplomatic distance between the two sides. The allusions to 'sorrowful events' and 'daily killings and ruin in the Holy Places' contained in the Pope's *Auspicia Quaedam* encyclical epistle, issued three full weeks after the Deir Yassin massacre of 10 April 1948, came far too late and were too vague an expression of moral indignation to have an impact on developments at the time.

The Vatican undoubtedly found itself in a quandary. On the one hand, it was extremely concerned at the prospect of zionist dominion over the Holy Land. On the other hand, it did not relish the idea of Arab control over Palestine. At the same time, it had to resign itself to the failure of 'Christianity' to establish permanent hegemony there. Thus for the next few months the Vatican was to adopt a cautious, diplomatic, wait-and-see attitude.

3

From Incredulity
to Resignation:
1948–1950

On 30 May 1948, two weeks after the proclamation of the state
of Israel, and nearly a month after the Pope's encyclical epistle
Auspicia Quaedam, the four spiritual leaders of Jerusalem's Catholic
community sent the Vatican the following emphatic protest at
Israeli military operations:

> As of 12.00 p.m. of 8 May, the city of Jerusalem enjoyed the
> benefits of the truce.
> In the evening of Thursday 13 May, breaking the truce
> without any warning and for no apparent motives, the Jews
> resumed their attack on the Holy City.
> As of the morning of Saturday 15 May, they occupied by
> force the guest-quarters of Notre Dame de France Monastery
> of the Assumptionist Fathers, the Convent of the Reparatrice
> Sisters and also the French and Italian Hospitals, disregarding
> the protests of the directors and the fact that the French, Vatican
> and international crosses were hoisted.
> On Tuesday 18 May, they also occupied the Dormition
> Monastery of the German Benedictine Fathers, the seat of the
> Apostolic Delegation and the Greek Convent of the Holy
> Trinity, all located on Mount Zion. They transformed these
> convents into fortified posts, from which, as of that moment,
> their mortars and other armaments open fire unceasingly and
> indiscriminately on the city of Jerusalem.
> The Holy Sepulchre, like many other convents and churches,
> has been damaged. Priests, monks, nuns, women, children —

all non-combatant civilians — who had found refuge in the
convents, have been killed or wounded in this very city of
Jerusalem, this city which the entire world respects and
venerates. The Arab military, both volunteers and regular
troops, have promised to respect the Holy Places, the convents,
the churches and the Red Cross institutions. Until today they
have been respectful of their given word, and, in cases in which
they entered some convent, they only did it to defend the Holy
City from the attacks of the Jews who attempted to penetrate
into it and disseminate death. If the Arabs opened fire on the
guest-quarters of the Notre Dame de France and the Convent
of the Reparatrice Sisters — *which the Jews had already destroyed
and burnt down to a large extent* — this was only to reply to their
adversaries who used these places to shoot on them and on the
Holy City. The Jews have transformed these convents, as they
have done also with their synagogues, with the Hebrew
University and the Hadassah Hospital, into operative bases from
which they repeatedly attack the Holy City in order to come
into the possession thereof and to plunder it, a destiny already
experienced by Haifa and Jaffa.

Our protests to the consuls of France, Belgium and the United
States (members of the Truce Committee nominated by the
Security Council) and to the International Red Cross have not
brought about any results despite the promises made to us.[1]

The statement was signed by Vincent Gélat, apostolic
administrative of the Latin Patriarchate, Mons. Assaf, vicar-general
of the Greek Catholic Patriarchate, Mons. Alberto Gori, the
(Franciscan) custos of the Holy Land, and Mons. Jacques
Ghiragossian, the patriarchal vicar of the Armenian Catholic
Church. It is believed to have been supported by Mons. Gustavo
Testa, apostolic delegate for Palestine, Trans-Jordan and Cyprus,
who had just arrived in Palestine, expressly charged by the Holy See
with overseeing the protection of the Holy Places.

The following day, the Christian Union of Palestine addressed
an appeal to 'Religious and Political Bodies throughout the World'.
It reiterated the accusations formulated in the above memorandum;
listed all the casualties among civilians who had taken refuge in
religious institutions and during the battles for their occupation by
zionist forces; and affirmed that, in contrast to the Israelis, the Arab
Command had issued formal instructions to all its posts to respect

the Holy Places 'and had kept their word until now' except where they 'entered a certain convent in self-defence'. Listing the damage caused to churches, convents and institutions by zionist attacks, the signatories — representing seven Christian communities, five of them Catholic[2] — also noted that when the Armistice Committee and International Red Cross representatives (at the instigation of the religious leaders) had protested at the infringement of the truce agreements by the zionist forces, they were told that 'the Stern Gang, which is working separately, broke the cease-fire agreement, and that the Jewish Agency had no control over this group':

> We then realized that the terrorists were controlling the Jewish movement. In consequence of which, the International Red Cross and the Armistice Committee declared that it was beyond their power to enforce respect for the agreement. In this way the Holy City was turned into a battlefield... Because of this dreadful situation we, the representatives of the Christian communities, deem it our solemn duty to raise our voice in protest against the violation of the sanctity of our churches, convents and institutions... We therefore appeal to all those in power and to the civilized world to compel the Jews to respect the Holy Places and the religious institutions and to desist from making them into military bases and targets.

The appeal received wide and detailed coverage in the Catholic press.[3] The attitude of the press during this period varied from hesitation and lack of comment on the new situation emerging in the Holy Land, to some lingering hope that the zionist state was merely an ephemeral phenomenon, to outright denunciation of the profane nature of the new entity, to straight reporting of events and developments in Palestine. The *Osservatore Romano* and the Italian Catholic Action daily *Il Quotidiano*, however, denounced the fighting in the Holy Land as sacrilegious and blasphemous, leaving little doubt that responsibility lay with the zionists. The *Osservatore Romano* also urged Christians not to 'abandon' the Holy Land 'spiritually', while *Il Quotidiano* urged the Church to take effective and immediate action. This paper also launched a Franciscan appeal to mobilize an international militia to guard the Holy Places.

In the US, Catholic papers such as the *Tablet, Sign, Catholic World, Catholic Worker* and the *Social Justice Review* expressed anxiety and distrust on theological grounds, as did *Commonweal,* whose commentary, however, also contained a series of pragmatic political questions: Would Israel be able to curb its extremists? What would be its relations with the USSR? What would be its final boundaries? *America* was ambivalent in recalling both Arab and Jewish claims to Palestine, but concluded that 'the Jews have staked their claim and do not intend to abandon it... The extermination or subjugation of Israel would not sit well with world opinion.'[4]

Reports from Palestine, however, were important in forming Catholic public opinion. As already mentioned, the protests of Christian communities in Palestine were given wide coverage. Significantly, the Franciscan Delegation to the Holy Land (Delegazione in Terrasanta) in Rome was receiving 1,000 applications a day from volunteers responding to its appeal for an international militia to guard the Holy Places. The initiative never materialized, probably for political reasons, but the scale of the response was a clear indication of the anguish felt by Catholic readers at the ominous news from Palestine.

Alarm reached a peak in the summer of 1948. On 24 June and 5 and 27 July, Mons. Antonio Vergani, vicar-general of the Latin Patriarchate of Jerusalem for the Galilee, reported to the Vatican State Secretariat on the extensive damage caused to ecclesiastical property under his jurisdiction in the course of the zionist military attacks in Tiberias and its surroundings and in Haifa. Among the points raised in his memoranda, Mons. Vergani said:

As of 25 May, strong Israeli forces arriving in Galilee plundered all [Arab] villages and expelled the Arab population from the area.

The monastery and other quarters of the Franciscan Custody of the Holy Land in Tiberias had been forced open various times between 5 May and 5 June and a large part of the sacred objects and apparel was stolen, the Vatican flag stripped to pieces and books and documents torn up and dispersed.

The school and convent of the Franciscan Sisters in Tiberias were forced open and damaged, the chapel profaned, the statues and furniture vandalized.

The Sanctuary and Hospice of the Beatitudes on Lake Galilee: the religious personnel — Franciscan monks and nuns — were evacuated by force to Tiberias for 24 hours, during which furniture, apparel and even personal objects and food provisions were all stolen. The Israeli military remained in the church, in front of which a mortar was placed. The sacred effigy was taken off the cross and was never returned.

Capernaum: the church and the hospice were plundered by the Israeli military, who evacuated the religious personnel by force to Tiberias on 5 June. The guardian, whose cow was stolen, was left for ten days without food. The church on Lake Galilee had permitted Arab refugees from the area to hide therein the few objects which they managed to save from their plundered homes. These have all been stolen by the Israeli troops, who also broke the marble window and the stone cross at the entrance to the church.

At Tabgha [Lake Galilee] the religious personnel were taken prisoner and not permitted to go out of two dark cells in the hospice for several weeks.

Mons. Vergani's memoranda, which were released to the press on 17 August 1948, concluded with the following note:

The occupation, carried out with the use of force, without previous approval by the ecclesiatic authorities, has opened the way to continual expropriation of ecclesiastic properties which will have strong repercussions in the Christian world. Moreover, this occupation constituted a clear violation of the armistice agreement.[5]

CNEWA Secretary Mons. Thomas McMahon dispatched a letter to the United Nations, quoting from Vergani's memoranda, and also referring to other reports from Palestine on the maltreatment of Christians and the desecration of the Holy Places, and urging the UN to undertake an immediate investigation. His letter closed on a note of warning:

It is our considered opinion that if these overt acts continue, or are explained by ascribing them to irresponsible forces, then the entire Christian world is justified in its apprehension over the disregard of Christian spiritual and material interests in the new-born state of Israel.[6]

At this point the Israeli and zionist propaganda machinery embarked on a massive campaign to counteract the negative effects of the reports from Palestine. Israeli embassies in the various capitals brought strong pressure on the press to publish statements refuting the accounts of vandalism and violations of the extra-territoriality of ecclesiastic properties. However, news of repeated violent episodes continued to arrive from the Holy Land. On 24 September 1948 another report on the plundering of Christian institutions in Haifa was sent to the head of the Custody of the Holy Land by Fr Pierpaolo, the superior of Haifa's Franciscan Convent.

The fact that Israeli forces were breaking into Church institutions was undoubtedly a serious matter, and it defeated the Church's attempts to provide shelter for uprooted and persecuted Arab civilians in areas of combat. But it should be remembered that this was merely one aspect of the grave war crimes being committed at that time in Palestine. Hundreds of thousands of civilians were being driven from their homeland by force, their villages were being shelled, attacked and sometimes destroyed. A refusal to leave often entailed violence against defenceless populations.

On 2 June, following the alarming memorandum by the Christian Union of Palestine, Pope Pius XII addressed a meeting of the College of Cardinals on 'The War in Palestine'. He asked the Christian world:

> *not to look on with indifference or with barren indignation while the Holy Land is still trodden by troops at war and subject to aerial bombardments.* [He added:] We do not believe that the Christian world could allow the devastation of the Holy Places to become complete, the great Sepulchre of Christ to be destroyed. May it be God's will that the peril of this horrendous scourge be finally dispelled.[7]

During the following weeks the Vatican strenuously supported the UN mediator Count Bernadotte's efforts for a revision of the partition plan, including his aim to incorporate Jerusalem into an Arab state (later modified to a scheme of a *corpus separatum* according to his progress report to the UN of September 1948).

Admitting to having received numerous urgent appeals over the past months regarding the situation, the Pope finally issued another encyclical letter on 24 October, this time devoted entirely to Palestine. Entitled *In Multiplicibus Curis*, it said:

> Among the multiple preoccupations which beset us in this period of time, so full of decisive consequences for the life of the great

human family, and which make us feel so seriously the burden of the Supreme Pontificate, Palestine occupies a particular place on account of the war which harasses it. In all truth we can tell you, Venerable Brethren, that neither joyous nor sad events diminish the sorrow which is kept alive in our soul by the thought that, in the land in which our Lord Jesus Christ shed his blood to bring redemption and salvation to all mankind, the blood of man continues to flow; and that, beneath the skies which echoed on that fateful night with the gospel tidings of peace, men continue to fight and to increase the distress of the unfortunate and the fear of the terrorized, while thousands of refugees, homeless and driven, wander far from their fatherland in search of shelter and food.

To make our sorrow more grievous, there is not only the news which continually reaches us of the destruction and damage of sacred buildings and charitable places built round the Holy Places, but there is also the fear that this inspires in us for the fate of the Holy Places themselves, scattered throughout Palestine, and more especially within the Holy City.

We must assure you, Venerable Brethren, that, confronted with the spectacle of many evils, and the forecast of worse to come, we have not withdrawn into our sorrow, but have done all in our power to provide a remedy. Even before the armed conflict began, speaking to a delegation of Arab dignitaries which came to pay homage to us, we manifested our lifelong solicitude for peace in Palestine, and, condemning any recourse to violence, we declared that peace could only be realized in truth and in justice; that is to say, by respecting the rights of acquired traditions, especially in the religious field, as well as by the strict fulfilment of the duties and obligations of each group of inhabitants.

When war was declared, without abandoning the attitude of impartiality imposed on us by our apostolic duty, which places us above the conflicts which agitate human society, we did not fail to do our utmost, in the measure which depended upon us and according to the possibilities offered to us, for the triumph of justice and peace in Palestine and for the respect and protection of the Holy Places.

At the same time, although numerous and urgent appeals are received daily by the Holy See, we have sought as much as possible to come to the aid of the unhappy victims of the war, sending the means at our disposal to our representatives in Palestine, the Lebanon and Egypt for this purpose, and encouraging the formation among Catholics in various countries of undertakings organized for the same purpose.

Convinced, however, of the insufficiency of human means for the adequate solution of a question the complexity of which nobody can fail to see, we have, above all, had constant recourse to prayer, and in our recent encyclical letter, *Auspicia Quaedam*, we invited you, Venerable Brethren, to pray, and to have the faithful entrusted to your pastoral care pray, in order that, under the auspices of the Blessed Virgin, matters may be settled in justice and peace, and concord may happily be restored in Palestine. As we said on 2 June to members of the Sacred College of Cardinals, informing them of our anxieties over Palestine, we do not believe that the Christian world could contemplate with indifference, or in sterile indignation, the spectacle of the sacred land... trampled over again by troops and stricken by aerial bombardments. We do not believe that it could permit the devastation of the Holy Places, the destruction of the great Sepulchre of Christ.

We are full of faith that the fervent prayers raised to Almighty and Merciful God by the Christians throughout the world... will render less arduous to the men who hold the destinies of people the task of making justice and peace in Palestine a beneficial reality and of creating, with the efficient co-operation of all those interested, an order that may guarantee security of existence and, at the same time, the moral and physical conditions of life conducive to spiritual and material well-being, to each of the parties at present in conflict.

We are fully confident that these prayers and these hopes, an indication of the value that the Holy Places have for so great a part of the human family, will strengthen the conviction in high quarters in which the problems of peace are discussed, that it would be opportune to give Jerusalem and its outskirts, where are found so many and such precious memories of the life and death of the Saviour, an international character which, in the present circumstances, seems to offer a better guarantee for the protection of the sanctuaries. It would also be necessary to assure, with international guarantees, both free access to Holy Places scattered throughout Palestine, and the freedom of worship and the respect of customs and religious traditions.[8]

Even in the changed circumstances of today, *In Multiplicibus* remains a fundamental statement of the Catholic Church's stand on Palestine. The encyclical affirmed that Palestine was of special, unrelinquishable concern to the Church; the Pontiff went out of his way to state that he 'had not failed to do his utmost' for the 'triumph of justice and peace' — a justice certainly not conceived in terms of the zionist policies which relied on achieving their goal through superior military force. *In Multiplicibus* also noted a particular concern for the Palestinians, 'homeless and driven far from their fatherland' — a definition that remains valid to this day. The issue of the Holy Places is dealt with at length in a later chapter (see pages 71-90). It is nevertheless worth noting here that the encyclical also demanded certain guarantees for the Holy Places 'scattered throughout Palestine', although priority was given to Jerusalem and its surroundings. Finally, there was a veiled warning that 'the Christian world could not contemplate with indifference the trampling of the sacred land by troops and the destruction of the Holy Places' — a clear though implicit attempt to press the Israeli government to accept the Bernadotte revision plan, viewed by Israel with the utmost hostility.

The document also implicitly traced the future direction of action on the part of the Holy See. In fact, as zionist military superiority was determining new realities on the ground, Vatican activities in regard to Palestine were to be increasingly focused on two issues: the Holy Places and the question of the refugees.

In February 1949 the Pope took the significant step of appointing Mons. Alberto Gori, the Franciscan custos who had signed the May 1948 appeal of the Catholic leaders in Palestine, as Latin Patriarch of Jerusalem. In the meantime, the UN having failed to implement its proposal on Jerusalem, various alternative plans were being examined by the Palestine Conciliation Commission. On 7 April the Israeli government informed the commission of its refusal to accept a territorial internationalization of the Holy Places. The maximum that it was ready to concede was a 'functional internationalization', i.e. international control over free access to the shrines and their conservation. One week later, on 15 April 1949 (Good Friday), the Pope issued yet another encyclical letter on Palestine in which he rejected Israel's position outright and exhorted Catholics the world over to pressure their governments 'by every legal means' to support the Church's demands for a return of the refugees to their homes and for a full territorial internationalization of Jerusalem and its surroundings.

The *Redemptoris Nostri* opens with an expression of the Pope's pleasure at an armistice having been agreed, although, he warns, it 'is not a true peace'. It goes on to say that the Holy Father has continued to receive pleas from innumerable refugees, together with 'many protests against the grave damages suffered by religious institutions and by churches and other places of worship, with very saddening devastations of Catholic institutions'. His plan for 'a true peace in that region so dear to the heart of every Christian' includes the following points:

1. an international regime for the city of Jerusalem and its surroundings, as already requested in the *In Multiplicibus*;
2. the safeguarding of all Holy Places, in every part of Palestine, with a guarantee of free access and of 'tranquil sojourn' for pilgrims, who should not 'find the Holy Land profaned by places of worldly and sacrilegious diversion';
3. liberty for all Catholic places of worship, charitable institutions and educational centres;
4. the conservation of all the rights that Catholics have acquired through many centuries in Palestine;
5. justice for those Palestinians driven from their homes through their return 'to rebuild their life in peace'.

The text reads:

> The Passion of our Divine Redemptor... calls upon the minds of Christians to turn with intense emotion towards that land which, through divine council and because it was the earthly homeland of the Incarnated Verb and witnessed his life and death, was bathed with his precious blood. But this year, the pious memory of those Holy Places profoundly saddens us because of their critical and uncertain situation.
>
> Already last year, through two encyclical letters of ours, we warmly exhorted you, Venerable Brothers, to convene public and solemn prayers in order to hasten the cessation of the conflict that bloodied the Holy Land, and obtain a just solution which would ensure full freedom to the Catholics and the conservation and tutelage of the Holy Places.
>
> As today the hostilities have ceased, or at least have been

suspended, following the armistice agreements recently concluded, we offer our ardent thanks to the Very High... But the suspension of the hostilities is still a far cry from the effective establishment in Palestine of tranquillity and order. In fact, we continue to be assailed by the laments of those who rightly deplore damage to and profanation of sanctuaries and sacred images, the destruction of peaceful homes of religious communities. We still receive the pleas of so many refugees, of every age and condition, who are forced by the recent war to live in exile, dispersed, in concentration camps, exposed to hunger, to disease, and to dangers of every kind.

...The situation of these refugees is so uncertain and precarious that it cannot be further prolonged. Therefore... we warmly appeal to all those who should provide for a solution that justice be rendered to those who were forced by the tumult of war to leave their homes and who desire nothing else than to reconstruct their lives in peace.

That which our heart and the heart of all Catholics wishes most ardently, especially in these holy days, is that the splendour of peace should finally return to shine upon that land where he who was announced as the Prince of Peace lived and shed his blood...

We have repeatedly invoked this true and lasting peace; and, in order to hasten and consolidate it, we have already declared in our encyclical letter *In Multiplicibus* that it would be highly opportune that for Jerusalem and its surroundings... there should be established an international regime...

Now we cannot but renew our declaration in this sense, in an invitation to the faithful, in every part of the world, to act with every legal means in order that their governments and all those who possess a power of decision on such an important problem, should be persuaded that the Holy City and its surroundings must be given an adequate juridical condition, the stability of which, in the present circumstances, can be ensured and guaranteed only through common accord between the peace-loving nations who are respectful of the rights of others.

But it is also necessary to provide for the tutelage of all the Holy Places, which are to be found not only in Jerusalem and its surroundings but also in other cities and villages of Palestine. Because no few of them have been, during the recent war, exposed to grave dangers and have suffered considerable damage, it is necessary that these Places... should be conveniently protected by a juridical statute, guaranteed by some form of international agreement or commitment.

We know how much our children wish to again undertake the traditional pilgrimage towards that land which the almost universal upheavals have long brought to a halt... But in order for this to happen it is necessary that all measures be adopted in order for the pilgrims to have access to the shrines, carry out without obstacles public manifestations of piety, stay there without dangers and preoccupations. Nor do we wish that the pilgrims should feel the pain of seeing that land profaned by places of mundane and sinful amusements...

Also the many Catholic institutions of which Palestine is full... should, as is their right, continue to practise without restrictions their activities... Finally, we must make present the necessity of guarantees for all those rights in the Holy Places which were acquired centuries ago and have always been defended with decision, and that our predecessors have solemnly and efficiently reaffirmed.

Exhort your faithful therefore to take ever more to heart the cause of Palestine and to present to the competent authorities their desires and their rights. And especially to implore with insistent prayer the help of him who guides men and nations. May God safeguard the whole world, but especially that land, bathed with the blood of the Divine Redemptor, so that above the hates and the rancours the charity of Christ should triumph as it alone can bring tranquillity and peace.[9]

Catholic opinion worldwide responded to the Pope's appeal, particularly in the US. In a statement issued on 27 April 1949, the American hierarchy reiterated Pius XII's call. Cardinal Cushing made a forceful plea along the same lines at a mass rally in Boston. The entire Catholic press carried the Pope's pronouncements, often accompanied by editorials giving prominence to the view of the Holy See. Cardinal Spellman, already the *eminence grise* behind much Vatican activity in regard to Palestine, co-ordinated the campaign in New York City. His 'right-hand man' was Mons. Thomas McMahon, the CNEWA's executive secretary, whose activities extended far beyond those of the official charitable mission which constituted his formal position. In fact, McMahon was seen by all parties at the time as more than just an executor of papal directives, i.e. he was instrumental in *formulating* Vatican policy and in securing strong support in the Holy See for his views.

On both the question of the Holy Places and that of the refugees, McMahon's stand was in the sharpest contrast to zionist policies and goals. His position on the first of these issues did not, however, conform to that of the major Arab parties either. He insisted on the need for the full restoration and growth of the Christian population in Jerusalem in order to prevent the shrines becoming mere 'museum pieces'. For Jerusalem to develop into a vital centre of Christianity, McMahon believed that a full territorial internationalization of the area was necessary: this would provide the climate and security for the growth of a Christian population. His actions behind the scenes, on the level of both national US pressure and international negotiations, were oriented in this direction.

In September 1949 the Palestine Conciliation Commission recommended a compromise plan to the UN: the Holy Places were to become the responsibility of a UN commissioner, backed up by a system of international courts to deal with disputes while the civilian administration of the Jerusalem area would be divided between Israel and Jordan. As the UN debate was about to begin, Australia presented a draft resolution seeking, instead, to reaffirm the international provisions of the 1947 partition plan. The Vatican explicitly supported the Australian initiative and this time succeeded in recruiting crucial Latin American votes to support its position. On 9 December the General Assembly in fact rejected the commission's plan, and adopted the Australian draft. The vote was warmly welcomed by the Vatican. However, opposition from both Israel and Jordan meant that the resolution was never implemented.

Mons. McMahon's stand on the question of the Holy Places, fully supported by the Vatican, was adopted on the basis of Christian interests. On the issue of the Palestinian refugees, however, the position of the Church in general, and that of active organizations such as the CNEWA and Mons. McMahon in particular, strongly supported the Arab stance. The Catholic press rejected from the outset the Israeli version according to which the mass flight of Palestinians from their homes was 'voluntary', and presented instead a picture of the 'exodus' much nearer to the truth than that described by any other sector of the media. Reports from the area explained clearly that native Palestinians had been forced to flee, and there were extensive descriptions of the miserable living conditions of the refugees.

In November 1948 the US Bishops Conference decided to send Mons. McMahon to Palestine as a special representative of the American hierarchy to investigate the question of the refugees. The mission received the Pope's full blessing. McMahon returned in March, 'Weeping at What he Saw', according to the headlines in the press. He reported on his visit to the Pope, and to the US Bishops Conference, and launched a vast emergency drive to collect funds for the refugees.

Although only a small percentage of the refugees were Catholic, the relief effort on the part of Catholics was impressive. Over 2,000 priests, nuns and lay workers volunteered for work in the refugee camps, where they set up rudimentary health, educational and other social services. Two hundred and sixty-eight pontifical centres were established in refugee concentrations, and by 1954 31,000 children were enrolled in pontifical schools. Out of a total of $10,391,000 in aid contributed by private agencies over $6 million came from Catholic Church sources. Even more important, the religious personnel were in many cases a constant source of testimony on the situation of the refugees, and thus directly or indirectly added their voices to the demand for more concerted action in favour of their repatriation. For lay opinion as well as for the Church hierarchy, the Christian stake in the Holy Land inevitably implied solidarity with the 'Arab refugees', as they were called at the time.

In June 1949 Pius XII set up the Pontifical Mission for Palestine to consolidate and strengthen worldwide Catholic relief efforts in the Middle East. Mons. McMahon was appointed president of the mission. His nomination was seen as evidence that the aid programmes to the refugees, beyond their immediate humanitarian goals, were also intended as the expression of a political trend on the part of the Vatican. But at the time, there was little the Vatican could do other than maintain its non-recognition (and thus non-legitimization) of Israel, continue its ongoing struggle for the internationalization of Jerusalem and keep up its material aid to the refugees.

4

Palestine and the Vatican's Cold War Policies: the 1950s

The years following the end of the Second World War were pervaded by the Cold War spirit. The Vatican, with Pope Pius XII still at its head, took a leading role in the anti-communist crusade. It adopted an unambiguously hostile attitude towards the fact that East European countries, all with large Catholic populations, had joined the Soviet orbit. In France and Italy the Church was the natural ally of US and related pressure groups in their fight against marxist parties. By the 1950s, with the Korean war at its height, the Catholic Church in both Europe and the US was fervently engaged in promoting a Cold War climate. In the US, Senator Joseph McCarthy and his witch-hunt became the political by-product (and symbol) of this trend, but Archbishop Spellman of New York was its major religious spokesman. In both Europe and Asia, Catholics who showed the least sympathy for leftist — or even progressive — positions were threatened with ex-communication and assured of purgatory after death. In Vietnam the local hierarchies, backed by the Vatican, were preparing the exodus of Catholics from the North (due to become independent) in support of the continuing French, and later American, domination of the South. Catholic assessments of international affairs were undoubtedly coloured by the East-West conflict.

In the Middle East, however, things were a great deal more complex. Notwithstanding strong US and Western support for the state of Israel, the Church generally shared the evaluation of one trend in Western diplomacy which considered the zionist state as 'atheist', 'socialist' and hence 'pro-communist'. Soviet support for the UN partition plan, the USSR's hasty recognition of Israel, the fact that a large part of the population had recently emigrated from East European countries, Soviet and Czech aid in the form of arms for the Israeli army in 1948-49 and the predominance of kibbutz members among the Labour zionist leadership all contributed to reinforce this conviction. By 1949 a Russian Orthodox archimandrite had come to Israel, and the Knesset passed a bill which gave the Soviet Union full control over all Russian mission property in the state. At the same time, the zionist state was thought to be a breeding-ground for 'dangerous left-wing developments', on account both of its own domestic trend, and of events at the regional level. Not only was there a suspicion that Israel offered a foothold for Soviet influence in the Middle East. There was also the related idea that secularism breeds socialism and communism, whereas religion is the latter's natural and most efficient enemy.

Ignoring the true theocratic nature of the zionist doctrine which lay just below the surface of the liberal/socialist/democratic appearances of the zionist state, and the opportunistic character of Israel's foreign policy at the time, the Church saw as its natural allies in the Middle East those regimes that could be counted upon to resist the inroads of communism. The suggestion was that of an alliance between Islam and Christianity — both natural enemies of communism — which could stem the tide of marxist influence in the region. In this context, the Church shared the view that the presence of hundreds of thousands of Palestinian refugees in the Arab countries, and the resentment provoked among the Arab masses by Israel's behaviour, would necessarily have a destabilizing effect on the anti-communist Islamic nations. This in turn would favour Soviet penetration and the rise of a leftist-tainted nationalism and/or an anti-Western fundamentalism. In addition to the suspected implications of similar developments on the global level of world politics, the Church's special concern also derived from a concrete preoccupation over the fate of Christian communities and Church interests and property throughout the Arab world. In the past, Christian, and particularly Catholic, churches had often — rightly or wrongly — been associated by the region's Muslims with Western colonial domination. Thus they were particularly vulnerable to attack in view of the Western governments' support for Israel. At the same time they also feared the consequences of social upheavals and of the strengthening of the secular/leftist trends in the Arab nationalist movement, to the detriment of their own economic and social interests.

Combined with humanitarian concerns, the question of the Holy Places and the traditional motivation of anti-zionism, these factors all helped to keep alive an ongoing tension between Israel and the Catholic Church. Although the Pope did not issue other official documents on the question of Palestine following the *Redemptoris Nostri* encyclical letter of April 1949, the Vatican's stand remained anchored to the positions expressed in it. Even though by 1950 most Arab states had signed armistice agreements with Israel, and negotiations between King Abdallah of Jordan and the Israeli government had culminated in a tacit agreement on the division of Palestine, the resulting situation was viewed by the Church — and rightly so — as one 'which, however, is not a true peace'. Vatican diplomacy continued to press Western governments, in particular the US, to meet not only Vatican demands for the inter-nationalization of the Jerusalem area, but also Arab demands regarding, first, repatriation of the refugees and, second, Israel's renunciation of the territories not specified in the UN 1947 partition plan, and acquired through the use of force.

The question of Palestine was thus the only issue on which there was a marked divergence between Vatican and official US policy, otherwise locked in a Cold War embrace and strategic alliance. On the other hand, the Church's position on Jerusalem influenced America's and the Western powers' stand on the issue, preventing the latter from according formal recognition to the Israeli government's transfer of the capital from Tel Aviv to Jerusalem. The Vatican's pressure in regard to the questions of refugees and borders was evidently less successful. That such pressure continued well into the 1950s, however, is revealed by the following entry made by Israel's premier and foreign minister Moshe Sharett in his personal diary on 10 November 1953:

I have been reading the report of Ya'acov Herzog [then the foreign minister's special adviser on Jerusalem as well as the director of the Jerusalem department at the Israel Ministry of Religious Affairs] on his conversations with [Mons. Thomas] McMahon, the emissary of the American Church, and in fact of the Vatican in the Middle East. *There is no change whatsoever in the Vatican's position, on the contrary it is even more rigid and intransigent.* The Vatican insists, and is not ready to accept any compromise, on the promulgation of three associated principles, all linked to one another, which it considers impossible to renounce: the 1947 borders, the repatriation of the refugees and the internationalization of Jerusalem. Both in the Middle East and on the international scene it is not afraid of giving the impression (due to these demands) of being an element that does not contribute to peace. It does not care if a return to the 1947 resolution means a new war, as long as such a return occurs.

...According to McMahon the total number of refugees amounts to 750,000... about 350,000 of whom... have found work, although very few have really integrated... The refugees' will to return is as resolute and strong as before.[1]

The Israeli government tried to allay the Vatican's hostility by taking various measures to repair the damage caused to Church institutions during the war, and by offering evidence of 'normalization' as far as the life of the Christian communities in Israel was concerned. However, Palestinian Arabs who remained within the territory which became Israel after the war were subjected to rigid, oppressive military rule. Arab villages whose inhabitants had been evacuated by force during the war were declared 'abandoned' and destroyed, so as to prevent the return of the refugees and establish Israeli sovereignty over their lands. At the very time that McMahon was visiting the area six villages were razed to the ground according to Sharett's notes.

The inhabitants of the two Arab villages of Biram and Ikrit in northern Galilee (some of whom were Christian) were also prevented from returning to their homes and lands. During his official talks, McMahon protested at these facts and the underlying policy. Ya'acov Herzog asked Christian leaders to support Israeli denials of maltreatment of the Arab population. Sharett wrote:

Herzog reports that the meeting, held in his presence, between McMahon and [the Greek Catholic bishop of Galilee] Hakim and others was very successful in contradicting his [McMahon's] claims in regard to the situation of the Arab minority in Israel.[2]

One would have to consult the McMahon papers to check whether the 'success' reported by Herzog really consisted in McMahon's having been persuaded by Hakim's pro-Israeli arguments. In any event, the extent to which the Vatican's stand was frustrating for Israel, and its effects on the latter's international relations, are revealed by another entry in Sharett's diary two days later:

At the Foreign Ministry we discussed Brazil's proposal that it should mediate between us and the Vatican in regard to the issue of Jerusalem. The painful point in that proposal is the suggestion that Jerusalem should be demilitarized on both sides of the [cease-fire] line. The army chief of staff [Moshe Dayan] is against it...

The principle of demilitarization has been mentioned in connection with guarantees for the immunity of the Holy Places in wartime by [Vatican secretary of state] Cardinal Tardini during a meeting in Rome with the Brazilian minister at the embassy [in Israel], Fabrino.

It is clear that the Vatican will not be satisfied with [international] control of the Holy Places alone. It probably considers the demilitarization proposal as a preparatory phase for the full territorial internationalization [of Jerusalem and its surroundings]. But the Brazilian proposal is that our agreement to demilitarization should be followed by the Vatican's recognition [of Israel] and an end to the conflict [between the Vatican and Israel]. This could mean UN recognition of Jerusalem as the capital of Israel. If this were so, the demilitarization would not damage our sovereignty but would help to reaffirm it. We all agreed on this interpretation. I added that a historic compromise between Jerusalem as the capital of Israel and Jerusalem as the city holy to Christianity must necessarily cost us a bitter price, and demilitarization is not too high a price...

This notwithstanding, I believe that it is still too early to enter into binding negotiations on this basis. It would be better to wait and see if after the UN General Assembly a change takes place in the currently frozen stance of the US on the issue of the transfer of the [Israeli] Foreign Ministry to Jerusalem. In this case, a compromise with the Vatican will become less urgent, although it will continue to be important. If no such positive change occurs in the US position, it will be even more important to try and arrive at a compromise with the Vatican through Brazil. For the time being we ought to play for time with Brazil: not responding negatively on demilitarization, but not hurrying to commit ourselves either. We will tell them that we are examining the matter and suggest that they could meanwhile obtain answers to our questions, e.g. do they see any prospect of Jordanian consent?[3]

The absence of any further reference to the subject would seem to indicate that the Brazilian initiative died there. A comparison of the two entries in the Sharett diary quoted above, made at a distance of two days from one another, suggests that the Brazilian government was trying to gain prestige as a mediator but that its proposals fell short of the Vatican's demands on Israel. These were not limited to the question of the Holy Places but were part of a 'package deal' that also included the twin issues of borders and the refugees. In any event, even as far as the Holy Places were concerned, it is doubtful whether the Vatican would then have agreed to trade recognition of Israel's sovereignty over Jerusalem for nothing more than demilitarization. The Israelis, on the other hand, although more clearly aware that it was the Vatican's veto that prevented them obtaining UN recognition for [West] Jerusalem as the capital, were reluctant to concede even a symbolic demilitarization in exchange, and were hoping to press the US into a disengagement from its commitment to the Catholic Church on this issue. This hope was not to be realized. The American embassy remains in Tel Aviv to this day, and official meetings between Israeli government leaders and American officials were held outside Jerusalem until well into the 1960s. But the Israeli leadership was obviously relying on its long-term policy of establishing *faits accomplis* to change the situation. Israel's politico-military establishment was already drawing up plans for the occupation, at an 'opportune moment', of the Jordanian-held part of Palestine, including Arab Jerusalem.

Throughout this period and until 1955, Catholic public opinion remained generally unsympathetic to, or critical of, Israel, although the question of Palestine generally received scant attention. These were tumultuous years throughout the Middle East, with one *coup d'état* following another at short intervals in various Arab states, while Israel engaged in military attacks on Palestinian and Arab villages across the cease-fire lines. Catholics throughout the region were divided into two groups: those who 'de-Westernized', becoming fully integrated into the national life of their respective countries and taking part in developments in the various nationalist movements, and those who, according to Fr G.C. Anawati, were 'frightened by the revolutionary trends' and isolated themselves in their communities, or preferred to emigrate. All pronouncements on Middle Eastern affairs were therefore made with the utmost caution, although it was often implied that the unresolved Palestinian question lay at the root of the crises.

Following the Egyptian-Czech arms deal of 1955, zionist campaigners launched their attempts to capitalize on the anticommunist policies of the Catholic Church. Efforts were made to persuade the Vatican, and the national Church hierarchies, to accord recognition to Israel as an essential element in protecting Western interests in the area against Soviet expansionism. These attempts, however, met with only limited success. If there was any temptation to recognize Israel on the part of the Pope, it was quickly dismissed.

On 26 October 1955 Sharett noted in his diary that:

Elias Sasson [Israel's ambassador in Rome] reported on an interesting development which seems to have taken place in the Vatican: according to a reliable source, the Pope might be ready — without changing his position on Jerusalem — to establish diplomatic relations with Israel... Elias will verify the matter through the bishop of Milan.[4]

The Sasson report must have been denied, or at any rate had no follow-up. There is no further mention of it in the Sharett diaries, nor is there any confirmation of the report from any other source.

Nevertheless political developments in the Middle East in the mid- and late-1950s led to a greater diversification of attitudes within the Church towards Israel on the one hand, and the Arab world on the other. Significantly, the tripartite aggression against Suez in October 1956 drew little if any response from the Holy See.

On the peripheral level, the American Church, which had never been pro-zionist, took comfort from its support of President Eisenhower's condemnation of the Suez aggression and his demand for a British-French-Israeli retreat from the position and areas occupied within Egyptian territory. None the less, perhaps for the first time a major division appeared in the US Catholic press between those who maintained traditional, firm anti-zionist positions and others who now, seduced by Israel's military collaboration with 'Western powers', accompanied their criticism of Arab policies with expressions of sympathy for the zionist state.

Thus for the syndicated diocesan weekly, the *Register*, 'although territorially minute, Israel has the potential to become a major bulwark of Western civilization in the struggle we are now waging with the communist empire'. The *Social Justice Review* also suddenly discovered 'that Islam is as powerful and dangerous a foe as it was centuries ago'. Other organs, such as *Pilot*, *Sign* and *Ave Maria*, considered, instead, that the crises in the Middle East ought to be traced to the West's lack of support for Arab nationalist aims in Palestine and that it was up to the West to make an effort to win back Arab friendship in order to block any further drift towards leftist or radical policies. A reversal of US policy towards the Jewish state was needed, and Christianity, inasmuch as it was associated with the West, had to exercise self-criticism: 'The great symbol of Christian arrogance in Muslim eyes was the imposition of the Jews on the Muslim world, and that, for which the Americans and the British are responsible, remains the fundamental obstacle to any reconciliation.' The two major US Catholic periodicals, *America* and *Commonweal*, adopted opposite stands. *Commonweal* said that action to counter Soviet influence in the Middle East should not involve a repudiation of Israel, and even went so far as to support Israeli requests for US arms and increased assistance. *America*, on the other hand, strongly urged withdrawing aid to the zionist state and a US commitment to unconditional support for the Arab world so as to restore its confidence in the West and 'save' the Middle East from communist domination.

Whereas the split emerging in the American church was between two trends, both of which were essentially related to imperialist thinking, the diversification of opinions and stands among European Catholics was becoming more complex and articulated. The division between pro-Israeli and 'pro-Arab' Cold Warriors doubtless existed here too, and was particularly evident at the level of political Catholicism in Latin countries such as Italy and France. A typical example was that of the differing stands on the issue found among Italian Christian Democrat leaders, some of whom had wholeheartedly approved of the anti-Nasser campaign and the tripartite attack on Suez in 1956, while others had openly condemned it. Meanwhile in France, the Algerian war provoked a crisis of conscience among Catholic intellectuals in regard to Third World issues, and hence also in regard to Palestine. Over the next few years, many of these intellectuals were to become actively engaged in aiding the Algerian struggle. This involvement would in the future mean that they were not susceptible to zionist rhetoric, and make them sympathetic to the Palestinian position.

In Italy, too, the Algerian conflict was having an effect. As of 1957 the Catholic mayor of Florence, Giorgio La Pira, was strenuously engaged in organizing the 'Mediterranean Colloquia' scheduled for the following year. These were billed as an attempt to achieve 'reconciliation between Algerians and French, Arabs and Israelis' through the establishment of a meeting-place for those cultural trends in Christianity, Judaism and Islam who were disposed to examine the possibilities of a dialogue. In fact, the Colloquia were conceived as an opportunity for Arab and Third World nationalist movements in general to make their voices heard in the West. La Pira's initiative was attacked by both the Catholic and the secular Right, and equally by the marxist Left. Although it did not receive the requested official blessing of the Vatican, it was nonetheless supported by some mainstream Christian and Catholic sectors of diverse orientations in Europe and the Middle East. Among others, it had the support of the Italian Episcopal Conference newspaper, *L'Avvenire d'Italia*. Even an initiative as mild as that of the Colloquia (which provoked a hostile reaction from zionist quarters) indicated, however, to what extent the Suez war had determined a (predominantly psychological) shift in public opinion in regard to zionist statehood in Palestine. Though generic and mostly theoretical, the use of terms such as 'the Arab-Israeli conflict' and 'peaceful solutions' indicated in fact that any residual hope or illusion that such statehood was an ephemeral or passing phenomenon had by now been swept away and eliminated. The Catholic Church and Catholic opinion were particularly marked by this discovery, which contrasted with much of their thinking in the past. On the other hand, following its massive military show of force, Israel was about to launch an offensive of a different kind, aimed at rekindling Christian feelings of guilt over the past persecutions of the Jews in Europe. This guilt complex, together with the budding seeds of liberalism and ecumenism, long suffocated under Pope Pius XII's authoritarian and conservative pontificate, were now to be channelled towards attempts at a theological-political legitimation of the Jewish state.

The death of Pope Pius XII in 1958 put an end to a 20-year-long pontificate during which the question of Palestine had been one of the Holy See's major, and often central, concerns. The Pope's policy on this question was fully in line with the traditional attitude of the Catholic Church, which opposed zionist statehood in the Holy Land. It was thus distinct from the great majority of Protestant Christianity, which saw political zionism as a 'messianic phenomenon', thereby providing a cultural and 'spiritual' cover for the self-interested policies of the Western powers, particularly Britain and the US. Once defeated on this question, the Vatican under Pius XII continued to view Palestine as an issue of supreme consequence for the Church. It repeatedly attempted to influence the conduct of its 'secular allies' on the issue, while denying legitimation to Israel and the *faits accomplis* achieved through the use of force. It is equally true that, in the attempts to implement its policy (intended mainly to conserve Christian influence in Palestine and throughout the Middle East, but also conscious that the prevailing injustice would inevitably damage this influence), the Holy See did not make full use of the only weapon available to it: a vigorous denunciation of the evil of discrimination and of the violation of law and justice, in a constant attempt to create a body of public opinion that would press for the restoration of an authentically moral world order. The Church's renunciation of its 'prophetic' role is a global argument which falls outside the scope of the present book. What should be stressed is that, notwithstanding its weaknesses, the pontificate of Pius XII, in line with that of its predecessors, laid down some basic rules and conceptions which the Church could not shake off in the following years, in spite of internal and external pressures. Pope Pius XII's three encyclical letters on Palestine, in particular, were landmarks in committing the Vatican to certain fundamental guidelines on the Holy Land (and its population, as well as the Holy Places).

5
Zionist Counter-Offensive: 1959–1965

Pope John XXIII threw the gates of the Catholic Church wide open onto the world, thus ending a long period of anathemas and dogmatic restrictions. It would probably be unfair to say that he closed them before the question of Palestine. The fact remains, however, that throughout his pontificate, from the end of 1958 to the summer of 1963, the 'Good Pope' was to refer specifically and publicly to Palestine only twice, both times in relation to the Holy Places and in a purely religious context. On 17 April 1960, in a letter to Fr Sepinski on the occasion of the 400th anniversary of the Franciscan Convent of the Holy Saviour of Jerusalem, the Pope appealed to Catholics to support a fund-raising campaign 'in favour of the Holy Places'. On 10 June 1962, during a Pentecost homily, a vague tone of longing and preoccupation seemed to underscore his words:

Whereas, on the one hand, we are happy to feel ourselves united in Christ in the hope of a good and fruitful apostolate that, like Jesus' passage through the streets of Jerusalem, meets with the acclamation of the crowds for his teachings and his miracles, on the other hand, we also have to declare our sadness in regard to evidence which... touches the heart.

We are thinking of the present conditions of the Holy Places where Jesus imparted his teachings: Jerusalem, Samaria, Judea 'and yonder to the ends of the Earth'.

Palestine, where his voice was heard, preserves hardly any trace of his earthly passage. It is from there that his teachings began to circulate, and the two Testaments resounded throughout the world... Jerusalem, the Holy City of the divine promises, the lands which surround it and the regions which border on it remain largely estranged from the sacred mission which was first announced to them.[1]

These words seem to betray remorse at the 'secularization' of the Holy Land, from a purely Christian/religious point of view, but nothing more. Following the Suez war and the Israeli retreat from Gaza and Sinai, the question of Palestine had entered a phase of political stalemate. The Arab world was going through another period of internal strife (the union and subsequent break-up of the United Arab Republic (UAR) between Egypt and Syria, a succession of *coups d'état* in Syria and Iraq) and the territory of Palestine — and Jerusalem — seemed definitively divided between Jordan and Israel.

During this period, there is no trace of any Arab activity aimed at encouraging the Vatican to take an interest in the fate of the Palestinian 1948 refugees, then mainly under Jordanian rule. When asked by the author whether this was the reason for Pope John XXIII's apparent lack of interest in an issue which only a few years before had seemed to occupy the foreground of the Holy See's activities, the Pope's private secretary and closest collaborator Mons. Loris Capovilla (later to become archbishop of Loreto) replied, after having conducted 'accurate, though rapid, investigations':

It is evident that the Palestinian question was also on the agenda during the 'quiet' years of the pontificate of John XXIII. The Pope dealt with it through the secretary of state; the State Secretariat dealt with it through the pontifical delegates in the Middle East. The documents are sealed in the Vatican archives.[2]

Mons. Capovilla also pointed out that Pope John's celebrated encyclical letter *Pacem in Terris*, with its general recommendations regarding respect for UN resolutions, international law and human and political rights as well as its condemnation of the use of force and of injustice, ought to be read as applying to the question of Palestine. Such an interpretation would imply a harsh judgement of Israeli policies of which, however, there was not the least sign in public gestures or pronouncements by the Holy See at that time.

On the contrary, Israeli manoeuvres were for the first time making some inroads, though partial and circumscribed, in the Catholic Church. In the late 1950s and early 1960s a widespread campaign to rekindle Western/Christian guilt feelings in regard to the nazi holocaust was undertaken by the Israeli leadership. It centred around the trial in Jerusalem of the nazi war criminal Adolph Eichmann. Far from aiming to stimulate a process of authentic catharsis related to the drama of the European Jews and to the perverted theological roots of 'anti-semitism', the zionists aimed to capitalize *a posteriori* on Christian responsibility for anti-Jewish persecution in the past in order to obtain a political legitimation of the Israeli state. Hearings at the Eichmann trial were partly geared to relaunching the controversy over Pope Pius XII's insufficient condemnation of nazi crimes during the war. While putting the Vatican on the defensive on this issue, the efforts of individual Catholics who had attempted to rescue Jews, sometimes at the risk of their own lives, were highlighted. Liberal Catholics (now in revolt at more than one aspect of the previous Pope's conservative and dogmatic pontificate) often fell for these arguments. They failed to see that what was actually, though subtly, requested of them was the legitimation of a political entity based on the dispossession of another people, the Palestinians.

In part, the zionist effort was given a head start by the personal history of the new Pontiff. During the Second World War Pope John XXIII had been apostolic delegate in Turkey. He was known to have intervened actively in favour of the persecuted Jews, and on various occasions in favour of those who had escaped the persecutions and were trying to reach Palestine through Turkey. His anti-nazi sentiments were beyond question, and his open, straightforward personality suggested a man who must secretly have been unhappy at his predecessor's reticence. After the war, he became apostolic nuncio in Paris, where he met with Jewish leaders and often expressed his sympathy for the victims of the holocaust. All this, together with his strong ecumenical convictions and his marked preference for reforms and for an understanding attitude towards modern ideas and trends of thought, made him, as Pope, an easier target for pro-zionist pressure from both inside and outside the Church. In practice, it cannot be said that Pope John XXIII actually ceded to this pressure on any concrete matter of policy beyond the opening of the Vatican to wider and more active contacts with representatives of pro-zionist Jewish organizations and even of the state of Israel.[3] The latter, however, played on the 'change of climate' to insinuate, at the level of public opinion, that a gradual change of policy was in the making.

The shift in climate, and the transformation of the attitude towards zionism into a bone of contention between conservatives and liberals inside the Church, became particularly evident in the early 1960s in two important Church communities: those in France and the US. In the former, developments were also connected with the post-war consolidation of large pro-zionist Jewish communities in important towns such as Marseilles and Strasbourg, as well as in Paris. In the US, on the other hand, the background was intensely political. It was bound up with the election to the White House in 1960 of John F. Kennedy as America's first Catholic president, on behalf of the traditionally pro-zionist Democratic Party.

In previous decades, the Catholic Church in the US, while not always identifiable with pro-Arab positions and often self-centred in its attitudes, had, with a few rare exceptions, been firmly anti-zionist in regard to the question of Palestine. Through its dignitaries such as New York's Archbishop Spellman, the apostolic delegate Cicognani, and Mons. McMahon, it had played a considerable part in shaping the Vatican's policies on Palestine. The hierarchy-controlled press had likewise managed to create an almost unanimous stance against zionist statehood in Palestine among its own public opinion. A concerted zionist attempt to encroach on this unanimity had not seemed to have much effect. Now, however, clear divisions were starting to appear. It was no accident that Bishop Cushing of Boston, the spiritual mentor of the Kennedy clan and formerly a man of decidedly anti-zionist views, 'opened up' to the pro-Israeli lobby. Among the new generation of liberal clergy, encouraged by the 'new direction' in the Vatican, Catholic personalities emerged who were to take openly pro-Israeli positions. Two of them, Mons. John Oesterreicher and Fr Edward Flannery, would play a particular role during the Second Vatican Ecumenical Council, where the issue of whether zionist statehood in Palestine should be given a theological legitimation by the Catholic Church was to be at the centre of a heated behind-the-scenes debate.

The convocation of Vatican II was decided upon by Pope John XXIII shortly after his election as Pontiff. It represented a huge project for the renewal of the Church at all levels, on the basis of a wide-ranging debate among all the currents of thought inside the Church. The news of its convocation sent waves of enthusiasm through Catholic communities in every part of the world. For decades the Church had seemed to be estranged from social, political and cultural developments. Now, however, liberals and conservatives, 'Third-Worldists' and 'Euro-centrists', rigid dogmatists and reformists were preparing for an ideological confrontation which, they felt, would determine future relationships both inside the community of believers and between the latter and the modern world. Among the wide range of theological, liturgical and disciplinary issues to be discussed, a particularly thorny issue was the theological reinterpretation of the role of the Jews *vis-à-vis* Christianity.

In fact, it was widely felt among both Jews and open-minded Christians that a critique and reform of existing theological concepts ascribing to the Jewish people a collective and permanent guilt in the martyrdom of Jesus were not only necessary but long overdue. Such traditional concepts, which depicted the Jews as a reprobate and accursed people which, having rejected Christ, was in turn to be eternally rejected by God, lay at the root of widespread, popular judeo-phobic superstitions and prejudices which had given rise to and facilitated the spread of racist ideologies, and the accompanying persecution, over the ages. It was felt by honest reformers that the elimination of such anachronistic concepts could bring about a liberatory catharsis and help prevent the resurgence of future, old or new, racisms based on religious premises.

Such a revision posed no few problems for the Church. Conservatives within the hierarchy opposed it on theological grounds related to the concept of the 'Chosen People' — Catholic tradition saw this mantle as having been spiritually inherited by Christianity as of post-biblical times. But the major problem was that of the immense pressure exercised by zionist lobbies aspiring to include a reference to the 'historical ties between the Jewish people and the land of Israel [i.e. Palestine]' in the revised texts. Obviously, the very mention of a relationship between the Jewish people and Palestine in terms of a 'divine promise' could then also be used to legitimize the zionists' occupation of the Holy Land and their claims to Palestine on religious and 'spiritual' grounds. Strong resistance among Arab Christianity to such a trend quickly developed, leading, among other things, to a tactical alliance between Arab Christians and the Vatican Council's conservative wing.

A statement on the Jews, to be presented within the framework of a schema on ecumenism, had already been prepared by the Secretariat for the Promotion of Christian Unity prior to the opening of Vatican II in 1962. Yet, due to the heated behind-the-scenes debate, it was not put on the agenda during the first session. Instead, a draft was distributed to the Council Fathers during the second session in November 1963. By that time Pope John XXIII was dead and had been succeeded by Giovanni Battista Montini, Pope Paul VI. Subsequently, the text was revised and detached from the original schema. Rephrased and reformulated, it was officially distributed to the Council Fathers on 21 September 1964. After discussion, an amended version was passed on 16 October 1965 as part of a 'Declaration on the Relationship of the Church to Non-Christian Religions', which also included a section on the Church's relationship to Islam. Some of the original sections dealing with a theology of the Jews were incorporated in the schema on the 'Doctrine of the Church' (*De Ecclesiae*). Here, too, the debate resulted in a compromise reflected in a succession of paragraphs that were later to give rise to contradictory interpretations.

Before dealing with the texts themselves, however, a few background remarks are needed. Pope John XXIII had been deeply marked by his experience of the Second World War. He was profoundly sensitive to all human suffering and wisely conscious that anathemas only perpetuated further injustice and sentiments of revolt. In his efforts to absolve the Jewish people from collective responsibility in the 'deicide' and to extirpate from Catholic theology all racist superstition and prejudice, he was undoubtedly inspired by his own 'prophetic' vision of a world in which racism and discrimination were no more in any way to be legitimized. His wish for the statement on the Jews to be incorporated into the schema on ecumenism could have meant that he conceived the whole idea perhaps less as a 'compensatory' gesture towards contemporary Jewry than as an act to redeem Christianity from past guilt, but above all from future errors. The fact that he placed the issue in the hands of Cardinal Augustine Bea seems to support this view. Of German origin, Cardinal Bea had been a long-time associate of Pope Pius XII. As such, he was on the one hand keenly interested in absolving the Church from accusations that it had not reacted strongly enough to the persecutions, and was therefore favourable to the proposed innovations. On the other hand, he was an extremely cautious and fundamentally conservative prelate, who firmly resisted all pressure designed to 'politicize' the issue. Such strong pressure undoubtedly existed, but in innumerable interviews and press conferences Cardinal Bea clearly and unambiguously rejected the zionist attempts to interpret the declaration's drafts as tending to legitimize the state of Israel. His assistants, such as Mons. Oesterreicher and Fr Cornelius Rijk, were to prove much less discreet.[4]

It was, however, on the 'practical' level that the Church, starting with the Pope and the Secretariat for the Promotion of Christian Unity, abandoned its traditional caution and opened the way to political misinterpretation of theological discussions. In fact, the dealings and behind-the-scene negotiations undertaken by the Church bodies were carried out invariably not with Judaism, but with zionist organizations and groups whose claim to represent world Jewry, and above all the Jewish religion, were at best a fraud. In reality, Judaism, especially Orthodox Judaism, was not remotely interested in dealings with the Church, or with Christianity in general, towards which its attitude remained that of abhorrence, or, at best, of traditional detachment. No rabbinical council or religious synod ever met to discuss a change of attitude. Nor, on the other hand, in view of the polycentric structure of Judaism, would such a convention have had any validity, unless perhaps approved *a priori* by specially sanctioned innovations. For Orthodox Jewry, which constituted the majority of Jewish believers, an easing of inter-religious tensions resulting from a theological change in the Church's attitudes might have been seen as encouraging mixed marriages and other forms of 'assimilation' by Jews living in a Christian environment. These were, and remain, anathema to Orthodox communities who believe that their survival in religious terms, in a world which has become increasingly secularized, depends on seclusion and exclusiveness. No few criticisms were therefore addressed from these quarters towards the 'heretic' Jews who had undertaken the negotiations with the Vatican.

By agreeing to deal with zionist organizations and groups such as the World Jewish Congress (WJC) (which handled most of the negotiations) and the American Jewish Committee, and even directly with representatives of the state of Israel, in regard to what were purely religious matters, the Vatican *de facto*, although repeatedly denying it, contributed to a 'politicization' of the issues at hand. In the first place, it legitimated the zionist claim to represent

Judaism and speak in its name. Second, by doing so, it actually negated its own claims to an 'ecumenical', interreligious dialogue. Third, it exposed itself to not-unjustified criticism from Arab quarters, concerned with the possible effects on the Vatican's political stance in regard to the question of Palestine. Finally, it perhaps inadvertently played into the hands of the zionist practice of creating *faits accomplis*. In a formal sense, the texts approved by the Vatican Council were far from satisfactory in terms of the initial zionist or even Jewish expectations. Yet the very fact that zionist and Israeli representatives were involved in negotiations over the various drafts, and the network of contacts they established with the Church hierarchy during the dealings, have served the zionist purpose of giving credibility to the idea of a 'change of climate' in zionist-Catholic relations among grassroots Christian public opinion, thus widening the arena for zionist propaganda and pressure in regard to Palestine. The first revised text of a theology of the Jews approved by the Vatican Council was incorporated into the schema on the 'Dogmatic Constitution of the Church'. Fundamentally, it reaffirmed the traditional view of the Jewish role as the *Praeparatio Evangelica*, i.e. as preparing, in its historical/biblical evolution, for the final revelation of Christ, in whom Jew and Christian were eventually to converge in the new People of God. But the last paragraph, dealing with the post-biblical Jewry, foreshadowed the later declaration:

> Finally, those who have not yet received the Gospel are related in various ways to the People of God. In the first place we must recall the people to whom the testament and the promises were given and from whom Christ was born according to the flesh (cf. Romans 9:4-5). On account of their fathers this people remains most dear to God, for God does not repent of the gifts he makes nor of the calls he issues (cf. Romans 11:28-29).[5]

Was the land of Palestine to be considered among the 'promises' and 'gifts' to the Jewish people from a 'non-repentant' God? The text does not say so explicitly, but in leaving such a delicate and fundamental question open, it granted the zionist lobby a weapon which, in the final analysis, could easily be directed against the interests of the native Arab population of Palestine.

The same concept was later incorporated into the statement on the Jews in *Nostra Aetate*. As already mentioned, of the four versions drafted in almost five years of discussions, the final version was the one which most clearly showed the marks of compromise between the opposing trends. Inevitably, therefore, the resulting text was somewhat of a disappointment to *all* parties. Admittedly, it repudiated 'anti-semitism', stressed the elevated position (from the Church viewpoint) of the Jews among the people who do not recognize Christ, and established that 'what happened in [Christ's] Passion cannot be charged against all the Jews, without distinction, then alive, nor against the Jews of today... [Therefore] the Jews should not be represented as rejected by God or accursed.' However, it refrained from a clear statement absolving the Jews from the charge of deicide and, above all, avoided any expression of remorse for the negative attitudes and consequent injustices of the past. In presenting the text to the Council Fathers, Cardinal Bea repeatedly stressed that, 'there is no national or political question here. In particular, there is no question of a recognition by the Holy See of the state of Israel, nor of the relations between the Arab states, Israel, and the movement called zionism'. In practice, however, the reference to God's 'gifts' and 'promises' would, in the course of the subsequent interpretative dialogical process based on the statement, be picked up and used by the zionists to their own advantage. Significantly, this implication was to emerge on the eve of, during and after the 1967 war. As a zionist writer has put it:

It was the trauma of the Six-Day war, when the mere silence of Catholics threatened the disruption of all further dialogue, that moved Catholics to realize the vital position of contemporary Israel in the religious consciousness of the Jews. If Catholics were to continue a dialogue with the Jews, they would have to understand this aspect and integrate it in their understanding of Jews and Judaism. Consequently, Israel, as a topic of study, began to appear on the agendas of dialogical workshops and lecture series.[6]

As usual, zionist manoeuvring was subtle, far-sighted and tactically shrewd, and in any case relentlessly constant. In the early and mid-1960s, when the *Nostra Aetate* was discussed and approved, only the inner circle of the politico-military zionist establishment knew of the preparations for a war intended to expand Israel's domination over the entire territory of the 'promised land', and beyond. There is nothing to suggest that Catholic liberals in general had any inkling of the trap that their 'Jewish' interlocutors were preparing for them. Both Pope John XXIII and Pope Paul VI would undoubtedly have presided more cautiously and scrupulously over the proceedings and contacts had they had any suspicion as to the true political motive behind 'official Jewry's' apparently innocent plea for a theological revision. Moreover, it was not until some ten years later that the '1967 trauma' was unmasked, thanks to documented disclosures, among others from highly qualified Israeli sources. These revealed the meticulous preparations since the early 1960s, in terms of preparing public opinion in addition to political and military justifications, for what was to be an extremely carefully planned attack.

Such developments could not, at the time, have been predicted by the majority of the Council Fathers. Yet they were certainly perceived, at least intuitively, by the representatives of Arab Christianity present at the assise. Their struggle to limit any advantage to zionism from the current debate was partly successful, in that, contrary to zionist ambitions, the statement on the Jews did not explicitly recognise the 'mystical link' between Judaism and Palestine, nor mention as relevant the creation of the state of Israel. In the climate of renewal prevailing in the council, however, their efforts were seriously hampered by their tactical alliance with the ultra-conservative groupings, whose position on this specific issue was determined solely by their attachment to anachronistic theological concepts and by their opposition, on principle, to reform.

The declaration was approved on 16 October 1965. Two days previously, Cardinal Bea explained again to the Council Fathers the methods employed for its discussion and revision, insisting that every effort be made 'to ensure that the exclusively theological nature of the document should be clearly expressed, in such a way as to exclude by every possible means a political interpretation thereof'. The cardinal specifically pointed out that:

> there is no reference here either to zionism or to the state of Israel... No interference by any authority or political logic can be tolerated... We must pursue the renewal of our attitude towards the Jewish people in the spirit of the charity of the Lord even at the risk that someone, for his own political ends, might *abuse* the declaration.[7]

The final version of the statement on the Jews contains three main points:

1. Recalling the Jewish origins of Christ and the heritage transmitted to Christianity by the Jewish people, the council recommends the mutual study and research of the respective theological patrimony and deplores the injustice committed everywhere against human beings, and in particular the hatred and persecutions of the Jews. The union between the Jewish people and the Church is part of Christian aspirations. Therefore in the catechism, in prayers and in daily speech, it is important not to present the Jewish people as reprobate and not to attribute to it [responsibility for] what was perpetrated during the Passion of Christ.

2. God is the father of all men, therefore respect must be paid to the opinions and doctrines of all (this applies to the Muslims as well).

3. Every form of discrimination is condemned. Therefore the very foundation of any theory that establishes differences between man and man, and between peoples, in regard to human dignity and the ensuing rights, must vanish. All honest men, and Christians in particular, must refrain from any act of discrimination or persecution for reasons of race, colour, social condition or religion.[8]

Needless to say, future events could not have been foreseen by those who drafted and approved the declaration. A 'spirit of prophecy' was decidedly absent from this session of the ecumenical assise. Otherwise it might have inspired at least the representatives of Arab Christianity to drop their hopeless battle against the statement as such, and attempt not only to reinforce its anti-racist and anti-persecutory contents, but also to demand that it be accompanied by a request for a parallel and equally strong commitment on the part of the Jews to the same concepts. Such a daring and imaginative initiative might have had far-reaching implications in its effects on world Judaism, and encouraged a break with zionist rhetoric.

Against the intentions of its instigators, the statement on the Jews in the *Nostra Aetate* thus laid the foundations for closer Catholic-zionist relations. This was especially true in those countries where large zionist-dominated Jewish communities pressed the Catholic episcopates to undertake joint activities. National Secretariats for

Catholic-Jewish Relations were created in Europe and the United States. In training courses for Catholic teachers, conferences, lecture series, seminars and workshops, many of them jointly sponsored by Jewish organizations, the theme of the state of Israel was at least insinuated and later began to appear openly on the agenda. Inevitably, a network of pro-zionist lobbies began to develop in and around the Church.

Not surprisingly, the same cannot be said to have resulted from that part of *Nostra Aetate* which deals with relations between Catholics and Muslims. There are many different reasons for this: theological, political, practical. Suffice it to say that, on the one occasion in which an attempt was made to approach the question of Palestine through the channel of Muslim-Catholic relations, it ended in failure (see pages 133-5).

The zionist counter-offensive aimed at achieving Catholic legitimation for Israel was particularly intense at this time. No account of these years would be complete without mention of Paul VI's pilgrimage to the Holy Land in early January 1965.

In announcing the forthcoming visit the Pope was careful to refer to religious motivations only: the inspiration needed for the final session of the Vatican Council, the ecumenical significance of his meeting in Jerusalem with Greek Orthodox Patriarch Athenagoras, and so on. And throughout his tour of the Holy Places, Paul VI in fact scrupulously adhered to this declared goal. His allocutions, interwoven with Evangelical quotations, never contained the slightest reference to the local or regional political situation. A reading of his speeches today, at a distance of some twenty years, leaves no doubt, moreover, that the major aim of the pilgrimage to the Holy Places (the first undertaken by a Roman Pope in the history of the Church, and thus assured of maximum coverage in the media) was to reassert the interest of Christianity, and of Catholicism in particular, in the question of Jerusalem and Palestine, on religious grounds. Without explicitly saying so, but through every biblical reference used, Paul VI thus affirmed a continuity with the interests which lay at the centre of Pius XII's exhortations and policies on the Holy Land. Indeed, the present Pope had been a close collaborator of Pius XII, especially at the Secretariat of State.

But Paul VI was too experienced a diplomat not to realize that even his extremely brief and formal meeting with the Israeli authorities (above all, with the Israeli president Zalman Shazar), and the fact that the major part of his pilgrimage took place in Jordanian-controlled territory, would inevitably lead to speculation regarding future relations between Israel and the Holy See. The Vatican firmly denied that any change had taken place or was imminent in these relations (or 'non-relations'), and the Pope's collaborators and spokesmen repeatedly underlined the impact made on the head of the Church by his meeting with the masses of Palestinian refugees in the Jordanian-controlled part of Jerusalem. An impression nevertheless prevailed among Vatican observers that the ice had somehow been broken and that the Church's uncompromising rejection of zionist statehood in Palestine had come to an end. With time, both versions would prove correct. In the following years, contacts would become more frequent than in the past, and Israeli officials would be received in audience by the Pope. But tension remained, and although the tone and language employed towards Israel would be 'softer', the Holy See was not to go back on its basic and long-standing conditions for the formal recognition of Israel.

6
The 1967 War
and its Aftermath

As Israeli troops moved to attack Egypt on Monday 5 June 1967, Pope Paul VI addressed the following message to UN Secretary-General U Thant:

> We are profoundly concerned and saddened by the turn of events in the Middle East. As we pray that divine mercy may preserve this region and the world from suffering and destruction, we appeal to you to make every effort in order that the United Nations may prevent and stop the conflict. In the name of Christianity, we express the fervent hope that if the situation should worsen — and we are firmly confident that such a sad eventuality will not take place — Jerusalem will be declared an open and unviolable city by reason of its particularly sacred and holy nature.[1]

On the same day, the Vatican secretary of state Cardinal Cicognani addressed the following message to Mons. Zanini, apostolic pro-nuncio in Cairo, for transmission to the Egyptian government:

> Profoundly saddened and anguished by the news of the battles raging along the frontiers; highly concerned, at the same time, about the possible repercussions and consequences, the Holy Father appeals from the depth of his heart to the sentiments of humanity and the responsibility of the president of the United Arab Republic and to his prestige among the Arab peoples, so

that he may find the means, in honour and justice for all, to stop... the armed conflict. In this way these populations will be saved from suffering and the world will escape the new danger of a bloody scourge.

His Holiness implores the parties to the conflict to silence their resentment and their challenges and to make an effort to find a solution to the crisis by having recourse to the international bodies. He expresses the hope that all will be concerned to preserve the Holy Places by declaring Jerusalem an 'Open City'. He prays to the Almighty that the precious gift of peace will not be irrevocably compromised.

I request the pontifical representatives in Lebanon, Syria, Iraq and Jordan to carry out similar moves through the respective governments.[2]

Simultaneously, Cardinal Cicognani sent a telegram formulated in identical terms to Mons. Sepinski, apostolic delegate to Jerusalem, for transmission to the governments of Israel and Jordan.

On 6 June, in response to the Pope's call, the French Episcopal Council issued a declaration which was read out during a specially organized mass at the church of St Germain des Prés by the bishop of Paris, Mons. Marty:

To the rattle of arms we oppose the cry of conscience. We reject the law of violence and the fatality of war. In face of the unleashing of passions and explosions of racism, we call for the fraternity of peoples. Through God, peace is possible among men... We ask all those charged with governing the peoples to do everything possible to re-establish and consolidate peace.

In the land of Christ, men are fighting, suffering and dying: may Christ give us mercy and free us from the scourge of war.[3]

The following day the UN Security Council approved a unanimous resolution calling for the immediate cessation of hostilities. On 8 June Paul VI addressed the following note to the presidents of Egypt, Israel, Iraq and Syria, and the king of Jordan, imploring them to respect the UN decision:

Motivated by the duty of our ministry, animated by an equal concern and love for all peoples, anguished by the idea of the suffering, mourning and ruin which the war brings upon individuals, families and nations, we address ourselves to Your Excellency (or Majesty) as to the other heads of the states which are parties to the conflict, and in God's name we implore you to accept the request of the United Nations for an immediate cessation of the fighting, so that the violence of arms can be replaced by confident, reasonable and honourable negotiations and the much longed-for peace may return to these regions.

We assure Your Excellency (Majesty) that we invoke the Almighty to assist you in the grave decisions that you must make, and in the choice of ways which will compensate you with the gratitude of all those who possess humane sentiments.[4]

On 11 June the Pope pronounced yet another allocution on the Middle East war, in front of the crowds assembled in St Peter's Square for the Sunday Angelus mass:

On what must our attention focus if not on the situation in the Middle East, and in the world as it is after the recent conflict?

We must thank God for the cessation of hostilities, but we cannot but be saddened by the suffering and devastation, and above all by the passions, the dangerous ideas and the rancour that the war leaves behind it.

Peace is blessed in the souls but who knows for how long? We must work, hope and pray *in order that the conscience of peace be founded upon justice and not upon force*, that it be inspired by reason and not merely by calculations of self-interest. Our human and Christian sense must once more be engaged to alleviate the suffering left behind by the war.[5]

On the same day, the *Osservatore Romano* published a front-page editorial, entitled 'Jerusalem':

While in the Middle East, thank God, the war draws to an end, the news reaching us from Jerusalem merits reflection. Once more the Holy City has been the theatre of tragic events. Once more blood has stained the stones that another blood dedicated to peace.

The facts of these last days have thus added another link to an already long and cruel chain.

Newspapers, press agencies and eye witnesses all agree that the battle of Jerusalem, although it lasted only a few hours, was a harsh one. The number of victims is not yet known. It is known, however, that mortars and artillery from both sides hit the city, causing casualties and damaging, among others, the Cathedral of the Dormition, near the Senacullum in the Israeli zone. In the Arab zone, the Church of St Anne, built by the Crusaders, has been devastated by grenades. The Holy Sepulchre was under fire for a long time. The great Mosque of Omar has not come out undamaged either.

All this has to be stated with regret, all the more so because the destruction of these last days could have been predicted. It could have been avoided were it not for the fact that, over the last two decades, goodwill has failed, whereas it could have contributed to make of ancient Zion once and for all a spiritual island in which all men, of all languages and all races, could have come to live together as brothers and honour in God Almighty the Father in whose name we are all brothers.

The public has perhaps forgotten it, but those who follow international problems will remember that on 29 November 1947, at the moment at which the United Nations decided upon the creation of the state of Israel, it also decided that Jerusalem and its surroundings should constitute a *corpus separatum* under international rule. One year later, on 11 December 1948, the 22nd session of the General Assembly nominated a Conciliation Commission charged with preparing a plan for this *corpus separatum*. The commission prepared an 'arrangement' which proposed the institution of a simple 'international control', thus abandoning the principle of 'international rule' as it should be and as it had been requested by the General Assembly. The General Assembly, convened at Lake Success in December 1949, did not deem it its duty to retain the 'arrangement' in question. It affirmed, on the contrary, that the fundamental principles of the resolution of 29 November 1947 'constituted a just and equitable way to regulate the question' and subsequently ordered the council to set up the statutes of Jerusalem.

The resolutions concerning the internationalization of Jerusalem were later confirmed by the United Nations but unfortunately they were not implemented.

The situation of Jerusalem — and anyone who has visited the Holy Places in these last three years knows how dramatic it is — remained as it was after the 1947-48 conflict, at the moment of the creation of the state of Israel. It is well known that peace was not achieved then, but rather an armistice. A demarcation line, not a border, was established which corresponded to the positions occupied by the two parties at the moment of the cease-fire. The old city remained in the hands of the Arabs; the new in the hands of the Israelis. And an absurd barrier had [thus] been established, remaining inviolable for 20 years and giving rise to many bloody incidents every year while this state of affairs, so contrary to the natural order, continued.

This line was broken by the violence on 6 and 7 June this year, bringing new mourning and new ruins.

Was all this necessary? Was it inevitable that there should be new killing?

It is with profound sadness that we invoke the three encyclical letters and the exhortation of Pius XII published between May 1948 and November 1949, imploring for Jerusalem and other Holy Places in Palestine a stable peace, founded upon an international regime which would ensure the protection of the Holy Places and free and unhindered access to them for all.

Jerusalem could have been, materially and spiritually, a meeting-place and not a symbol of contradiction and of hate, a cause for periodically repeated violence.

Has such a perspective been overtaken by the facts? Not at all. At the moment at which arms are silenced and in which negotiations are about to begin — even though, as the world expects, they will be long and difficult — Jerusalem will again become a burning issue, if it is true, as the press unanimously reports, that no one in the Arab world wants to believe that the city is 'lost' to Islam.

On the other hand, while no one challenges the strength of the spiritual and historical bonds which link Judaism and Islam to Jerusalem, one cannot forget that the Christian world considers Zion as its unique, its great Holy Place. It is there that Israel and Ishmael can meet and retire in meditation. But it is also there that Christians must be able to meet without offending their monotheistic brothers. And in the ever-living reality of the Old Testament, the terrestrial road to redemption follows the way traced by the steps of the Son of Man.[6]

For the first time since the 1950s, the Vatican had thus taken up again in regard to Palestine the two traditional themes of 'peace with justice' and the internationalization of the Holy Places. In fact, Paul

VI went even further, and demanded for Jerusalem not only the status of an 'international regime' but also that of an 'Open City': 'a shelter for the non-combatants and the wounded, a symbol of hope and peace for all'.[7] He returned to the theme during a consistorial allocution on 26 June, this time including among his concerns the question of the Palestinian refugees:

> As of the first announcement on the conflict, we implored the governments, through our representatives, to avoid whatever might aggravate the situation. Once hostilities broke out, we tried, in vain, everything possible to prevent destruction and the suffering of the populations and to save at least Jerusalem from the evils of the war, demanding that all interested nations accept the UN-decreed cease-fire. After the conflict, we have taken steps to heal, at least a little, the many wounds. We renew our appeal: grave questions remain to be solved — *the condition of the Palestinian refugees, especially, profoundly saddens us. The question awaits a remedy through a just and generous solution.* The difficult and complex territorial problems which have long awaited a reasonable solution and which the armed conflict has now highlighted so tragically, must be dealt with without delay, for the good of humanity itself. The Holy City of Jerusalem must remain forever that which it represents: the City of God, a free haven of peace and prayer, a meeting-place where all reach elevation and concord, with its own guaranteed international statute.
>
> ...We believe that it would be illusory to wish to construct peace upon any ground other than that of justice, of the recognition of human rights, of the acceptance of others' rights in the same way that one's own rights demand recognition. Peace and concord are inseparable from justice and truth.[8]

Shortly before pronouncing this allocution the Pope received the text of the following declaration by Cardinal Léon Etienne Duval, archbishop of Algiers:

> At the moment in which the painful problem of the Near East is the subject of debate at the Extraordinary Assembly of the United Nations, all Catholics, in union with all believers, must address God, in prayer, so that a just solution, the foundations for a true peace, may prevail.

The human implications which characterize this problem are so grave that no one can remain unmoved by them, in particular as far as concerns the fate of the multitude of Arab refugees, Muslim and Christian, whose tragic situation has remained unsolved for [the past] 20 years, and whose number has now been increased.

Equally grave is the fact that recent events threaten to compromise the efforts at mutual comprehension which is a duty for all believers at the present time, in which materialism threatens to submerge the world.

The difficult solutions which are to be established must not consecrate [the principle] of hegemony through the use of force. Any form of racial hatred should be banished from the attempts to reach a just solution. It is now imperative that the Palestinian question, for far too long avoided by the highest international bodies, should be faced and dealt with at its roots.

A land [that is] sacred to the three great monotheistic religions, Palestine must be the land of reconciliation. Among the symbols of this reconciliation are the Holy Places of Judaism, Christianity and Islam, which must be placed above all national rivalries in respect of the acquired legitimate rights.

In this grave hour, it must be remembered that nothing is impossible for God. May the prayers of all converge towards him whose wisdom should inspire the leaders of this world and give them the necessary light and courage, in order that the demands of international morality be respected and that justice, especially towards the Third World, should progress.[9]

Even as the Pope was appealing for a peaceful solution based on justice for the Palestinians, Israel was preparing for a future annexation of the West Bank and Gaza, including East Jerusalem which was effectively annexed to Israel. The mass deportations and destruction continued for most of 1967,[10] with entire quarters of Arab Jerusalem demolished and their inhabitants driven away. On 22 July 1967 Paul VI received a delegation of Egyptian Christian dignitaries who handed him a letter from Cardinal Patriarch Stephanos I Sidarouss of Cairo and a message from Patriarch Cyrillus VI of Alexandria, the two major spiritual leaders of the Coptic-Catholic and Coptic-Orthodox communities in the Middle East.

After thanking the Pope for his 'fatherly solicitude for the suffering people in recent weeks', Stephanos I went on say (20 July):

The recent clashes and raids which have caused new victims among the civilian population show that fire continues to smoulder in the ashes, so that the consequences cannot be foreseen.

Moreover, the incomplete and contradictory news — which are [sic] in contrast with the line always followed by the Holy See concerning the problem of Jerusalem and the Holy Places — make us anxious and give us a great deal of concern.

In our country, Egypt, there is the unhappy impression that, because of certain misunderstandings, the West may have forgotten the traditional ties of friendship which have united it with this country through the centuries.

That is why we believe that the voice of Your Holiness, as the universal Father of the great human family and thanks to the moral authority which you exercise everywhere, could contribute still more towards relieving the sufferings caused by the conflict, clarify the situation, and arrest every decision likely to aggravate the conflict.

Your Holiness recently declared that you are disposed to undertake any steps, at no matter what time and even if beyond the traditional protocol, to urge men of goodwill to work for a solid and durable peace.

We are persuaded, Most Holy Father, that if your voice could be heard one more time, among either the responsible people of the international organizations or heads of state in the countries concerned, to find the way to an equitable conciliation, it would surely meet with the approbation and unanimous consent of peoples throughout the world.

Although we completely understand how delicate and complex the present situation is, we nevertheless know that no circumstance has ever prevented Your Holiness and your predecessors of venerable memory from making the voice of justice and truth heard — *as His Holiness Piux XII did on the occasion of the occupation of Belgium, Luxemburg and the Netherlands.*

The whole world knows that Your Holiness is closer than ever to those who suffer. That is why every intervention, suggestion or appeal to the principles of justice and humanity which you judge opportune and useful... will bring encouragement and the hope of better days to this people.[11]

There was a dramatic, pressing sense of urgency, almost of despair, in this message. However, the Pope responded in cautious, diplomatic terms to the cry of alarm raised by the Egyptian Copts:

> We are particularly grateful for your having exposed to us your thoughts on the question of Jerusalem.
>
> We wish to say that we were engaged, within the bounds of our possibilities, to prevent the Holy City becoming a prey, at the moment of danger, to the war regime. And in making that attempt we were conscious of the aspirations of all those who consider her the City of God and a symbol of peace and reconciliation.
>
> This is one of the reasons why we think that the Holy Places must be protected by guarantees such as modern international law should offer for the defence of everyone's rights.
>
> You would understand without difficulty that we consider it our duty to concern ourselves with the Holy Places and to adopt a vigilant attitude towards them, in particular in the very difficult present situation. The Holy See will always act in favour of the Holy Places, in such a way that the legitimate interests of the various parties concerned should not be prejudiced.
>
> We should like to assure Your Holiness that we continue to be very near, through our aid and our sympathy, to all those who have been victims of the recent conflict. As we have said on many occasions, our great desire is that the delicate and complex questions which are on the agenda at present may reach a useful and at the same time honourable and peaceful solution which would reaffirm the rights of justice and the needs of equity, and would re-establish among all the sons of one God ties of veritable fraternity.[12]

Paul VI's response revealed a balanced attitude towards the parties in the conflict, not going beyond expressions of solidarity with its — unnamed — victims and hope for 'a just and peaceful solution'. To dissipate the 'incomplete and contradictory news' in regard to Jerusalem, however, the Holy See issued a new memorandum clearly intended to show that the Vatican did not accept Israel's occupation of the Arab part of the city as a valid solution to the status of the Holy Places. This memorandum was sent to all the parties in the conflict as well as to the UN:

1. The recent events in the Middle East have again given rise in all its sharpness to the problem of the Holy Places of Palestine, a problem always followed by the Holy See with the keenest attention.

2. In view of the threats that the conflict has brought to the Holy City of Jerusalem, His Holiness Pope Paul VI dispatched, as of 5 June 1967, a message to the secretary-general of the United Nations, and, at the same time through the pontifical representatives in the United Arab Republic, in Jerusalem, in Lebanon and in Syria, to the governments of these countries, with a view to obtaining an immediate end to the hostilities.

3. Unfortunately, on that very day, the battles were extended to the city of Jerusalem. The material damage caused to the sacred buildings has not been, thank God, too serious, the main one concerning the Church of the Dormition on Mount Zion, and that of St Anne which houses the grand seminary of the Melchites.

4. The Holy See, in its permanent concern to preserve the area in which are to be found the majority of the Holy Places, then embarked on a further step. It intervened with many governments in order to ensure that members of the UN Cease-fire Observers Commission and the consuls in Jerusalem should be charged with assuming, on behalf of the UN and in view of ulterior decisions, at least the control over the Old City of Jerusalem. But this plan was soon negated by events.

5. Receiving numerous pilgrims in the Vatican during the general audience of Wednesday 7 June, the Holy Father expressed his view on the subject of the Holy Places in the following terms: 'And we shall add another word to repeat our most earnest wish that the Holy Places may be safeguarded. It is in fact of the utmost concern for all the descendants of the spiritual race of Abraham — Jews, Christians and Muslims — that Jerusalem be declared an "Open City" and that, disengaged of any military operation, it should be spared all war actions such as have already hit it and even more still threaten it. We address an urgent appeal, in the name of all anxious Christianity, and, moreover, in the name of the entire civilized humanity, to the governments of the nations in conflict and to the heads of the battling armies: that Jerusalem should be saved the state of war, that the Holy City should remain a shelter for the defenceless and wounded, a symbol of hope and peace.'

6. Meanwhile, immediately he was informed of the unhappy condition of the populations hit by the conflict, the Sovereign Pontiff dispatched the president and the vice-president of Caritas Internationalis and ordered the dispatch of many planes carrying urgent food and medical aid.

7. On the eve of the debates at the General Assembly of the United Nations on the Middle East crisis, the Holy See's UN observer acted in favour of the Holy Places, according to instructions. It is partly thanks to his efforts that the question of Jerusalem was inserted in the so-called 'Latin American' resolution, which, however, did not receive a sufficient number of votes to be approved.

8. The Holy Father returned to the question of Jerusalem in his allocution in the secret consistory of 26 June 1967. He expressed himself in these terms: 'The Holy City of Jerusalem must remain forever that which it represents: the City of God, a free haven of peace and prayer, a meeting-place where all reach elevation and concord, with its own internationally guaranteed statute.

9. In this spirit, the Holy Father dispatched to the Holy Places, at the earliest possible opportunity, a prelate from the Secretariat of State, Mons. Angelo Felici, then under-secretary of the Sacred Congregation for Extraordinary Ecclesiastical Affairs, with the aim of monitoring the exact state of affairs and the provisions of the local activities. The on-the-spot observations by the envoy of the Holy See have given him a better understanding of the complexity of the problems concerning the Holy Places in the present situation and the difficulty of finding a solution capable of reconciling and satisfying all points of view.

10. The Holy See, in accordance with what it sees as its right and duty, will continue to take an active interest in the Holy Places, whose nature is sacred not only to the Christian world but to the whole great human family. In particular, it will not cease to intervene in view of securing a special statute for the Holy Places, with guarantees of a nature such as would deliver and protect them from the vicissitudes of the political situation.[13]

In response to zionist accusations that 'as long as the Holy Places were under Jordanian domination the Holy See had accepted the situation as a *fait accompli*, but now it proposes an international statute in order to take Jerusalem away from its new occupiers', the *Osservatore Romano* published an editorial on 6 July, firmly recalling the various phases of the Vatican's commitment to the idea of Jerusalem being transformed into a *corpus separatum*. After quoting from three of Pope Pius XII's encyclical letters on Palestine, thus reaffirming their validity as policy statements for the Church, the editorial went on to say:

> The transformation of Jerusalem into a *corpus separatum* serves the cause of peace and that of the reconciliation of peoples related to each other by blood and by affinity of origins but divided by the hate that violence feeds and reinforces.
>
> And let no one say that the question should be considered as overtaken by events, as one Italian paper declared yesterday. [So far is it from being] 'overtaken by events' that the president of the United States himself, in a recent declaration published on 28 June, demanded that the Israeli government undertake no unilateral action in regard to the status of Jerusalem.
>
> Jerusalem is a Holy City, above all for the Christians; but equally for the Muslims and the Jews. The reasons that led the United Nations to decide upon the internationalization of the city remain valid, because they are based on truth and justice. The fact that Jerusalem is no longer 'divided' does not change anything in reality. At this moment it is simply and only a factual situation. The internationalization of the city in which the most important Holy Places of the three religions re situated would greatly contribute to an easing of tension.
>
> ...In the course of these last years the word 'internationalization' has been misinterpreted: it has been identified with a tutelage or surveillance of each Holy Place in order to preserve its integrity, to ensure that the traditional ceremonies take place unimpeded, [and] that free access be secured for all.
>
> This is not the internationalization foreseen by the United Nations in 1947 and indicated by the Holy See as a condition for peace [and for] reconciliation among various peoples, as a meeting-place free of all mortgage, be it light or heavy, of any decision of a unilateral nature which could oppose tomorrow that which is promised today.
>
> On each occasion which presented itself over the past years, the Catholic Church has not ceased to insist — [both] publicly and through diplomatic channels — on the necessity of establishing the *corpus separatum*. Today it expresses the wish that the spiritual and universal values of Jerusalem be taken into

careful consideration and that, for the sake of peace for all, this crucial problem be faced and solved.[14]

Paul VI was to return to the subject in his Christmas allocution on 22 December 1967, though in a somewhat minor key:

The recent resolution of the UN Security Council to send a representative of the secretary-general seems to us to constitute a first positive step in the search for *a solution which, if it is to be lasting, will have to be just and reasonable.*

As can easily be imagined, we have been solicited by various parties, and by authoritative persons, to prevent the conflict turning into a peaceless cease-fire, full of hatred and of potential future claims, equally damaging for international life, and to act in a way that would help to reach a solution... especially concerning the question of the [Occupied] Territories, [which are] a theatre of bloody clashes.

We hope and trust that the United Nations initiative will receive the sincere support of all those responsible and lead to fruitful results.

[Both] *the old and the new refugees deserve particular attention.* Their problem aggravates the regional crisis. To these poor and helpless victims goes our sympathy and also the aid which we have never failed to provide.

As to the Holy Places, 'a question [that is] still unresolved due to a state of affairs which is very complex and whose exterior aspect is visible to all':

Suffice it to say here that, in accordance with its duty towards Christianity, the Holy See has paid great attention to the possible initiatives concerning this grave problem on the international level. We have discussed it with the qualified leaders and we have asked that inquiries be made to reach at least the beginnings of a solution. We have informed the Orthodox and Anglican hierarchies of our intentions, as well as the governments who have relations with the Holy See, and the General Secretariat of the United Nations.

Overall, the question presents, in our opinion, two essential aspects which are indivisible. The first concerns the Holy Places as such... to guarantee the freedom of worship, the respect, the conservation and the access through special immunity as part of a statute... which should be guaranteed by an international organization, taking into account the historical and religious aspects of Jerusalem.

The second aspect regards the free enjoyment of the legitimate religious *and civil rights of the persons, institutions and activities of all the communities living in the Palestinian territory*.[15]

Throughout 1968 the Pope, aided by Vatican diplomacy, continued the frenetic efforts to transform the aftermath of the 1967 war into an opportunity to achieve a lasting solution to the stalemated question of Palestine. After the war, Jerusalem and its surroundings, with its Holy Places and Christian communities, came under unilateral Israeli control. The government effectively annexed East Jerusalem to Israel, its statements leaving little doubt that it would avoid all future compromise on the subject. Nevertheless Arab opposition to the internationalization of the Holy City remained adamant. Combined with Israeli intractability, this Arab attitude (based on what was seen as the exclusive right to an 'Arab Jerusalem') made the situation extremely complex, and the Vatican's mediation highly arduous. As in 1947-48, the Holy See's preoccupation with a solution to 'the problem of the refugees' — although genuinely motivated by humanitarian concern as well as by the farsighted understanding that no true peace could be achieved in the region unless the Palestinians who had been driven from their homeland were allowed to return — was also connected to this problem. By firmly insisting on the refugees' right to return, the Vatican was undoubtedly also hoping to enlist some Arab support for its international pressures in regard to Jerusalem. The Arab regimes' inability to transcend their own rhetoric, however, played straight into the hands of the zionists whose goal was the 'Judaization' of Jerusalem.

On Christmas Eve 1968 the Pope again devoted a central part of his allocution to the situation in the Middle East, and in particular to that of the 'old and new' Palestinian refugees, 'whose homeland is... the homeland of the Saviour'. For them Paul VI demanded 'dignity, their rights and their legitimate aspirations', i.e. a peace based on the 'irreplaceable principles of justice and solidarity':

Almost every day there are clashes, acts of violence, attempts, reprisals. This is a source of anxiety and sadness for us because it reveals the agitation of the spirits, ever more dense with rancour, adversity and passions which prevent a serene and generous vision of reality which could lead towards the search for an honourable solution.

Authoritative voices have made themselves heard, pointing out the gravity of the present situation. In fact, while there is talk of an arms race, and while the decisions taken by the highest international bodies are waiting to be implemented and encounter difficulties, *a just and definitive solution must urgently be found for... the refugees, both the old and the new, whose miserable condition saddens us profoundly.* And [in the absence of such a solution] the populations despair... of a peaceful solution.

...Faithful to our mission to serve and bring peace, inspired by our love *for all the populations, especially the ones who suffer most, whose homeland is this blessed land which was the homeland of the Saviour, we do not cease to recall the irreplaceable principles of justice and solidarity which constitute, also for these populations, the substance of a real peace and a guarantee for the dignity, rights and legitimate aspirations of all.*

We cannot, however, pass over in silence the great responsibility which will weigh upon the nations, even those which are not directly related to these regions, if they succumb to temptations of egotistic calculations, or the will of power or supremacy, if everything possible is not done to heal a situation [that is] so dangerous for millions of persons, and — God forbid — for humanity itself.[16]

Inside Israel, there was growing irritation with the Vatican. At the same time, hopes for a peace agreement were fading. In particular, the Holy See's hope of seizing upon the opportunity of renewed international activities and negotiations to achieve a positive solution for the question of Jerusalem was losing ground. True, its efforts were to continue, but the strong initial impulse, and the optimism which seems to have animated the Pope's interventions in this phase, were already declining. Israel, on the other hand, needed to keep tension alive in the region in order to force the international community to accept Israel's gains in the 1967 war.

On 28 December 1968 Israeli commandos raided Beirut airport, destroying 13 Lebanese civilian aircraft. The pretext was that of retaliation for a Palestinian attack on an El Al plane at Athens airport. But behind it lay the spearhead of the long-planned zionist aim of destabilizing the only Christian-dominated Arab country. The very same day, Paul VI sent a telegram of support (destined to infuriate the Israelis still further) to Lebanese President Charles Helou:

> We wish to express to Your Excellency our affliction at the grave event which took place in Beirut. We strongly deplore violent acts from wherever they come and which cannot but aggravate a situation already so tense.
>
> Formulating the wish that Lebanon, in conformity with its noble traditions, will not be dragged into the way of violence which would render impossible a peaceful solution of the present controversies, we exhort all men of goodwill to pursue without discouragement their efforts, assured of our moral support.[17]

On 6 January 1969 Dr Nahum Goldmann, president of the WJC, whose executive was meeting that week in Rome, was received, at his request, by Paul VI. According to a communiqué issued by the WJC, but *not* in the Vatican press, the Pope:

> expressed to Dr Goldmann his esteem for the Jewish people and his wish that opportunities for collaboration between the Church and the Jewish people, as between the Church and other peoples, may be created in the service of the causes common to humanity. While expressing his displeasure at the misinterpretation of his recent statement on events in the Middle East, His Holiness underlined his opposition to all acts of violence... and expressed his support for all means leading to the achievement of a peaceful solution founded on justice which would permit all the peoples of the Middle East to live together in peace and harmony.[18]

On 31 August 1969, during a Sunday general audience at his summer residence at Castelgandolfo, the Pope pronounced yet another anguished allocution on the situation in Palestine. A few days earlier an Israeli Jew of Australian origin, later declared to be 'a mentally deranged tourist', had attempted to burn down Jerusalem's al-Aqsa Mosque, one of the holiest shrines of Islam.

> Our thoughts go today to the Middle East, to those lands which cannot but retain our attention, being so related... to the history

of civilization and of Christianity, and most especially to the Holy Land.

They are in such a state of tension and conflict that it is to be feared that other conflagrations might follow the very short war of 1967...

Meditating upon the events of these days, we have the impression that instead of advancing towards peaceful solutions, events seem to reveal, under certain aspects, those dark symptoms which preceded the unleashing of the Second World War, exactly 30 years ago.

May God wish that it should not be so! We wish, however, to implore the governments and the peoples — as did then our venerated predecessor Pius XII who, alas! was not listened to — to do everything in their power to prevent, while there is still time, the first rash steps which could push [the situation] towards the tragic path of new wars and new ruins.

...*A recent episode which we strongly deplore has been added in these last days to the painful series of perturbations in this region. As you know, we refer to the fire which has damaged the Mosque of al-Aqsa*, in the Holy City of Jerusalem, where the places sacred to all three monotheistic religions are located. This time it is the Muslims who have been hit in their religious sentiments and who have been moved by the devastation of a place dear to the tenacious and jealous veneration of millions of men. We understand their bitterness, but we hope that it will not aggravate the situation in the Middle East, already so tense and delicate, and we express the wish that it will not degenerate into further violence or into more ferocious hate. This could damage even further the cause of justice and peace which is a supreme duty for all.[19]

The previous day, Cardinal Duval of Algiers had also made a statement relating to the attack on al-Aqsa:

The criminal arson attempt on the Mosque of al-Aqsa provoked indignation in all human consciences: all sincere believers felt that they themselves were under attack because the contempt for the Holy Places constitutes a threat to the faith in God and can benefit only atheism or religious indifference. The Christians, especially, have suffered from this hateful act, because the Mosque of al-Aqsa, due to the memories associated with it, is the symbol of the spiritual links which unite the Church of Christ to the Muslim community. May the prayers of the faithful rise to God that the Palestinian question find a solution in line with the requirements of justice and of international law and in order that Jerusalem may truly become the city of peace.[20]

Pope Paul VI also sent a message deploring the arson at al-Aqsa to King Hassan II of Morocco on the eve of the Islamic Conference convened in Rabat on 22-24 September.[21]

Two weeks later, however, on 6 October 1969, the head of the Church received Israeli Foreign Minister Abba Eban at the Vatican. An official communiqué issued after the meeting and published in the *Osservatore Romano* of 6-7 October 1969 explained:

> During the conversation, which lasted about one hour, the Holy Father and the minister reviewed the various problems related to the present situation in the Middle East, notably: the problem of peace and understanding between the peoples of this region, the questions — particularly close at heart to His Holiness — regarding the refugees, the Holy Places and the sacred and unique character of Jerusalem, as well as those regarding the different communities who live in the Holy Land.
>
> His Holiness thus had the opportunity to confirm and illustrate the positions of the Holy See on these problems, positions exclusively inspired by the superior motives of religion and human and Christian charity, as by the desire to see a just and lasting peace in the Middle East as well as a fraternal and fruitful co-existence in the recognition and the respect of (religious and civil) rights for all.
>
> The Holy Father listened with great attention to what the minister amply explained to him about Israel's efforts to achieve such a desired peace and on the different questions cited above, as well as on the situation of the Jews in the Arab countries and other problems of a humanitarian nature.
>
> His Holiness renewed — as he has always done in his talks with the representatives of other people engaged in the conflict — the offer of his full and cordial collaboration.

According to Georges Huber (writing in *La Liberté* of 11-12 October 1969):

the visit has not changed the Holy See's attitude in regard to the

recognition of the state of Israel, at least not for the time being...
However, if the Holy See does not recognize Israel *de jure*, it
recognizes it *de facto*, as is demonstrated [on one level] by the
audience accorded to Mr Abba Eban and, on another level, by the
meeting between Pope Paul VI and the president of Israel, Mr
Zalman Shazar, during his pilgrimage to the Holy Land in
January 1964.

Judging by the Pope's later pronouncements, however, Abba Eban
does not seem to have made much headway in his talks at the
Vatican.[22]

On Christmas Eve 1969, in what had by now become a tradition
with Pope Paul VI, the Pontiff again devoted a part of his speech to
Palestine:

On this Christmas Eve we cannot forget the peoples of the
Middle East, and in particular those of the land where the angels
chanted in the Holy Night, in the land which witnessed the
childhood, life and death and resurrection of our Saviour.

We think of all those who suffer daily from the conflict, *of the
refugees who remain without a home and a homeland.* We address our
good wishes to them and we shall not fail to continue to give
them our paternal aid.

We wish to address a special thought to the Christian
communities of the ancient land of Palestine, whose problems
and difficulties of all kinds cannot but affect us intimately. The
ranks of the faithful to Jesus have been and are illuminated in that
sanctified land by his prophecy and his sacrifice. This situation
gives us cause for reflection and leads us to the following
question: will not the majestic and beautiful religious shrines
which evoke the life of Christ one day be deprived of the living
presence of their ecclesiastical communities?

Thus on this Christmas Eve, *the bitter considerations in regard to
peace which has not been achieved are associated with the thought of the
Church in the Holy Land.* Both stimulate our action and our prayer
to Christ Our Lord.[23]

A week later, on New Year's Eve, the Pope addressed the
following message to all heads of state in the Middle East, including
the Israeli president Zalman Shazar:

Vatican City,
31 December 1969

The peace which we invoke today for the entire world, together with all men of goodwill, is particularly desired by us for those regions which constitute the birthplace of very ancient civilizations and which are sacred for those grand religions for which peace is one of the most sublime values.

To all those responsible for the nations at present in conflict we wish to address our wishes and our encouragement, echoing those of all the peoples, that they unceasingly and with wise and generous determination explore all ways to reach a just and peaceful solution, to be achieved through loyal negotiations.

Our special thoughts go out to all those who suffer from this conflict, *and especially to the refugees. We are confident that their fate and the recognition of their legitimate aspirations for justice and humanity* will be taken into account by those who are responsible for this very painful situation.

May the Very Supreme implement the prayer that we address to him today, as a new year dawns — [one] that we hope will bring peace and concord to all nations.[24]

On 16 January 1970 the Israeli president responded to the Pope's appeal with vague phrases, saying Israel was inspired in its 'search for peace' by 'its spiritual traditions' and 'painful historical experience'. However, a solution to the problem of the Palestinian refugees was possible only *after* the establishment of 'a lasting and constructive peace' based on 'fraternal and fruitful co-operation' with the Arab states, and on a solution to the alleged 'persecutions from which the remainder of the great Jewish communities suffer in the Arab countries'. In other words, Israel was adamant in its refusal to recognize the rights of the Palestinians. Its 'solution' was founded on the idea of a dispersal of the refugees throughout the Arab world within the framework of an exchange of populations, and, if need be, of compensation. Thus the response to Paul VI's plea, in conformity with the Israeli interpretation of UN Security Council resolution 242,[25] was totally negative.

By now, however, it was no longer possible to ignore the Palestinians. Notwithstanding its chaotic nature and its often erratic methods, the Palestinian Resistance was beginning to hit the headlines. Christian awareness could not lag far behind.

7
The Holy See and Palestinian National Rights: 1968–1972

As we have seen, until the mid-1950s and as of the 1967 war, the question of the 'legitimate aspirations' of the Palestinian 'refugee populations' was one of the Holy See's major concerns. Indeed, in terms of emphasis and frequency in its public pronunciations, it was second only to the issue of Jerusalem. The rise, as of 1968, of the Palestinian Resistance posed new problems for the Vatican. On the one hand, it underscored the failure of all the 'goodwill' efforts, in particular those undertaken by the Church leadership itself, to find a peaceful solution to the problem. It also proved the correctness and farsightedness of the Holy See's warnings as to the eventual consequences of the international community's ignoring the centrality of the Palestinian question. On the other hand, terrorism was starting to become an issue.

Events in Jordan in September 1970 ('Black September'), when the Jordanian army drove out the Palestinian Resistance after violent clashes, put the Vatican in something of a quandary.

At his general audience in the Vatican Basilica on 23 September 1970 the Pope made the dramatic announcement that he would refrain from delivering his usual general audience because of the 'state of affairs in the Middle East... so grave and threatening that we cannot speak... about anything else with a quiet heart':

We think of the thousands of dead and wounded, and the hostages who still do not know what their fate is to be; we think of the many new ruins and the unbearable sufferings of the people. But even more we are afflicted by the mark of civil war

91

which has been added to that long and implacable conflict. Our pain is worsened by the increase of bitterness of spirit, and the aggravation of the dangers. These can take on enormous proportions and generate incalculable catastrophes.

...So far as we are able, we will aid every attempt at finding a reasonable solution to the crisis. And above all, together with you and with the Church, we will call down God's mercy and assistance.[1]

Four days later, Paul VI said:

It is not our custom to speak about things which do not concern us; but the events in these regions seem to assume an importance, at least [a] potential [importance], for the peace of everyone. Moreover, these events have their focal point in the land of Jesus which is very dear to us and to all Christianity. Therefore we consider it our duty to reflect on the seriousness of the situation and to show our compassion for the victims of the conflict, which this week has assumed violent and bloody forms which are very distressing. We have also tried to give help and we are grateful to those who... are trying to bring the conflict back to a truce and to negotiations.

We wish to say once again that only feelings of justice, charity and peace guide our concern and interest and that neither material interests nor selfish calculations inspire our action. We... have no other aim but to help the weak, the civilian population and above all the refugees, to defend human rights and to persuade all sides to lay down their arms and to try to find wise, honest and peaceful ways of resolving this complicated and tragic happening.[2]

The apologetic tone used by the head of the Church to express thoughts and sentiments which one would normally have deemed not only a religious leader's privilege, but also his duty, suggest that the Holy See had come under fierce attack following Paul VI's 'intervention' four days earlier.

Six months later, however, the Pope again had recourse to a public address, this time calling attention to the source of his authority and to the Holy See's particular interest when the issue of Palestine was on the agenda. On Sunday 14 March 1971, he launched a renewed and far from apologetic appeal to international organizations, to world leaders, and to those who could influence public opinion, to do all in their power to 're-establish peace'.

At present we are mere spectators of the unhappy situation in the Far East and in the Middle East; but we cannot remain indifferent or silent. Our heart is stricken at the violence, suffering, destruction and threats of these theatres of war. We take upon ourselves, because of our ministry, the anxieties and aspirations of the peoples involved in these unending conflicts...

It is necessary to reaffirm the rights of the various nations to their independence, legitimate integrity and the inviolability of their territory. All parties must effectively respect agreements entered into to ensure a peaceful order in territories which are now theatres of war. *The greatest consideration must be given to the refugees and the population who are victims of the abnormal conditions caused by the present conflicts.*

Speaking more particularly of the situation in the Middle East, which would require a much longer discourse, we feel that we must protect a grave right and duty, not merely in our own name but also in that of the whole of Christianity. We refer to the recognition of the special claims on the Holy Places in Palestine, of the continued presence of Christians in that troubled land, and of the status of Jerusalem, where one cannot deny a very special convergence of a multitude of historical and religious rights.[3]

At that time, the Rogers Plan[4] was under discussion and UN mediator Gunnar Jarring was shuttling back and forth between Middle East capitals. For the Holy See, the new opportunity to raise the question of a final settlement for Jerusalem was not to be missed. Thus the Pontiff's speech was followed by an unequivocal editorial note in the *Osservatore Romano* which expressed the mounting concern felt by the Church hierarchy over developments in Jerusalem, where non-Jewish communities found themselves ever more circumscribed, and their very existence put in question. Under the headline 'Jerusalem and Peace', the paper wrote on 22 March 1971:

The recent negotiations initiated by [UN mediator] Ambassador Jarring between Israel, the United Arab Republic and the other Arab states are at present — we hope temporarily — blocked. As efforts to revive the negotiations are under way, the cease-fire expired on 7 May. It is the wish of all that the hopes raised in the last few months will not again give way to the violence of war.

In this context, while each party tries to acquire a better negotiating position... the fate of Jerusalem remains an extremely delicate point.... Any political agreement on all other questions might find this issue an insurmountable obstacle, a stumbling-block, if the sense of justice of those responsible does not suffice to impose respect for the rights of the minority communities who today feel that their very existence and development are threatened by a policy which seems designed to suffocate them little by little, and if Jerusalem does not become the city with which the believers of the three great monotheistic religions, Jews, Christians and Muslims, may identify.

This is why attention must be directed at the present moment to the problem whose consequences, if not brought under control in time, may cause irreparable damage to the cause of peace in the Middle East.

The unhappy division of the city which followed Great Britain's withdrawal from Palestine in 1948, and the non-implementation of the United Nations resolutions regarding a constitution for Jerusalem and its surroundings as a separate entity (*corpus separatum*), i.e. as a city which should belong to all, has had its sequel in the Israeli occupation of the 'Arab part' of the city during the war of 1967, an occupation which the Israeli parliament, under the pretext of 'unification', quickly transformed, in practice, into an annexation. This [Israeli] will to establish its sovereignty also over the Arab part has subsequently been repeatedly reasserted through legislative measures, fiscal decrees and town-planning provisions which impose on Jerusalem an ever more unilateral and particularist character, to the disadvantage of the non-Jewish population (Muslim and Christian), which is forced, under the pretext of urban expansion, to limit its residence to ever narrower and more restricted spaces, and ultimately to look elsewhere for a future which it feels can no more be realized in its own country.

As is already the case with the plan for the internationalization of Jerusalem, the resolutions of the UN Security Council and General Assembly, ordering that the 'status' of Jerusalem not be touched and that all measures taken against this status be cancelled, have not been respected. *It remains true, however, that these resolutions testify that a very grave state of affairs is being established illegally, on the basis of the logic of* faits accomplis.

The expropriation measures [decreed by Israel] suffice to give an idea of the radical manner in which a character that does not conform to its historical and religious nature and to its universal vocation is being imposed on the city. In January 1968 300 acres of land were confiscated in the Mount Scopus area and are already largely built up with Jewish residential quarters. In August 1970 another 1,200 acres were confiscated in the Arab zone of Jerusalem and around the city, in order to implement the 'Greater Jerusalem' plan. Another plan for the Old City of Jerusalem is under consideration, according to which about 6,000 Arabs will be displaced and numerous buildings confiscated.

One cannot but feel a profound apprehension in the face of such grave changes. Even in Israel itself these plans have given rise to well-founded criticism, and not just from a town-planning point of view. The Jerusalem press has equally reproached the government for having prepared and implemented these projects hastily and in contrast with the peace initiative outlined by US Secretary of State [William] Rogers, in order to affirm through [the creation of *faits accomplis*] its scarcely veiled intention to establish permanent Israeli sovereignty over the whole city. These intentions have been given official confirmation by the Israeli minister of urban planning, who has declared explicitly that 'the plan is aimed at Judaization'.

On 21 February, despite open opposition by technicians and architects, the Jewish municipal council of Jerusalem approved the Ministry of Urban Planning's plans for the construction of peripheral neighbourhoods. Thus a true girdle of buildings will rise on the hills encircling the Holy City, comprising 20,000 dwellings for some 75,000 Jews.

Unfortunately, these projects and their implementation do not favour peace. Those who really work for a definite peace in the Middle East must not remain indifferent. Together with other projects which the press is beginning to hint at, they tend to confirm the need for an international body which would truly guarantee Jerusalem its particular character and the rights of its minority communities.

The article in *Osservatore Romano*, undoubtedly inspired by the

Vatican State Secretariat, became the object of fierce attacks in the
Israeli press. The *Jerusalem Post*, labelling it 'cheap journalism',
attributed the information contained in it to 'Arab Christian sources
hostile to Jerusalem', and went as far as to suggest that 'no
authorized Vatican personality had endorsed it before publication'.
In particular, the mention of the internationalization of Jerusalem,
'whereas the question is only that of recognizing the rights of all
the religions in the city', raised an uproar in Israeli government
circles. The Vatican replied indirectly to the Israeli attacks through
the major French Catholic paper *La Croix*, in an article on 2 April
1971 entitled 'Compassion without Justice in Jerusalem means
Nothing but Folklore':

> It must be recognized that the Arab population of Jerusalem has
> been systematically, scientifically, rigorously pushed to leave
> Jerusalem, [whether] through offers of emigration (without a
> right to return) to Australia, Canada and elsewhere (and many
> young people have had to accept these offers, the future being
> barred for them in their own country), or through more radical
> methods such as the confiscation of lands and homes, forcing
> them to swell the ranks of the refugees and those of the 'dis-
> placed'.
>
> Through a series of *faits accomplis*, undertaken in violation of
> the rights of the people, the city has been emptied little by little
> of its Arab population, without the victims' complaints or
> protests being able to find any support.
>
> And it is to be feared that when the Israelis decide to consult
> the population on its feelings towards the annexation, there will
> no longer be an Arab majority in Jerusalem, because the exodus
> of the Arab population will have been met by a corresponding
> increase in the imported Israeli population.
>
> It must be understood, therefore, how sensitive and critical
> Arab opinion inevitably is in this issue, and why it sees certain
> elements as collaborating with Israel when they appear to co-
> operate with these... policies.

Under the headline 'Sympathy for the Palestinians', the
Osservatore Romano of 15 April 1971 reported the Pope's Good
Friday address of 9 April. In it, the head of the Church had returned
once more to the question of the Christian communities in
Palestine, who 'are in need, more than ever, of our spiritual, moral
and material support'.

On 24 June, in an allocution to the College of Cardinals, Paul VI further affirmed:

Then there is the Middle East, where the Holy Land is at the centre of the conflict. We cannot but look to that Holy Land with passionate interest and with a sort of prophetic instinct, to wish it peace, true peace. It is clear to all that this peace cannot be the fruit of a military victory; it is also clear that there can be no simple formula for attaining it. It is the complexity of the situation that renders it extremely delicate and difficult.

...Besides the protection of the Holy Places, there is also that of the Christian population and the interest also of the non-Christian Arab and Jewish population of the region, so that they may be enabled — despite a composite character — to live there in freedom and normality. Then there is the question of Jerusalem. It seems to us, we repeat, that it is in the interest — and hence it is the duty — of all, that this city, enjoying as it does a unique and mysterious destiny, should be protected by a special statute, guaranteed by an international legal safeguard, and that it should thus be enabled to become, no longer an object of implacable controversy and endless dispute, but a meeting-place of concord, peace and faith. To this end we are seeking to carry out — in a spirit of respect and friendship — a work of persuasion...[5]

As this heated debate between the Vatican and Israel was under way, the Holy See remained in close contact with US diplomacy over the negotiations. On 6 May Paul VI accorded an audience to US Secretary of State William Rogers, on his return from a tour of the region's capitals. The prolonged discussion concerned:

the crisis in the Middle East and the efforts to advance peace negotiations. The Holy Father [according to the official communiqué] expressed his serious hopes that the initiatives undertaken would lead to positive results and bring about a definite solution in justice and peace for all the peoples of that region. *Special mention was made of the question of the refugees, and that of the Holy Places.*

Once again, the two issues were mentioned almost in the same breath. According to press reports of the time, the Pope was not overly optimistic as to the prospects of a solution.

In summer 1971 the situation of the Palestinian Resistance in Jordan became ever more critical. By the end of the year, the remaining Resistance bases which had survived the 1970 Black September battles were to be liquidated, and the movement's militants forced to move to Lebanon. At the same time, in the Israeli-occupied territory of Gaza, Israel crushed the Resistance still active in the refugee camps.

On 22 July the leaders of the Christian communities in Algeria issued an 'Appeal for Justice in the Middle East', calling for solidarity with the Palestinian cause. The appeal was signed by the Catholic archbishop of Algiers, Cardinal Léon Etienne Duval, by the president of the Reformist Church (Protestant) of Algeria, Pastor Pierre Rochat, by the director of the Christian Communities Committee of Algeria (CCCA), Pastor Jacques Blanc, and by the Catholic bishops of Laghouat, Mons. Jean-Marie Raimbaud, and of Constantine, Mons. Jean Scotto:

> In these days in which in the midst of an almost total silence the Palestinian people, already deprived of its territory, endures ever more cruel sufferings, we, the Christian leaders of Algeria, appeal to the believers to devote their prayers fraternally to the men and women martyred today in their flesh and in their dignity, and call upon them to show their solidarity with a people threatened by despair. We further call upon all human conscience to remember the responsibility of each person towards the construction of peace. We affirm that peace in the Middle East cannot be based on the extermination of the Palestinian people but requires the recognition of the existence of this people and the participation of its representatives in the determination of its future.[6]

Two months later, during the meetings in Rome of the Holy Synod of the Bishops called by Paul VI to debate the theme of 'Justice in the World', the voice of the Palestinian cause sounded through the allocutions of three major exponents of Middle Eastern Catholicism. On 21 October Cardinal Patriarch Stephanos I, speaking for the Coptic Patriarchal Synod of Egypt, demanded that the Church take a stronger stand in favour of justice in Palestine:

Christians everywhere should be concerned about the conflicts and injustices prevailing in the country where Our Lord lived. The evils there have repercussions on all neighbouring countries. Expulsions and confiscations of property, even massacres of innocent people, are rampant in the land where Christ lived.

Little has been done to alleviate the plight of the refugees in a country where in the past Muslims, Jews and Christians lived peacefully side by side. Now the Jews assert that 'might is right'...

The pilgrims who go to the Holy City of Jerusalem are shocked by the changes they find since their last visit. New buildings replace the old from where masses of people have been expelled, where there used to be sacred places and all that can recall Christ's life is obliterated. There is no real freedom as long as every believer — whether Christian, Muslim or Jew — is not free to visit the places he holds sacred.

Justice should concern itself first of all with the weakest, the oppressed and exiles. But if the oppressed of the Second World War now become the oppressors, will this help establish peace? The problem of the East gets little attention from the West — partly because of the difficulty the West has in understanding the East at all. If the West feels a sense of guilt for past injustices, will it help matters if it tries to make up for them by tolerating the new injustices being perpetrated? Religious, cultural and social discrimination does not make for peace. The Church must take a stand in order to give hope to the weak, courage to those who work for peace and support to those who seek justice.[7]

On 22 October Patriarch Giacomo Beltritti, Latin patriarch of Jerusalem, reported to the synod on the general assembly of the Latin Bishops in Arab Countries (CELRA) held in Beirut from 30 August to 4 September 1971. He presented a document prepared for the Rome synod by the assembly and listing the following requirements in regard to the 'problems of the Holy Land':

1. The reinstatement of the rights of all those who have been stricken and of the [Palestinian] refugees who number no less than 1,500,000.

2. The safeguarding of the rights of minorities and especially of Christian minorities: 100,000 in Israel and the West Bank, and 80,000 in Jordan. Many have been forced to emigrate.

3. In accordance with the desire expressed by the Holy See on many occasions, Jerusalem's sacred and universal character should be preserved intact. The rights of all religions and communities should be safeguarded in Jerusalem with a guarantee of an international nature.

In making these statements which were destined for the synod, CELRA was motivated by feelings of love of justice and concern for the true well-being of all the citizens of the Holy Land.

Patriarch Beltritti also mentioned his long stay in Palestine [from 1926] and repeated the need for the Synodal Fathers to co-operate in putting an end to the Palestinian tragedy by bringing pressure to bear on the leaders of the countries involved and exhorting the faithful to pray that peace may return to the Holy Land.[8]

The following day, Fr Pietro Azzi, superior-general of the Lebanese Maronite Order, stated that 'a particular interpretation of the Old Testament prevents Christians from understanding the question of injustice in its true light'. Referring to European and American theological interpretations of the 'election of a nation' (i.e. Israel), Fr Azzi reproached those who accepted these interpretations with being 'incapable of actually understanding the dramatic situation in the Middle East':

The official Church, however, has not been misled, as is testified by the repeated appeals of the Sovereign Pontiff in favour of a just peace in the Middle East [and, on 23 December 1968, of] *'the irreplaceable principles of justice and solidarity which constitute for these peoples the pattern of a real peace and a guarantee for each of them of his dignity, his rights, and his legitimate aspirations'*.

One does not need to live in the Middle East to realize how justice is trampled underfoot; one does not have to visit the Palestinian refugee camps, where living conditions are inhuman, to realize how human dignity is being flagrantly violated with the result that the young people who grow up in these camps, robbed of their identity and of their homeland, inevitably carry bitterness, hatred and revenge within them, not to mention the real and profound oppression of these refugees on the religious, political and economic levels in their host countries.

It is in order to save this people in exile which aspires to justice that we bring you, Venerable Fathers, our personal testimony, in order that with all available means, the Christian people throughout the world should be made aware of this problem and united with the Supreme Pastor, who has never ceased to demand the safeguarding of the inalienable rights of all men. Only thus shall we be able to save ourselves from the implacable cycle of violence and injustice, always ready to be unleashed by narrow-minded and exclusive nationalism.[9]

There was no immediate, specific, official, public response from the head of the Church to these passionate, urgent appeals for justice from the major representatives of Catholic Christianity in the Middle East. But on Christmas Eve 1971, following the closure of the synod, Pope Paul VI spoke to the College of Cardinals on the subject of 'Nations in Conflict':

In this context we have not forgotten the Middle East, especially the land we Christians like to call the Holy Land and which is brought to our minds in so many ways these days: the country of Jesus.

Although there is reason for satisfaction that the clash of weapons had been almost entirely silent in that area of the world for almost a year and a half, there are grounds for justified trepidation in the fear that the uncertain cease-fire may suddenly come to an end without having produced the results for which it was chiefly proposed and accepted. This was the voluntary search for a peace agreement or at least for the firm beginnings of an understanding, *through sincere talks which would take due account of the rights and legitimate interests of all parties, among which would be included, in the position proper to them, the people who have been forced by the events of recent decades to abandon their lands.*

For our part, in our meetings with the authorities of the nations concerned, we have never ceased to give encouragement to every noble endeavour towards an extension of the truce and towards a just and honourable understanding. We are convinced of the urgent necessity of a peaceful and wisely balanced solution of the Middle East problem, a solution which of course cannot be imposed by recourse to further war or by means of a military victory.

With regard to Jerusalem in particular, we do not now intend to add further considerations to those which we have repeatedly set forth in the past. Those considerations confirmed the need for a special statute, guaranteed internationally, which would do justice to the pluralistic and altogether special character of the Holy City and to the rights of the various communities which are situated there and which look to it as their spiritual centre.[10]

The text reveals the Pope's conviction that no peace agreement or even 'the firm beginnings of an understanding', was possible without the inclusion of the 'rights and legitimate interests of... the [Palestinian] people who have been forced... to abandon their lands'. Notwithstanding the somewhat Byzantine formulation chosen to express this conviction, the Vatican's position on this central question once again not only denoted a firm continuity with its past policies, but also ran far in advance of all other Western, including European, positions.

The question of Palestine was at the root of two papal pronouncements in the course of 1972. Both concerned the subject of terrorist actions which had followed in the wake of Black September. On 1 June, the feast of Corpus Christi, Paul VI announced the text of a telegram he had sent to the president of Israel, deploring 'the terrible massacre which took place tonight at Tel Aviv airport',[11] and invoking God 'unceasingly for the cessation of the conflict of hatred and blood which strikes the human conscience and Christian feelings'. On the same occasion, the faithful, gathered in St Peter's Square, were exhorted:

to pray... that peace may return to the world and that this growing method of crime and cowardly and cruel delinquency may be so condemned by everyone that men may return to being more civilized, better, and also more Christian.

During a general audience on 6 September the Pope expressed his condemnation of the killing of Israeli athletes by a group of Palestinian guerrillas at the 1972 Munich Olympic Games.[12] However, there was also an attempt to express an understanding of the underlying causes:

We cannot speak at this... meeting without removing, as it were, a weight from our heart: the weight of the news that has arrived from Munich... and which could not be sadder or more grave. You all know how the episode of the Israeli athletes and... the Arab guerrillas... has ended in tragedy, in a miserable and painful slaughter.

We deplore this fact, which dishonours our times, times straining towards peace and brotherhood... And before the dead... we cannot but be very sad and express our distress and strong condemnation.

...And then we go further still in our thoughts. Why? What are the causes? And these too cannot but sadden us. If there is this craving to explode in such episodes, it is a sign that there is a great malaise, a great suffering of spirits, which becomes blind and indulges in these explosions of revenge and resentment.[13]

The Pope's rhetorical 'Why?' was to be amply answered a week later in a public declaration by the Catholic bishops of Algeria:

We think above all of the people of Palestine. Conscious of the extreme gravity of blind terrorism, we condemn it; but we judge it necessary to denounce the ill which lies at its roots. In the name of the principles of justice, we ask the Christians in the Western countries and all men of goodwill to reflect on the essential facts of the Palestinian question.

Due to the will of the Great Powers, people have been deprived of their homeland; an entire people of 2 million persons has been, for the last 25 years, deprived of its right to exist as a people; and during the period in which these people have been demanding that justice be done, all kinds of plans purporting to determine their fate are being concocted without even consulting them. A permanent state of war has been established, aggravating the sufferings of the poorest and leading to despair, with the consequent hatred and violence.

Peace cannot but be the fruit of justice. It demands the collaboration of all the nations. But it requires in the first place that the destiny of an entire people should not be decided without its own effective participation in the plans concerning it.

We deem it our duty to alert the Christians in order that they draw inspiration from the New Testament and from law, and that they should not let their judgement be misled by the sole criteria of force and efficiency.[14]

8
From 'Refugees' to 'a People': 1973–1974

On 15 January 1973 Israel's prime minister Golda Meir was received in audience by Pope Paul VI at the Vatican, at her request. The media hailed the event as 'historic': it was the first time (and in spite of the absence of diplomatic relations between the two parties) that the head of an Israeli government had been received by the Holy See. Moreover, the fact that the person in question was Golda Meir, who had repeatedly stressed her hostility towards the Arabs in general, and the Palestinians in particular ('They did not exist'),[1] could not but give rise to a wave of protests in and from the Arab world. Clearly wishing to minimize the importance of the visit, the *Osservatore Romano* of 15-16 January 1973 discreetly published the Vatican's official communiqué on the audience on its second page. It read as follows:

This morning, 15 January 1973, at 12.15 pm, His Holiness Pope Paul VI received in audience Her Excellency Mrs Golda Meir, prime minister of Israel, who was accompanied by the Israeli ambassador to Italy, Mr Amiel E. Najar.

The conversation, which lasted about one hour, centred on the situation in the Middle East and the particular problems regarding the Holy Land.

His Holiness, after having recalled the history and the sufferings of the Jewish people, exposed the viewpoint of the Holy See on the questions which most closely interest its humanitarian mission, such as the problem of the refugees and the situation of the various communities who live in the Holy

Land, as well as the questions regarding its more specific religious mission concerning the Holy Places and the sacred and universal character of the city of Jerusalem.

The prime minister underlined Israel's desire for peace and amply illustrated the Israeli position in regard to the possibility of reaching a peaceful solution of the Middle East conflict, thanks to negotiations between the parties, and in regard to the above-mentioned questions. She equally touched on the phenomenon of terrorism, as well as the particular situation of the Jewish communities in various parts of the world.

In formulating his fervent wish that justice and law should restore peace and co-existence to all the peoples in the Middle East, His Holiness has again expressed the Holy See's intention of doing all in its power towards the achievement of this aim.

Before distributing this communiqué to the press, Prof. Federico Alessandrini, director of the Vatican Press Office, made the following statement:

In regard to the visit that Mrs Golda Meir, prime minister of Israel, paid to the Holy Father, I wish to observe that it was neither a gesture of preference nor [one] of exclusive favour [on the part of the Vatican]. Paul VI has received, in fact, King Hussein of Jordan and other important personalities of the Arab world and countries. And the Holy See, as is known, has cordial relations with Egypt, Lebanon and Syria, as well as diplomatic relations with many other Arab states such as Tunisia, Algeria, Kuwait and Iraq.

Mrs Golda Meir requested the audience on the occasion of her trip to Paris. It was not preceded by any 'concerted move or planning'.

It does not mean nor imply the least change — in fact no such change has taken place nor is there any reason for a change — in the attitude of the Holy See concerning the problems of the Holy Land, an attitude which was confirmed by the Holy Father in his allocution to the cardinals on 22 December 1972. *Equally, the attitude of the Holy See in regard to Israel remains unchanged.*

The Pope agreed to Mrs Golda Meir's request because he saw it as his duty not to forgo any opportunity to act in favour of peace, for the defence of human rights and those of the communities, for the defence of the religious interests of all, and in order to aid most particularly those who are the weakest and those who are defenceless, *in the first place the Palestinian refugees.*

As to the defence and tutelage of the religious interests, it would be superfluous to recall that in this specific case the question regards the inalienable rights of the three monotheistic religions linked to the universal and pluralist character which is particular to Jerusalem.[2]

The statement provoked a furious reaction in Israel, where Golda Meir was attempting to present her mission as a success. It was soon discovered from press reports, however, that the conversation between her and the Pope had been extremely agitated. The Israeli prime minister had adopted an aggressive tone in replying to the Holy Father's reproach that a people who had suffered as much as the Jews must not inflict similar sufferings on another people, the Palestinians. In reply to Israeli attacks, the French Catholic paper *La Croix* was used once again to state, unequivocally, that 'the declaration of the Holy See's spokesman... had been reviewed by the State Secretariat before being subjected to the approval of the head of the Church, according to reliable Vatican sources'.[3] Prof. Alessandrini himself objected sharply that he 'wasn't in the habit of voicing personal opinions'. Undeniably, the audience granted to Golda Meir implied a qualitative leap in relations between the Vatican and Israel from a *formal* point of view. Yet the actual result of the visit seemed to have been more negative than positive as far as Israel was concerned. Or at least, this was the impression that the Vatican went out of its way to give at the time.

Throughout the following months the conflict inside the Catholic Church between zionist sympathizers and those Christian circles that supported the Palestinian cause reached new heights. Neither the Pope nor the Vatican as such intervened in the debate, at least not publicly and officially. It is difficult, therefore, to judge whether the extremely general nature (more so than at any time in the past) of the Pontiff's comments both at the start of and during the October 1973 war were to any extent inhibited by the fear of unleashing renewed disagreements in the ranks of the Church, or simply dictated by an awareness of impotence in the face of events, or once again determined by the attitudes of outside forces. On 7 October 1973 'the bitter news of the sudden resumption of war in the Middle East' elicited from the head of the Church expressions of 'sadness' and meditations on 'the incurable passion of man and his quick return to the old conviction that major disputes have no other solution than the furious confrontation of lethal forces'. On 14 October he issued the following 'anguished appeal':

...for reason to prevail... we remind it of its responsibilities, denouncing again the irrationality of war: particularly in the blindness of its excesses. Even war, for example, has certain moderating laws of its own: it is not right to involve civilian populations in its ruins, to deny prisoners or unarmed persons the safety due to them, or inflict reprisals on innocent human lives.

Moreover even all-out war aims, more than at a questionable victory of arms, at peace; at a peace which will make justice possible and prepare minds for a new equilibrium.[4]

On 10 December 1973 the (Palestinian) Justice and Peace Commission of Jerusalem issued the following statement on the occasion of the twenty-fifth anniversary of the Universal Declaration of Human Rights and the tenth anniversary of Pope John XXIII's encyclical letter *Pacem in Terris*:

1. In fact, while Palestinian patriotism has its roots in much older memories than those of the last 25 years, the formulation of the Declaration of Human Rights has greatly helped the growth of awareness in regard to our national identity: the declaration provides a guide to every people that looks for solid reasons for hope and construction.
2. This testimony concerns both the men and the assemblies who, for the last 25 years, have devoted their work day after day to the formulation of the juridical aspects of Human Rights. During a historic visit, Pope Paul VI emphasized his appreciation of the work of the United Nations.
A small people, long ignored, the Palestinians will never forget that men of goodwill, compensating, finally, for the desperate battle and the spilt blood of some of the best among them, have recognized the 'inalienable rights of the Palestinian people' and the legitimacy of its 'aspirations to equality of rights and to self-determination' as 'an indispensable element in the establishment of a just and lasting peace in the Middle East'

(UN General Assembly resolutions, 10 Dec. 1969 and 8 Dec. 1970).

3. A contemporary writer has written regarding our recent history, and in particular the present conflict: 'In this affair, each side has its rights. But nowhere does there exist a supreme court, a code of deontological doctrine on relations between peoples, which allows us to establish whose rights come first and to share out accusations or absolutions regarding sovereignty' (Maxime Rodinson, *Israel et le refus arabe*. We intend partially to deny this assertion. It remains valid, however, that the authority of the international organization which proclaimed the Rights of Man should be reinforced. 'More than ever', Paul VI has written, 'the people resent the gap which separates these generous resolutions from their effective implementation' (Message to the UN, *Osservatore Romano*, 9 Oct. 1970).

4. Delighted, this December 1973, at the prospect of the promises being implemented, we turn once again to the community of peoples, the witnesses to our long vigil.

Among these peoples, and particularly among the people of Israel, we pay tribute to those men for whom the [UN] declaration constitutes the sole sure foundation for peace and who will welcome with sympathy the political structure to be chosen by the Palestinian people upon its final liberation.

We know that the road to freedom, for which we have been preparing ourselves for years, side by side with our Muslim brothers, will be strewn with difficulties. For this reason we express the wish that the political Palestinian community be autonomous and free of ties which could compromise its goals, in order that it may have every possible chance to endure and expand, thus realizing one of the fundamental conditions for peace.

Finally, we express the wish that any negotiations starting under the auspices of such an anniversary should consist of a sincere and generous dialogue, illuminated by the principles of the [UN] charter and guided by concern for the men, women and children who in this part of the world aspire simply to happiness and to the dignity of being responsible for their own destiny.[5]

On 22 December 1973, as the Geneva Conference on the Middle East opened, only to close two hours later, Paul VI received several world figures at the Vatican: Ethiopia's emperor, Haile Selassie; the Sudanese president, Jaafar Nimeiri; the vice-president of Liberia, James E. Greene; and the foreign minister of Zambia, personally representing President Kenneth Kaunda. Curiously, the joint communiqué issued after the meeting was never published by the *Osservatore Romano*. It read:

> The African heads of state expressed to the Pope their points of view on world peace and security, and in particular on the search *for a just solution of the crisis in the Middle East, which should take into account the legitimate rights of the Palestinian people.*
>
> One of their major preoccupations is the question of Jerusalem, which must not be subjected to the exclusive rule of one religion. The solution for the status of the city should be founded on the basis of the United Nations resolutions.
>
> The heads of state affirmed that the cause of peace in the world is one and indivisible...
>
> The Holy Father expressed his gratitude and appreciation for the significant visit and took particular note of the views expressed by his illustrious visitors.
>
> The Holy Father confirmed, for his part, the Holy See's keen interest in questions relating to the Middle East. The Holy See is ready to contribute in every possible way to their just solution in collaboration with all those who are inspired by the same ideals.
>
> The Holy Father confirmed the Holy See's position on the Holy Places, and especially on Jerusalem.[6]

On 24 October 1973 Paul VI had expressed the hope for 'a truce, peace and reconciliation' in the Middle East. In an allocution to the consistorial assembly on 21 December the Middle East — and especially the Palestinian question — was again at the centre of his thoughts:

> That land has for many — too many — years been the theatre of a conflict that afflicts and endangers the very peace of a wider circle of nations, and perhaps the world. It is a conflict that has caused endless sorrow and suffering to many innocent and defenceless peoples, a conflict that makes an object and motive of hate and rivalry out of a land and a city that ought to be a symbol and reminder of unity of heart for millions and millions

of men and women who look to it as a beacon of faith and love. The ambiguous and unstable situation of non-peace and non-war that had dragged on for more than six years was brought to an end last October by the outbreak of fresh hostilities.

An intense and courageous initiative (for which we have already... expressed our appreciation) has led, first, to a cease-fire, and now to a peace conference, opening this very day in Geneva under the auspices of the United Nations. Although for the moment at least it is incomplete in its participants, it is opening the way to negotiations that allow one to hope for positive developments for the definite settlement of the long conflict.

...As in the past, the Holy See will continue to follow all developments in the situation with the utmost attention. It will likewise maintain contact with those involved and with all those who are able and who desire to contribute to a just solution. The Holy See is always ready to lend its willing collaboration in order that the efforts being made may be happily concluded in agreements which can guarantee for all the parties concerned a tranquil and secure existence and the recognition of their respective rights.

Together with a strong general interest in the question of peace for these tormented regions, *we have a special preoccupation with the condition and lot of those who have suffered the most, and are still suffering because of events from 1947 up to the present day. We are thinking in particular of the hundreds of thousands of people who are refugees from their land, reduced as they are to desperate circumstances or frustrated in other ways in their legitimate aspirations.* At times their cause is brought to world attention and even compromised by actions... which are in no case justified... And yet there is the question of a cause that demands human consideration and which pleads, through the voice of neglected and blameless means, for a just and generous response.[7]

Notwithstanding the evident over-optimism concerning the prospects of the Geneva Conference, and the use of 'humanitarian' terms to describe the problem of the 'refugees', the Pope's appeal is noteworthy: first, there was the mention of a solution based on the 'legitimate aspirations' of the Palestinians; second, there was the emphasis on a 'recognition of [the parties'] respective rights'; and third, there was the call for an understanding — in spite of '[terrorist] actions' — of 'a cause that demands human consideration', at a time when most of the West blindly followed Israel's denial of the 'existence' of the Palestinians. No less remarkable is the fact that these same attitudes were expressed by Paul VI at an audience he granted to a group of relatives of Israeli prisoners of war on 20 March 1974. The Pope expressed himself in the following terms:

> We would like to say to you and to all the relatives you represent, to those, too, who, in both camps, have been stricken by the loss or absence of their dear ones, or who have had to leave their homes: we are near to you in sorrow...
>
> And we wish, once more, to express our... severe disapproval of the great evil that is war, and our ardent desire to see *the solution of the causes that foster it, in a spirit of justice, understanding and reconciliation.*[8]

But it was on 16 July 1974 that Paul VI finally and unambiguously abandoned the definition of Palestinians as nothing more than 'refugees'. A letter from the Pope to the president of the Pontifical Mission for Palestine, Mons. John G. Nolan, written on the occasion of the twenty-fifth anniversary of its foundation, was published in the *Osservatore Romano* of 29-30 July under the significant heading 'Holy See's Participation in Sufferings and Aspirations of Palestinian People'. After recalling the circumstances under which the mission had been founded by Pius XII, and paying tribute to its activities, the letter continued:

> The mission's work for Palestine has been one of the clearest signs of the Holy See's concern for the welfare of *the Palestinians, who are particularly dear to us because they are the people of the Holy Land, because they include followers of Christ and because they have been and still are so tragically tried.*
>
> *We express again our heartfelt sharing in their suffering and our support for their legitimate aspirations.*

Months before the UN granted observer status to the Palestine Liberation Organization (PLO), the Holy See thus recognized and affirmed what Israel denies: that the Palestinians are 'the people of the Holy Land'. Politically, their 'legitimate aspirations' are thus to be interpreted as inseparable from this fundamental definition.

Significantly, most of the Western media chose to ignore the implications of this affirmation by the highest authority of the Church. Neither this fact, however, nor certain ambiguities which were later to emerge (even on the part of the Vatican), would be able to obscure the value of this 'historic' statement.[9]

In addition to the Holy See's ever-growing preoccupation with the question of the Palestinians, concern for the two other principal issues which have always characterized the Vatican's interest in the question of Palestine — Jerusalem and the fate of the Christian communities living in the Holy Land — were repeatedly dealt with by Paul VI in the course of 1974. Both were the subject of a written apostolic exhortation, *'Nobis in Animo' to the Bishops, Clergy and Faithful in the World on the Needs of the Church in the Holy Land* issued on 25 March, and of an Easter allocution on 10 April. Tension between the Vatican and Israel was developing on these issues as well. In fact, reacting to distortions of statements made by him in an interview with the Israeli newspaper *Ha'aretz* (5 February 1974), the Holy See's spokesman, Prof. Alessandrini, issued a note on the 'precise attitude' of the Church in regard to the issues concerned:

I cannot but confirm what has already been said, i.e. that while wishing for a just and peaceful solution of the entire conflict in the Middle East, *the Church, at the moment of dealing with the problem of Jerusalem in a concrete manner, desires that its own viewpoint on this problem should be opportunely made known.* In other words, it is necessary to consider today what the Pope has said in his recent discourses. In any case, the Holy See wishes that the faithful of the three monotheistic religions should feel themselves at home in Jerusalem... *It would be superfluous to stress that this response and the Pope's recent discourses exclude [the possibility of] the slightest change having occurred in the attitude of the Holy See.* On the other hand, although in the above-mentioned interview [i.e. in *Ha'aretz*] the humanitarian aspect of the drama of the refugees was underlined, this does not at all mean that I underestimated the aspirations and legitimate rights of the Palestinian people, which the Holy Father has mentioned many times. Consequently, *it is totally erroneous and gratuitous to affirm, as has been done on this occasion, that the comprehension of this drama [on the part of the Vatican] does not go beyond the limits of a 'reasonable humanitarian solution of the Palestinian problem'.*[10]

The polemics continued throughout April. On 12 April *La Croix* wrote that the Pope's recent statements:

have demonstrated, more clearly than ever, that the Pope considers on the one hand that the city of Jerusalem must be under a special statute based on international guarantees, and on the other hand that the Holy Places such as Nazareth, Bethany, the shores of the Jordan, etc. must enjoy, according to Rome's wishes, a special juridical tutelage. *This position is in contrast with that of the Israeli government, which refuses to consider any arrangement other than that of free access to Jerusalem and the other Holy Places, which would not put in question the political status to which the latter are subjected at present.*

The following day, Israel's chief rabbi, Shlomo Goren, attacked the Vatican's position as being 'of a purely political nature, without any regard for justice, religious integrity or historical rights'. These were harsh accusations, to which the chief rabbi added that 'never have the Holy Places been so well protected and so accessible to all as since their subjection to Israeli rule'.[11]

The Vatican avoided any further direct dispute with the Israelis, but did not retract its stand. On 18 August 1974 the Israeli security services arrested the Greek Catholic patriarchal vicar of Jerusalem, Mons. Hilarion Capucci, accusing him of arms traffic and contacts with the (illegal) Palestinian Resistance. Following a trial by a military court, whose competence to judge him was denied by the accused, Mons. Capucci was sentenced to twelve years in gaol.

The sentence was passed on 9 December. The following day the Holy See issued a communiqué to the press:

The Holy See has learned with profound pain and sorrow of the sentence passed on Mons. Hilarion Capucci...

This episode is a painful blow to one of the glorious Catholic communities of the Orient, the Melchite Church... Mons. Capucci has for many years exercised episcopal functions [in this Church] as a pastor of a region where, in the midst of the most diverse historical vicissitudes, the heads of the religious communities are traditionally accorded honour and respect, and also as a leader of the faithful who live in Jerusalem and in the

Holy Land. [These are] places dear to and venerated by believers and where the presence of Catholics is of particular concern to the Holy Father.

Unfortunately, this sentence cannot fail to aggravate tension... in a complex situation and in a territory where, notwithstanding repeated efforts, a just peace is still far away, and where the populations live in a climate of anxiety, conflict and uncertainty.[12]

9
Competing Lobbies within the Catholic Church

The promulgation in 1965 of the *Nostra Aetate* had led to a proliferation of organizational bodies and pressure groups (secretariats, commissions, committees, study groups, and so on) for the 'improvement of Christian-Jewish relations'. In turn, these bodies laid the foundations for the development of zionist lobbies in and around the Catholic Church, both on the periphery and at the centre. Significantly, however, it was mainly after Israel's occupation in 1967 of the West Bank (including East Jerusalem) and Gaza, and its affirmation as a regional military power, that such lobbies came into the open. As of that time, and throughout the 1970s, these lobbies, centred mainly in France but also in the US, have led a sustained campaign to legitimate not only Israel's existence but also its conquests and the policies of its governments.

Illustrative of these activities are articles, statements and declarations published in the media, particularly the Catholic section. In the US the American Bishops Conference has generally maintained, over the years, a balanced attitude, closer to the traditions of the Catholic Church and favourable in any case to the rights of the Palestinians. It was personalities such as Mons. Oesterreicher and Fr Flannery, and the institutes they headed, that were the leading spirits in the pro-zionist activities.

In France, the Bishop of Strasbourg, Mons. Elchinger, might be described as a crusading champion of the cause of zionism, at the head of an 'Episcopal Committee for Relations with the Jews'. Other Latin/Mediterranean countries such as Italy and Spain have remained largely unaffected by similar developments. In Northern

Europe, where the majority of Christians are Protestant, some combative but rather marginal Catholic elements have joined the zionist lobbies operating under the cover of 'Judeo-Christian Committees'. In prevalently Catholic East European countries such as Poland, where anti-Jewish feelings were strongest in the past, pro-zionist activities in Church quarters have been undertaken mainly by liberal sectors engaged in moderate forms of opposition to the communist regimes, in whose ranks many non-zionist Jews have reached prominent positions.

Pro-Zionist Church Groups in the US

Pro-zionist activity within US Church circles reached a peak in the late 1960s and early 1970s. In an article published on the *New York Times* Op-Ed page in May 1971, for example, Mons. Oesterreicher championed the cause of Israeli sovereignty over the Holy City. This was in blatant contrast with the Vatican's known position on Jerusalem. Mons. Oesterreicher's plea, entitled 'Justice in Jerusalem', read:

> Christians who have not yet understood the signs of the times and thus the meaning of Israel's rejuvenation, will have to reconcile themselves to the fact that Jerusalem is a Jewish city, in origin, destiny and significance.
>
> A Christian theologian must, it seems to me, see in the new state... a significant event. The living reality of the state will, for the most part, evoke his respect and admiration. More than that, if he understands what has happened and still happens there, he will become a champion of the state's independence and integrity.[1]

Mons. Oesterreicher seems to have taken upon himself the task of spurring American Catholics to legitimize a 'theological recognition' of zionism. In a booklet published on the occasion of the fifth anniversary of the *Nostra Aetate*, he further affirmed:

> To me, the state of Israel is the visible expression of the God-willed permanence of the Jewish people. As is Judaism, so is the state of Israel, a banner of God's fidelity...[2]

Yet at the very time of the booklet's publication, this 'banner of God's fidelity' was carrying out a harsh policy of repression in the Gaza Strip. (According to the *Middle East Newsletter* of June–July 1971, student demonstrators were shot, 12,000 people — relatives of suspected activists — were detained in concentration camps in the Sinai, and thousands more were deported to Jordan.) The Palestinian Christians who daily experienced harassment by the Israeli occupation authorities in Jerusalem and elsewhere did not exactly give their blessing to the alleged 'God-willed permanence' of Israel. All this was evidently of little importance, however, for the Catholic director of the Institute of Judeo-Christian Studies at Seton Hall University, Mons. Oesterreicher. The same could be said of Fr Flannery, executive secretary of the American Bishops Secretariat for Promoting Christian Unity, who has written along the same lines. In the opinion of Roy Eckardt, a Protestant theologian, Flannery stands 'in the forefront of Christian moral and theological support for Israel'.[3] According to a zionist Jewish writer:

> The fact that both Oesterreicher and Flannery head official Catholic institutions should not be underestimated in assessing the effectiveness of their work for Israel. Although their respective institutions were not established with the intention of promoting support for Israel... the authority, the public forum and the financial support which such institutions provide helped to propagate their pro-Israel views among the American Catholic public.[4]

Other zionist lobbyists among US Catholics may also be mentioned. Among them Fr Cornelius Rijk, director of the Vatican Office of Catholic-Jewish Relations, has played a particularly prominent role in building a bridge between the US zionist Catholic lobby and the Holy See.

Fr Flannery was directly involved in the preparation of a quasi-official document drawn up in December 1969 by the American branch of the Secretariat for the Promotion of Christian Unity. Drafted under the supervision of Cardinal Sheehan of Baltimore, the document demanded an 'updated' theology regarding the Jewish people, and consequently regarding the position of the state of Israel in the religious experience of the Jews:

> Fidelity to the Covenant was linked to the gift of a land which in the Jewish soul has endured as an object of an aspiration that

Christians should strive to understand... It would seem that Christians, whatever the difficulties they may experience, must attempt to understand and respect the religious significance of this link between the people and the land. The existence of the state of Israel should not be separated from this perspective.[5]

This document, which reflected an attempt to 'smuggle' zionist doctrine into American Catholic thinking, was withdrawn by the Vatican, and its publication was defined as 'inexcusable'.[6] Due to the insistent efforts of Fr Flannery, however, its basic points were to be reiterated in subsequent reports to synodal meetings of Catholic archdioceses where zionist influence was predominant, such as that of Cincinnati. In a report of October 1971, in fact, a document by Cincinnati's synod urged Catholics to 'understand the depth of the concern that most Jews feel for the state of Israel'.

The role of Cardinal Cushing, archbishop of Boston and the spiritual mentor of the Kennedy clan in this context, has already been mentioned (see page 60). In an address to an Inter-Faith Assembly in Massachusetts on 13 March 1969, Cardinal Cushing maintained that it 'was false to say that Israel is indifferent to Arab refugees, that Israel is not the rightful owner of Palestine, that Israel has expansionist designs or is guilty of atrocities or terror'.

On the whole, however, the positions of US bishops such as Cardinal Cushing and Cardinal Sheehan (of Baltimore) have not determined the attitude of the official American Church. Indeed, the existence of strongly contrasting views has led to the adoption of well-balanced stands. A good example is provided by an address on 2 March 1971 to the third annual meeting of the Jewish-Catholic Institute of Philadelphia by Cardinal Krol, bishop of Philadelphia:

At issue are: the just desire of nations to have their sovereignty, territorial integrity and political independence recognized; the suffering and indignities of more than a million and a half Palestinian refugees evicted from their homes; the restoration of territories occupied in the 1967 war... The way of peace demands that each of these issues be resolved through sincere negotiations... Our concern for the Palestinian refugees is not academic... Our concern for the Christian shrines and Holy Places is a deep one. Christian people are looking forward to some form of an international authority... They will not be resigned to the control of the Holy Places by a single nation.[7]

If Cardinal Krol's attitude was clearly at the opposite pole from that of Mons. Oesterreicher, Fr Flannery and Cardinal Cushing, so also was the resolution of the US Catholic Bishops Conference of 13 November 1973. After underlining the complexity of the Middle East situation and the dangers to world peace from the prolongation of a state of war in the area, the American Bishops demanded:

The recognition of Israel's right to exist within secure borders.

The recognition of the rights of the Arab Palestinians, in particular of the refugees: this necessitates, in our view, that they should be admitted as partners in all the negotiations, that their right to have a state of their own should be recognized, and that compensation be paid to them for damages suffered in the past not only by Israel but also by the international community members who were responsible for the partition plan of 1948.

The recognition of the need that the USSR and the US pursue a policy of moderation and of a responsible diplomatic engagement, in co-ordination with the UN initiatives.

International guarantees for the unique status of Jerusalem and its religious significance, for the character of the city, the life of its religious communities and the protection of their civil and religious rights.[8]

Subsequent official documents of the US Catholic Bishops Conference have maintained the same tenor. The US conference has been, incidentally, the only national episcopal body to have regularly issued resolutions on Palestine. Despite the efforts of the lobbyists, it has held to a firm attitude of support for 'the rights of the Palestinian Arabs to participate in all negotiations and to their own homeland'.[9] Nevertheless the zionist lobby in the American Church should not be underestimated; its effect on the level of both public opinion and local institutions is far from negligible.

The World Conference of Christians for Palestine
On 7-10 May 1970 the first World Conference of Christians for Palestine took place in Beirut with the participation of 400 delegates (Catholic, Orthodox, Anglican and Protestant) from 37 countries in America, Europe, Asia and Africa. It was to be the first of a

series of similar meetings, the last of which would take place in 1974. It was sponsored chiefly by the Middle East Council of Churches (MECC), but also had Catholic participation.[10] It was intended to constitute (as indeed it did for several years) a means by which the voice of the Palestinians could reach Christian public opinion worldwide and rally support to its cause.

The first session of the conference came at a time of great optimism for the Palestinian Resistance. Black September was yet to come, four months later... At the end of its deliberations, the conference issued the following message to world Christianity:

> While expressing solidarity with the Palestinian people in the struggle for its right to a free and independent life, and condemnation for all explicit or implicit forms of anti-semitism, we also vigorously protest at the multiple manifestations of anti-Arab racism. We invite you to combat such attitudes and all the political or religious justifications which may be given them, attitudes and justifications [which are] contrary to the evangelical requirements: where man is offended, Jesus Christ is insulted as well.
>
> Affirming that the Bible reveals to us a messiah whose kingdom is not of this world though he manifests himself in this world, we refuse all manipulations of biblical texts for goals of political power.
>
> [Since] the zionist political interpretation of these texts is in contrast with the spirit of Christianity, it seems to us unacceptable for the Christians, as it seems to us unacceptable for the Jews, faithful to the spiritual interpretation of the Old Testament. Such interpretation in fact leads to a legitimation through the holy scriptures of the grave injustices suffered by the Palestinian people and the other Arab peoples, and against which human conscience must revolt. Thus, the zionist state, like every politico-religious system, whether it leans on a living faith or not, is in contrast with the dignity and freedom of man.
>
> For this reason, we Christians meeting in Beirut invite you to participate in the building of a humane, secular and democratic society that respects all convictions.
>
> We Christians meeting in Beirut recognize that many non-Arab countries and great powers carry a very heavy responsibility for the injustice committed against the Palestinian people and the other Arab peoples. We radically oppose the

view that the Middle East's problems can be solved only through the balance of forces or through the intervention of the great powers, or through national or international policies which are in contrast with the rights of the Palestinian people, and especially with its basic rights to return to its homeland and to self-determination.

We declare that it is first and foremost up to the Palestinian people to conceive political solutions which would permit the co-existence of persons of different ethnic, religious and ideological origins and convictions in a free and democratic Palestine within the Arab world. We consider that the evacuation of the Occupied Territories is an indispensable first step towards peace. It seems to us that another step towards peace will necessarily have to consist in the disappearance of the zionist structures.

Similarly, we protest at the massacres, the tortures, the destruction of villages and homes, the expropriation of lands, and at all the arbitrary measures taken against groups and individuals, and at all the violations of the rights of civilians in wartime, etc.

In protesting against all forms of the exploitation of man by man, we cannot separate the struggle of the Palestinians from that of the poor and oppressed who struggle for their liberation and development throughout the world. We call upon all our brothers... to side with those who fight for the recognition of their human dignity. The establishment of new social and political structures, national as well as international, demands the elimination of the present systems of oppression and violence. As Christians, in obedience to the judgement of God and guided by his merciful grace, we commit ourselves, and we invite you, Christian brothers throughout the world, to gain a better knowledge of the Arab problems and to support the Palestinian people in its resistance and in its struggle, which constitute one of the most significant expressions of the struggle for the human individual and for freedom.

Through its debates, its resolutions and the echo of its appeals, the conference provoked a furious response from zionist lobbyists in the Christian Church intent on affirming Israel's 'rights' over Palestine. In Europe, where the echo of the conference's appeals was the strongest, the Christian-Jewish Friendship Groups reacted vigorously, issuing counter-documents which accused the promoters of the conference of supporting 'anti-Israeli violence', and of creating 'a new form óf passionate anti-semitism'.[11] The French zionist paper *Tribune Juive*, published in the stronghold of the Catholic zionist lobby in Strasbourg, thereupon accused the Vatican, and in particular Substitute Secretary of State Mons. Luigi Benelli, of 'wishing to liquidate all Christian-Jewish dialogue after having suppressed a pro-zionist document which recognized the permanent link between Palestine and the Jewish people'.[12] The Vatican issued a firm denial, revealing that the document in question was none other than that prepared by Cardinal Sheehan of Baltimore.[13] This document, the Vatican declared, was nothing but a proposed 'working paper', submitted by the archbishop of Baltimore to the Secretariat for the Promotion of Christian Unity, and rejected by it. The very publication of the document was, according to the Vatican note, 'inexcusable'. The Christian-Jewish dialogue, the note concluded, was continuing. The storm raised by this 'affair' subsequently led to the creation, in Paris, on 16 December 1971, of an International Catholic-Jewish Liaison Committee, designed to canvas support for the zionist cause on a world scale.

The pro-Zionist Church Lobby in France

On Easter Eve, 17 April 1973, the French Episcopal Committee for Relations with the Jews published a series of *Pastoral Orientations for the Attitudes of Christians Towards the Jews* which became the cornerstone of yet another attempt to 'smuggle' a legitimation of the zionist state in Palestine into Catholic theological doctrine under a 'religious' cover. After a storm of protests from Christians everywhere, members of the committee were forced to express reservations about their document, but it was not withdrawn.[14] In a counter-move, the archbishop of Paris, Cardinal Marty, gave a press conference on 18 April at which he personally declared that:

> the Palestinians, too, have the right to a life and a territory.
>
> I have seen too much of the misery reigning in the refugee camps during my trip to the Holy Land. That since 1948 human beings should live in refugee camps away from their land is certainly inadmissible for our civilization.[15]

Finally, the president of the episcopal committee responsible for the *Orientations*, Mons. Elchinger, bishop of Strasbourg and chief pro-zionist crusader in the French Church, was forced to pronounce on his positions in public. In *L'Eglise en Alsace* (May 1973) he wrote, with a view to 'avoiding inexact interpretations':

> In order for a Judeo-Christian dialogue to exist and develop, it is necessary that Catholics should make an effort to understand to what extent the 'return to the Promised Land' constitutes an aspiration of the Jewish soul. This does not prevent us from thinking that the mixture of religious and political motivations which characterizes zionism does not correspond to our Christian sensitivity.
>
> The interpretation according to which Mons. Elchinger intended the episcopal text to constitute an official recognition of the state of Israel is inexact. The document simply states the existence of that state.
>
> If we believe that, as a result of the criminal extermination perpetrated against the Jewish people, the universal conscience cannot refuse it a land in this world, the French bishops underline, at the same time, the importance and tragic character of the Palestinian issue and the urgent duty to end the situation of injustice of which the Palestinian populations are the victims.[16]

These ambiguous 'amendments' could obviously not satisfy those Christians for whom the French document constituted (as in effect it did) nothing less than an attempt to pass off what was actually a zionist resolution as a pastoral document legitimizing the state of Israel in Palestine. The entire Episcopal Conference of Algeria signed a statement rejecting 'the grave exegetic and theological ambiguities designed to create a negative confusion between Judaism and zionism'. They recalled that 'the Palestinian people's right to exist is an essential factor in the Middle East problem' and that 'the recognition of this right is a first essential step towards peace'.[17] Forty Jesuits from Lebanon, the US, Egypt, France and Holland, meeting in Beirut, issued a statement calling the French episcopal document 'a Catholic Balfour Declaration'. They termed Cardinal Marty's reservations 'insufficient', as were the 'assurances by Pope Paul VI that he intends to stay on the side of the oppressed against the oppressors'. In brief, they rejected the document *in toto*.[18] Cardinal Jean Danielou, a member of the

Académie Française and particularly close to the Pope, published a justification of the protests against the document in *Le Figaro* of 28-29 April 1973:

> In the first place, because to accord to the state of Israel a theological significance means to create a dangerous confusion between politics and religion, which the Vatican II Council wished to avoid... [Second, because the (French) text] engages in a controversial theology in regard to the role of the Jewish people in the history of salvation... It is false still to speak today of a particular choosing of the Jewish people. It is humanity in its entirety which was originally called upon by God — all the peoples today assembled in the Church... And moreover, this is the best way of giving rise again to anti-semitism...

Finally, the Vatican spokesman, Prof. Alessandrini, made a statement that practically disowned the significance of the document desired by the zionists:

> The Catholic Church stated its position on the relations with the Jews through the Vatican II Council in the declaration *Nostra Aetate* regarding the Church and the non-Christian religions, para. IV (1).
> As far as the Holy See's position on the Middle East conflict and its consequences is concerned, there is nothing to be added to the statements repeatedly reaffirmed, including Paul VI's last Easter message.[19]

The furious debate continued over the following weeks, with articles in the French Catholic press. Among others, there was one by Fr Yves Congar, O.P.[20] in favour of the document, and an interview with Mons. Pérezil, auxiliary bishop of Paris and a member of the episcopal committee which had produced the *Orientations*, expressing embarrassment and grave reservations over the document.[21] At Pentecost, the Catholic Bishops Conference of Egypt, representing all denominations and headed by Cardinal Patriarch Stephanos I of Alexandria, issued a severe criticism of the document. In an 'Open Letter to the Bishops of France', the conference stated:

> The publication [of *Orientations*] was aimed at French Catholics,

and from this point of view we appreciate the spirit of understanding, dialogue and brotherly charity which lies behind this step: it aims to combat the seeds of anti-semitism, whose origins — especially in the West — lie in the way in which the Christian message has long been presented.

However... by stating that its 'text' rests exclusively on religious grounds, the episcopal committee forgets rather too quickly that such a text is also situated in a particular moment in time and in a particular international context. This inevitably leads to the adoption of certain contradictory positions and judgements...

In particular, we should like to point out:

1. The unfortunate timing of this document, coming at such a crucial and difficult moment for the Christians of the Near East and even for those in our own country.

2. The serious exegetic (and theological) ambiguities which lead to a harmful confusion between judaism and zionism, between the Jewish people of the Old Testament and the state of Israel, seeming even to demand the acceptance of a *fait accompli* — the violent occupation of a 'land' — while ignoring the demands of justice and those repeatedly stated in International Law and [by] the United Nations which have been blatantly ignored for many years...

We should like to recall here the many interventions by the Holy Father Paul VI, particularly over the last two years, to ensure the sacred, supranational and universal character of the Holy City, guaranteed by an international UN statute...[22]

The debate subsided as public attention was diverted to the October 1973 war in the Middle East. But the conflict within the Church was far from over. On 4-6 December 1973 the International Catholic-Jewish Liaison Committee held its annual meeting in Antwerp (Belgium) under the joint presidency of Mons. Charles Moeller, general secretary of the Vatican Secretariat for the Promotion of Christian Unity, and Professor Zvi Weblovsky, an Israeli official appointed by the government of Israel as chairman of the Jewish Council for Inter-Religious Contacts in Israel. This fact needs no further comment. Neither do the topics discussed at the meeting: two papers presented by Catholic and Jewish scholars on the concept of 'People, Nation and Land' in their respective religious traditions; the Middle East situation and its implications for Jewish-Christian relations; the situation of Christians in Israel and the activities of certain missionary groups there; the situation of the Jews in the USSR; the recrudescence of anti-semitism and concerted action in combating it.[23]

As can be seen, the situation of the Palestinian Arabs under Israeli occupation was absent from the agenda. The meeting proved yet again the success of zionist tactics: the acceptance of a joint presidency by a Vatican official and an Israeli aide represented a political, not a religious, fact. Similarly, the topics chosen for discussion were political rather than religious. Yet officially the Holy See was to claim that the 'dialogue' was of a purely religious nature.

On 8 March 1974 the National Council for Jewish-Christian Friendship of France issued a resolution which said that they:

> recognize once and for all the legitimacy of the national and political existence of Israel. We intend fully to respect the conviction of our Jewish friends that the land was given to them by God... We request that the authorities of the Churches represented in this council should be informed of this position... We request that the fact that Israel's existence is in fact threatened should be taken into consideration. Neither the Jews nor the Christians can allow this existence to be put into question again... In particular, the statute for the Holy Places should not become a pre-condition for a settlement of the conflict; on the contrary, it could become its consequence. In the event that the need arose to change it, the Churches could place their trust in the Israeli authorities, who have proved their respect for religious freedoms.

On 10 January Paul VI received in audience the members of the International Catholic-Jewish Liaison Committee. He refrained, however, from the slightest allusion to the questions of zionism and Israel, or that of the Middle East in general. His allocution was neutral and centred on exclusively theological themes. He also recalled the help given by Pope Pius XII to Jewish victims of the nazi persecution. On 1 December 1974 the Vatican Commission for Religious Relations with the Jews, headed by Cardinal Johannes Willebrands, a Dutch liberal, issued a document on *Orientations and Suggestions for the Application of the Nostra Aetate*, nine years after its promulgation by Vatican II. The chief rabbi of Paris,

Meyer Yais, expressed his enthusiastic approval. He declared that
it was a document which 'goes much farther than the original
council text', in that it explicitly condemned, 'in the name of the
spiritual links and historical relations between the Church and
Judaism, every form of anti-semitism' and recommended 'the duty
of better mutual comprehension and of a renewed esteem between
Catholics and Jews'.[24] The main pro-zionist crusader, Mons.
Elchinger of Strasbourg, was also delighted at the new Vatican
document, which, he affirmed, 'approves of the initiatives in
various countries which... lay down the most favourable conditions
under which the new relations between Christians and Jews may
be elaborated and developed'. The French document of April 1973,
Mons. Elchinger pointed out, 'is part and parcel of these initiatives'.
The bishop of Strasbourg wanted to make the point even more
emphatically:

> It should be noted that on 23 December last, before the cardinals,
> the Pope evoked what Jerusalem represents for Judaism. He
> called Jerusalem 'the centre of love and ancient longing of the
> people whom God had mysteriously chosen, designating it in
> advance as *his* people, in which we recognize ourselves'.[25]

Evidently, the bishop had been trying to force an interpretation
of Paul VI's discourse which finds not the slightest confirmation
in any of the Pope's pronouncements on and requirements for the
fate of Jerusalem. In his attempt to support Mons. Oesterreicher's
thesis that 'Jerusalem is a Jewish city', and justify his own wish to
see the zionist possession of Palestine legitimated, Mons. Elchinger
was perhaps ahead of his time. But might he have actually expressed
what could be termed a strategic goal of the Vatican, or of certain
quarters of it — a goal that the Holy See was tactically trying to
conceal, for the time being, through the Pope's repeated formal
assurances to the Arab world and the Palestinian people?

A clear response to that question seems premature at this stage.
Nevertheless it is likely that the Holy See was playing along with
the gradual changes in the regional balance of power and waiting
for clearer indications as to the outcome, without actually
identifying with the positions of either side. Meanwhile,
notwithstanding the positive reaction from Rabbi Yais and Mons.
Elchinger, zionists and their supporters within Church circles
voiced widespread and loud disappointment over the new

Orientations and Suggestions. In response, Fr Pierre Marie de Contenson, secretary of the Vatican Commission, declared on Vatican Radio:

> Certain commentators... have deplored [the fact] that the document does not mention the attachment of the Jewish people to the Land, nor the significance that the Land may have in Jewish tradition. In order to understand the document's silence on this point, one must take its nature into account. This is a document which deals with the application of a council text, a document proposed by the Catholic Church to Catholics. It does not seem convenient that in such a document the Catholic authorities should risk including interpretations which the Jews give about themselves... It is not up to the Catholic Church to propose a definition of Judaism. It is up to the Jews themselves to say what they are. We must — and the document exhorts us to do so — listen to the Jews in order to understand them. The dialogue supposes a mutual listening.[26]

On the face of it, this statement, like similar ones in the past, seemed ethically correct. In substance what it said was that objective 'listening and understanding' do not necessarily mean becoming subjectively convinced of, or identified with, the arguments of the interlocutor. From a religious point of view, the Church appeared to warn the faithful that a dialogue with the Jews should not be taken as meaning preparations for a conversion to Judaism and its declared values. Among other things, such an interpretation would negate in advance the value of such a dialogue, and would ultimately represent a threat to the Church's own identity. But the statement stopped short of developing this and other related themes. Thus some important questions remained unanswered. For example, what about those Jews who neither define themselves as zionists nor accept the alleged theological or other role of the state of Israel as part of their Jewish credo? Why did the Church negotiate its 'relations with Judaism' with zionists only? True, the statement said that 'it is up to the Jews themselves to say what they are'. But in fact only zionist representatives and activists were listened to. Why did the Catholic Church not clear up its position on this point for the benefit of its own members?

The ambiguity inherent in the Church's stance was to surface later in 1975, when a UN General Assembly resolution equating zionism with racism provoked frenetic reactions by the zionist lobbies and led to heated debate on a world scale. In reality, the UN resolution's definition of zionism was anything but alien to the historical and traditional judgements of the Catholic Church on Jewish statehood in Palestine. But when the Vatican was pressed to pronounce its stand on the issue, Cardinal Willebrands (speaking in the name of the Holy See) reacted in the following terms:

> On 10 November a United Nations resolution on zionism was approved. I was astonished that they should speak in it of phenomena as complex as zionism and racism without specifying or defining the sense in which these words are used. In *Le Monde* of 12 November I found three linguistic-conceptual definitions of zionism and three others of racism, the constitutive elements of which do not at all coincide. So what can be the significance of a declaration that does not clarify the terms it deals with or explain the sense in which they are to be understood? This method of procedure, in my opinion, certainly cannot serve justice or the peace that we all hope for in the Middle East region.[27]

A quite different tone was adopted by Mons. Elchinger, who for the occasion had his signature flanked by that of the president of the Protestant Federation of France (a secular, not a religious body), Jean Courvoisier:

> We wish to express our profound anxiety in view of the UN resolution which declared that 'zionism is a form of racism and of racial discrimination'. We know that the word 'zionism' is given different interpretations. Also, to label zionism... as racism means to forget history, means to adopt the use of a language which has been the source of incalculable ills for the Jews throughout the world, means to commit an act against peace and to revive an ever latent anti-semitism. The Christian community is called to exercise a permanent vigilance on these various points. Conscious at the same time of the gravity of the problems of the Middle East, we shall not cease to ask that justice be achieved for all, Palestinians and Jews, with dignity and peace.[28]

This position was not, however, supported by all French Catholics.

The French Justice and Peace Commission issued a document of a very different tenor, the central part of which affirmed:

> The reality today is this: two peoples are engaged in a confrontation within the same country which each of them considers his... One of these peoples, the Jews reassembled in Palestine, gave itself a political structure, and by a decision of the United Nations this became the state of Israel. But as a result of this fact, wars have broken out and injustices have been created. The Palestinians have undertaken a struggle in order to defend their own right to political existence. Until this right is acquired, peace will not be achieved.[29]

The state of Israel has provided maximum support to the zionist lobbies within and around the Church, with evident political objectives in mind. Moreover, as of the 1960s, Israeli embassies have assigned specialized personnel to follow Church affairs. This has been particularly evident in Rome where, notwithstanding the absence of formal diplomatic relations between the Holy See and Israel, constant informal contacts have been maintained through a special attaché chosen on the basis of a personal training and history which would make him particularly well qualified to deal with Vatican officials and Church procedures.

The Absence of an Arab/Muslim Lobby

Nothing of this kind can be said to have developed on the Arab side in support of the Palestinian cause. Although certain Arab states have embassies accredited to the Holy See, contacts and the flow of information seem to have been, throughout the years, sporadic and non-systematic. Coherent support for the Palestinian cause has come through the years from the Egyptian Churches (whose problems, however, became more complicated following, and as a result of, President Sadat's visit to Jerusalem in 1977)[30] and from the Catholic hierarchy of Algeria. The disappearance, in practice, as of the Lebanese civil war, of the World Conference of Christians for Palestine, has deprived the Palestinian cause of a precious voice of conscience in their support in the West.

As to Muslim institutional bodies, it will be remembered that the *Nostra Aetate* declaration dealt not only with relations between Christians and Jews but also with those between Christians and Muslims. A commission for such relations has been set up within the framework of the Secretariat for Relations with non-Christians, yet this has had little effect on the issue under discussion. Even if we discount the fact that the power accorded to the Commission for Relations with the Jews has since the start (1974) been greatly superior (due to the preferential status of the Secretariat for the Promotion of Christian Unity in which it is situated), the Commission for Relations with the Muslims has not acquired the wide breadth and the character of an instrument for political advancement which the former has achieved. Furthermore, while in the case of the relations with the Jews the institutional instruments have been assigned to the control of Church dignitaries who are themselves ardent supporters of the zionist cause, in the case of the relations with the Muslims the mechanisms in question have been taken over by appointees of whom the same cannot be said, and who in some cases do not even conceal their preference and admiration for zionism and try to undermine the issue of Palestine.[31] It is not known whether any protest has been made to the Vatican about this state of affairs.

The Tripoli Seminar

Discussions, seminars and debates on a religious level have taken place on various occasions at the level of the Commission for Relations with the Muslims and involving experts from both sides. Not until 1976, however, was the question of Palestine brought up at a Seminar on Islamic-Christian Dialogue, held in Tripoli (Libya) on 1-5 February under the joint sponsorship of the Libyan government and the Holy See. The occasion was a bitter failure.

The seminar, evidently intended by the Libyan government as a spectacular event designed to enhance its own prestige, was attended not only by Muslim *ulemas* and Catholic ecclesiastics, as well as Orthodox and Protestant observers, but also, according to the official communiqué, by 'intellectuals, politicians and journalists from over 60 countries'. The Vatican was represented at the highest level by Cardinal Sergio Pignedoli, an experienced diplomat and the president of the Secretariat for Relations with non-Christians. According to the communiqué, the aim of the seminar was:

> to create a new atmosphere of mutual confidence between the Muslim world and the Christian world, working to clear away the various difficulties and after-effects resulting from periods

of divergence, discord and colonization, seeking their real causes and making joint efforts to eliminate them... to construct bridges of understanding and co-operation between those who embrace the two religions, to create an atmosphere that will assist understanding of the material and moral crises endured by man in the modern world, in order to find practical solutions for them.[32]

The seminar produced a declaration, drawn up by experts in both the Muslim and the Christian delegations, and corresponding to the subjects discussed. These included: faith in one God; racism; development; religious freedom; peace; religion and science; education; the Holy Scriptures; religious co-operation; the rights of all peoples to scientific development; and Lebanon. The paragraph on Lebanon stated:

the two parties denounce the subversion that has taken place in Lebanon and denounce its camouflage as a confessional conflict. They also denounce any attempt to partition Lebanon and any attempt to interfere with the tolerant co-existence of all the spiritual families of Lebanon...

Paragraphs 20 and 21 of the declaration dealt, or rather were supposed to deal, specifically with the question of Palestine. In practice, however, no agreement on the wording could be reached between the Muslim experts and those of the Holy See. The proposed paragraphs read as follows:

Paragraph 20: The two parties regard revealed religions with respect; consequently they distinguish between Judaism and zionism, considering zionism an aggressive racist movement, extraneous to Palestine and to the whole region of the East.
Paragraph 21: Respect for rights and for justice, and concern for peace, and faith in the rights of peoples to self-determination, lead the two parties to affirm the national rights of the Palestinian people and their right to return to their lands; to affirm the Arab character of the city of Jerusalem and reject plans to Judaize or internationalize it; [and] to denounce all attacks on the sacred character of the Holy Places. The two parties demand the liberation of all prisoners in occupied Palestine, and in the first place of all Muslim *ulemas* and Christian ecclesiastics; they also

demand the liberation of all the Occupied Territories and call for the setting up of a permanent commission to investigate attempts to change the character of the Islamic and Christian Holy Places.

The Vatican delegate saw to it that the text of the declaration was followed by a postscript saying:

At the close of the Seminar on Islamic-Christian Dialogue at Tripoli, the two delegations are happy to recognize the positive character of the results of this historic dialogue, expressed in the final joint declaration. As regards especially the two paragraphs 20 and 21 of the declaration, their content will be transmitted by the Christian delegation to the Holy See authorities, which alone are competent in the matter.

On 12 February the *Osservatore Romano* published the final verdict:

The Christian delegation to the Tripoli Seminar on Islamic-Christian Dialogue has transmitted to the competent authorities of the Holy See, according to the agreement with the Islamic delegation, paragraphs 20 and 21 of the text of the final declaration... After an examination of these paragraphs the Holy See has declared that it cannot accept them, as their content does not correspond, on essential points, to the viewpoints of the Holy See, which are already well-known.

The text of the declaration was thus published with the word 'omitted' by paragraphs 20-21.[33]

10
The Holy See and the Lebanese Civil War: 1975–1976

By 1975 world attention was coming increasingly to focus on the situation in Lebanon. On 9 July 1974 the Lebanese Catholic Episcopate had addressed the following 'Letter from the Assembly of the Catholic Patriarchs and Bishops of Lebanon to the Bishops of the Whole World'. The text is worth reproducing almost in its entirety:

As for a quarter of a century, this region of the world, the birthplace of faith for so many millions of believers, has continued to witness the horrors of violence, the misery of exile, the hatreds which generate injustice; at a moment in which it seems possible to hope that the remorse of human conscience will lead to the dissipation through justice of hate, the reparation through law of wrong, and the re-establishment of confidence through concord; we believe it opportune to appeal to you, brothers in the episcopate, and through you to your Churches and to your co-citizens throughout the world, especially in the West, and most particularly still in those countries which are most directly and primarily responsible for justice and peace among men.

Various events certainly justify such hopes in the hearts of men of goodwill, but it would be pure illusion to believe that the Arab-Israeli conflict is about to find a definite and complete solution. Threats continue, in fact, to weigh upon this region and upon our country and violence is being exercised under various forms.

The efforts made with a view to the disengagement of the armed forces do not constitute, any more than does the prospect of a possible conference in Geneva, a sure means of preventing the clashes continuing in other sectors and by other methods. Promising as the peace initiatives may be, it must not be forgotten that the long road ahead is strewn with obstacles and pitfalls. No one can be unaware that problems of crucial importance have not yet even begun to find a solution.

Our country, in fact, even at the moment in which peace messengers pass through it, is still the theatre of violent and aggressive acts which bring ruin and cause the death of innocent victims among the civilian population.

The Use of Double Standards
And in such painful circumstances... we are deeply pained to observe how those responsible for politics in the West, the promoters of its ideologies... [and] its mass media, frequently evaluate such human dramas using a double standard that works to the disadvantage of the Arab populations in general, and of the Palestinians and Lebanese in particular.

It is somewhat of a consolation for us to state that a growing number of noble exceptions to this rule are emerging. Nevertheless we feel the need to appeal once more to honest consciences in order that the situation be understood and judged with greater truth and impartiality. One must certainly condemn injustice, but it is just as important to respect criteria inspired by equity. The kind of condemnation expressed must be equal to the kind of oppression exercised. The graver and more flagrant the injustice, the more vehement and solemn must be the condemnation.

In this sense, it seems opportune to ask oneself, for example, which recourse to violence is more to be condemned, that perpetrated by individuals or that organized by a state. Morality certainly cannot but be outraged by crimes perpetrated against the fundamental rights of citizens, but when these rights are violated by regular forces, in carrying out an official state policy, is the offence to morality not more outrageous than when similar activities (of course always to be condemned *per se*) are carried out by small groups of uncontrollable rebels? And which country can claim not to suffer from such uncontrollable elements?

In such circumstances, one must establish a fundamental

distinction (as some have fortunately done) between the violence exercised by the oppressors and the violence perpetrated by the... oppressed. The former generally have at their disposal powers and resources which allow them systematically to impose a kind of methodical, permanent terrorism; the oppressed, then, consider it legitimate to turn to terrorist acts, as if to shake off the chains of this system of violence from which they are unable to free themselves. It is certainly deplorable that relations between men and groups in our times are still marked by such imprints, so humiliating for civilization. But when one sees how the West, in cases of violence, hastens to libel and condemn only the oppressed, one is necessarily filled with profound bitterness. This must be the explanation for those few instances in which these oppressed act as they do in order to attract the attention of so-called international public opinion which they judge to be so partial and so unjust.

A Right to Return versus the 'Law of Return'
A similar discrimination is illustrated by the West's attitude towards the problem of 'return'. There are many people who refuse to understand the determination of the Palestinians to return to their land. But very few people have the courage to question the validity of the 'law of return', invented in favour of the Jews of the world for a 'return' which can only be realized at the expense of unjust deprivations [for others].

Under what pretext may a Jew just emigrated from the Soviet Union enjoy a preferential right, based on racial privilege, entitling him to a dwelling erected on land recently confiscated from Palestinians and situated in a zone just annexed by the state of Israel, in defiance of the opinion of the international community and in violation of the Geneva Conventions? Such injustice is often committed. Why is it so rarely condemned?

Western public opinion is often moved by the fate of the Jews who wish to leave the Soviet Union, and invokes in their favour the Declaration of Human Rights. But this same declaration does not only recognize the right to leave a country, even one's own country; it also proclaims the right to return to one's own country. These are two faces of the same reality. In order to respect human truth, world opinion must support only those proposals for a solution to the Arab-Israeli conflict that foresee a return of the Palestinian people to its land.

A People and Values

Unjust violence, which must be eliminated everywhere, has existed... for far too long. The devastating consequences make themselves felt today as well. The Palestinians have recourse to it here and there and the world loudly condemns them, but how is it that the on-going violence of which the Palestinians are permanent victims is not being condemned more vehemently?

Despite ample documentation... this situation, which has lasted for a quarter of a century, is often passed over in silence. In order to excuse the oppression, repression is invoked, or in order to reduce the enormity of the abnormality, they call it 'reprisal'. We in Lebanon know what atrocious realities are being hidden under such fallacious euphemisms, which no longer mislead any but those who prefer not to know or to see.

And what can the future bring when both the past and the present are so charged with violence?

The Palestinians are far from confident. They fear, not without reason, arrangements which would institutionalize the loss of their rights, and hence make this loss definitive. They are suspicious of the mentality prevalent in the West which judges everything on the basis of double standards.

Hundreds of thousands of these Palestinians live with us on Lebanese soil and our civilian population shares with them the horror of the reprisals. The iniquitous fate of the victims of the violence is thus added to the unjust fate of the exiles.

We must speak to you of the future of this people. We think, in fact, that the future of the faith and of charity in this region of the world is linked to a just solution of the future of the Palestinians. How can one possibly love and have faith when the violence of arms is the supreme arbiter? How, on the other hand, is it possible to foresee the future of the Christian presence in these countries when the Palestinians remain at the mercy of outbursts of religious or racial fanaticism on the part of a state which pretends to be founded solely on ethical and religious principles? It has correctly been stated: 'full respect for the inalienable rights of the people of Palestine is an indispensable element for the establishment of a just and lasting peace' (UN General Assembly resolution, 8 December 1970).

The fate of Jerusalem and of the Holy Places is likewise linked to the recognition and respect of these rights. Our Christian delegation to Lahore [Conference of the Muslim Heads of State on 23 February 1974] spoke in these terms to the Muslim heads of state and to the entire Muslim world. We promise to speak to you with the same language and we keep our promise right here: we implement the role assigned to the Christians of the Orient to constitute a link of understanding and charity between the great spiritual families of East and West. It is only in such a framework that the efforts and forces that aim to achieve a dignified, stable and just solution which 'responds to the needs of the special character of this unique city of Jerusalem... and to the rights and legitimate aspirations of the adepts of the three great monotheistic religions' (Paul VI, 22 December 1973), particularly 'the legitimate civil and religious rights of the persons, places and activities of all the communities present on Palestinian territory' (Paul VI, 22 December 1967), may be joined together.

In fact, the problem of the Holy Places is a problem of a 'presence'. Our delegation to Lahore, quite correctly, stressed this aspect: 'Will there be any authentic significance to the Holy Places as of the moment in which no believers originating from the country in which the latter are erected inhabit these places any more? In the absence of these people, the Holy Places will be reduced to nothing but skeletal vestiges of a long-gone past... Because it is up to man to realize the presence; the stones alone would not secure it.'

In this sense, we believe it necessary for many circles in the West to develop an awareness... of the true position of the Palestinians, who aspire to see the establishment in Palestine of a state [that is] secular in its government and whose children, the adepts of the three great monotheistic religions, are profound believers. The testimony of life offered by the Lebanese experience allows us to believe in a more prosperous future for such a state were the fanaticisms of race, of traditions and of interpretations banished from it.

Repression is not Peace
Viewed in such a perspective, peace becomes possible. Together with Pope Paul VI, we are all convinced that peace is not only possible, it is a duty. This is how the politics of fear and that of the balance of forces, both rooted in the 'secret and sceptical conviction that peace is practically impossible', can be defeated.

The Arab-Israeli situation is a sad illustration of the words of the head of the Church, who rejects 'the equivocal tendency to confuse peace with weakness (not only physical but also moral), with the renunciation of true law and justice, with the flight from risk and sacrifice, with timorous resignation and submission to domination by others, of acceptance of one's own slavery'.

The Pope continues: 'This is not... true peace. Repression is not peace. True peace must be founded on the sense of the intangible dignity of the human person, which is the source of unviolable rights and the corresponding duties' (Paul VI, 22 December 1973).

We believed, Very Venerable Brothers, that it was our duty to send you this appeal at a moment in which the world seems to detect some rays of peace in the Orient. We firmly believe that it will be understood and accepted in the same spirit which inspired it. Is it not the task of the Church of Jesus Christ to work for the establishment of what was a messianic prospect for the psalmist: 'Mercy and truth are met together; righteousness and peace have kissed each other'? (Psalms, 85:10).

Each one of us and each group of our faithful is determined to contribute his part to this work. Permit us, Venerable Brothers, to invite all Church pastors throughout the world to focus upon this human drama that we have exposed to you, and whose solution is of grave concern to the future of so many men, and of so many sacred values.

'Peace', the Pope said, 'lives thanks to the consent, even though individual and anonymous, which people give it. The affirmation of peace must become not only individual, but collective and communal. It must become an affirmation of the people and of the community of peoples. It must become conviction, ideology, action' (Paul VI, 22 December 1973). In this evangelic and authentically missionary context, we consign to your good attention the terms of this fraternal message, certain that we shall find in you and through you, in the priests, the ordained and the faithful of your Churches, a favourable echo and a generous response to the hope that we place upon your devotion to the cause of peace...[1]

This moving document can be seen, *a posteriori*, as a cry of alarm in view of events which were at that time maturing under the surface. Since the late 1960s, and especially following Jordan's expulsion of the PLO in 1970, the shadow of the Palestinian situation was gradually extending over Lebanon. This was due to Israel's refusal to implement the UN resolutions on Palestine, to its attempts to force the Lebanese to reject the PLO presence on their soil, and its aim of destroying the Lebanese example of multi-confessional and pluri-ethnic co-existence proposed by the PLO as a basic model for a future democratic, secular state in Palestine. It is worth asking how much responsibility for the bloodshed that was to occur some months after the publication of the bishops' appeal may be attributed to the lack of active response on the part of Christianity as a whole — and of the Catholic Church in the West, including the Holy See, in particular — to that dramatic, desperate call.

By 1975 the violence in Lebanon was reaching new heights. The bishops had warned that it was 'pure illusion' to believe in an imminent 'definite and complete solution' to the Arab-Israeli conflict. Implicit in the warning had been the suggestion that by nurturing such an 'illusion', attention was diverted from the growing danger in Lebanon. These fears were now revealed as solidly grounded. On 22 July 1975, at the height of the civil war, the Lebanese Catholic hierarchy issued another document, 'considering it to be its duty to spread [information] abroad, in the hope of arousing [people's] conscience and of reinforcing the will for good'. But the tenor of this document was already very different.

1. Causes of the Crisis

1.1. External Causes

As all are aware, our region has for some time seen a disturbed situation which policy — international, regional and local — has rendered explosive, and which has exacerbated the tension of the Palestinian drama with its ensuing injustice and misery. Thus it is that a people, reduced to exile, has not found in the international conscience sufficient protection for its rights and has been forced to launch itself into a lasting and unavoidable revolution.

1.2 Internal Causes

Furthermore, the currents of this policy have found a particularly favourable background for their disturbing activity in the internal state of the country. This situation has indeed become dramatic from many aspects: moral decay; a lessening of a sense of responsibility at various levels of society; a display of corruption in most sectors of public life; a keen sense of frustration in many regions, animating the most diverse groups; a social crisis that knits together, in zealous imitation of each other, a haphazardly revolutionary Left and a tenaciously reactionary Right. And it is obvious that state neglect has brought the tension to a head in an already alarming situation. Once the security forces were paralysed, the army condemned to inaction and, to a great extent, the borders of the country kept open to intruders and foreigners, one could expect every imposition. Disorder became synonymous with liberty; the media could indulge in the most infamous accusations; human dignity decreased in worth and personal interest supplanted the search for the common good; selfishness prevailed, displayed by individuals, communities and parties; arms became toys in the hands of all. From then on, could one expect anything other than this explosion of instincts, silencing the voice of tolerance and stifling all brotherly feeling? And this was the dreadful series of humiliations, surprise attacks and even real invasions, spreading death and destruction, not even sparing our sanctuaries though, throughout our history, these had been respected by all.

Were it not for the courageous and wise intervention of ministers of religion and men of goodwill, there would certainly have been the most deplorable of religious confrontations between people of different religious persuasions. Even so, the list of the victims... is too long: people kidnapped, killed and disfigured, institutions ransacked and left in ruins — so many deplorable atrocities that have been forcefully condemned by us, but which have almost shaken faith in Lebanon's capacity to survive and to persevere in its humane mission of civilization.

1.3 Attention and Vigilance
Thanks be to God, since the coming to power of the new government, the situation is, on the whole, starting to return to normal insofar as security and stability are concerned. This government has had the good fortune to undertake to compensate the victims (something that we demanded for all from the outset), to take energetic initiatives, and boldly to

elaborate plans to deliver the country from its ordeal, but above all to place it once more on the path of development and prosperity. Nevertheless, the situation still demands an attentive and vigilant attitude lest a smouldering fire be kindled once again. This is why it is our duty to all that we should courageously seek the remedies for these terrible evils.

2. Where does the Remedy Lie?

Let us endeavour to analyse this state of affairs together. If we are powerless to alter the course of international politics it falls upon us at least to draw attention to the danger and to seek to find a remedy for those sources of tension which have provoked this deplorable explosion.

2.1 The Palestinian Problem

Within this perspective, it was with great satisfaction that we received the declarations of the Palestinian authorities, affirming their determination not to become involved in the country's internal politics, to avoid every source of friction as well as every slur upon the national dignity, and to respect Lebanon's sovereignty. Has Lebanon not made the cause of Palestine its own? And has not Lebanon, through the voice of His Excellency, the President of the Republic, and with all the means at its command, firmly stood up in all circumstances and at all levels in defence of this cause of the rights of the Palestinians to regain their homeland? We ourselves, furthermore, loudly proclaimed the justice of this cause when, a year ago, our conference addressed a message to this effect to all the Catholic bishops of the world. This has subsequently become an official document of the United Nations Organization.[2]

The rest of the document is devoted to an exposition of Lebanon's internal social and political problems. Evidently the mood inside the episcopate had somewhat changed since the previous year. In 1974 the Church hierarchy had unanimously adopted a prophetic tone in admonishing world Christian opinion on its duty to side with the Palestinians in the conflict in order to safeguard both justice and Christian faith in the region. Yet a mere twelve months later the Church seemed subjectively involved in, and subdued by, events. It is almost as if, once aware that their prophecy had become a reality, the religious leaders took fright at their own foresight. In fact, this sequence of events must have alarmed the Vatican to a far greater extent than would appear from official statements. Suspended as usual between, on the one hand, its illusory faith in international diplomacy and the trend towards *realpolitik*, and, on the other hand, its preoccupation with the religious implications of its actions, the Vatican seemed paralysed in the face of events in Lebanon. It was only in a public allocution on 21 September 1975 that the Pope made a brief first reference to the situation:

> And then there is Lebanon, which until now has been for us, too, and for the world, a model of fruitful, peaceful co-existence and of the collaboration between the Christian population... and the Muslim population. And now these populations are engaged in furious confrontations while only a loyal and friendly concord can assure the homogeneity and international vocation of this dear country.[3]

On 4 October 1975 the leaders of all the religious communities in Lebanon, both Christians and Muslims, met at the seat of the Maronite Patriarchate in Bkerke. The meeting, which was attended by the Maronite, Greek Orthodox, Greek Catholic, Chaldean, Syriac, Armenian Catholic, Armenian Orthodox, Sunni, Shiite and Druze spiritual leaders, resulted in a joint statement reaffirming the conviction that co-existence between Christians and Muslims in Lebanon was necessary, and rejecting any division of the country along confessional lines. After examining the recent events in Lebanon and deploring the acts of violence committed by different factions, the statement went on to say:

> [The religious leaders] warn all Lebanese, and all residents in the Lebanese land, against the negative effects of a situation which is liable to deteriorate and have the most regrettable consequences for the national unity and independence of Lebanon and the integrity of its territory, not to speak of the dangers that it may bring upon the Palestinian cause, and the Arab cause in general.
> ...they proclaim and guarantee their support for the Palestinian cause and insist upon the importance of the agreements concluded between Lebanon and the Palestinian brothers being implemented.[4]

On 3 November, as the Lebanese situation deteriorated still further, Paul VI addressed a letter to the Lebanese president, Suleiman Franjieh. The letter, which was handed to the president by the Pope's special emissary, Cardinal Paolo Bertoli, contained an appeal for peace and reconciliation. But it added:

> The Holy See, for its part, while supporting the efforts of the leaders of the parties concerned to ensure justice for the Palestinian people, expresses its good wishes for the safety of Lebanon, in respect of its sovereignty and freedom from all external interference.[5]

The Vatican's attitude towards the Lebanese-Palestinian question was, and would remain for some years, summarized in the terms adopted in these few lines. What it basically implied was the Holy See's wish to separate the issues of Palestinian rights (for which the Church repeatedly asserted its full support) from that of the presence of the armed Palestinian Resistance in Lebanon. The Vatican saw the latter as a threat to the delicate balance of power on which Lebanon's inter-confessional co-existence (in which the Christians had a major role) was based. It was consequently thought to be a factor liable to destabilize the entire pattern of Christian-Muslim relations throughout the region. The Holy See's position, however, was by no means identified with that of the Maronite political Right, nor did it ever give the least sign of approval or encouragement to the Maronites' increasingly close politico-military alliance with Israel, in view of the division of Lebanon along confessional lines. On the contrary, Rome seems to have exerted constant pressure on the more intransigent wings of the Catholic parties in an attempt to persuade them to desist from their isolationist plans. An example was contained in Paul VI's allocution on 30 November 1975, on the occasion of a mass celebrated at St Peter's Basilica in the presence of Lebanese Maronite Patriarch Antoine-Marie Khoreiche:

> Up to now, your country has offered an example of the concrete (unfortunately only too rare) possibility of a peaceful and fraternal life between very different ethnic and religious communities; of a society likewise open to the contributions of different civilizations and capable of harmonizing them while maintaining its unique identity. Today, dissent, radicalized to

the point of deadly and destructive battles, seems to threaten this dynamic balance. We are profoundly saddened by it, for you, for all your compatriots whom we love, for the Middle East which watches this [Lebanese] formula of co-existence between Muslims and Christians, [and] for all peace-loving men throughout the world. Therefore, in the name of the New Testament, we beg you... to facilitate the path of peace and reconciliation. And once again, in the name of all humanity, we implore those responsible to seize upon any remaining chance to promote the unity of Lebanon, rejecting violence from wherever it comes, putting an end to the fratricidal battles, taking up again the friendly contacts among all the believers, Christians, Muslims and Jews, and searching for sincere collaboration among all citizens.[6]

The Pope returned to the subject three weeks later, during the traditional Christmas Eve allocution to the College of Cardinals on 22 December 1975:

What is to be said, then, about the still serious and unsolved problem of the Middle East? Should we say once more how close it is to our heart, and how much it concerns us, for strong and particular motives? Or must we recall again the fundamental lines which, in the view of the Holy See, must guide its just and lasting solution, and make it possible?

Although we are conscious of the still very recent tragedies which led the Jewish people to seek protection in a sovereign state of its own — indeed, precisely because we are aware of this — we would like to ask the sons of this people to recognize the rights and legitimate aspirations of another people which has also suffered for a long time: the Palestinian people.

As for Lebanon:

Those who have been able to know and admire at close hand the example of peaceful co-existence given for a long time by the population of Lebanon, Christian and Muslim, are led almost naturally to think that the explosion of violent hostilities of which it has become the theatre can have no adequate explanation other than in the interference of forces extraneous to Lebanon itself and to its true interests. Our wish, our warning, which

goes to everyone, cannot, therefore, be but this: do not desire,
do not permit, the destruction, for obscure reasons, of a tradition
of tolerant co-existence and collaboration which should, on the
contrary, also set an example for other and more extensive forms
of civil and religious co-existence in the Middle East, if it is
desired — as it must be — that a real, secure and stable peace
will reign there and restore to those lands a tranquillity that is
also in the interests of the neighbouring peoples.

And in this painful hour, let us call Christians, in particular,
to pray for Lebanon, that God may grant all its populations to
find once more the spirit of brotherhood, the way of concord
and national reconciliation.[7]

In early 1976 the Palestinian-Lebanese situation was the subject
of a highly significant statement issued by Cardinal Joseph
Bernardini, president of the National Conference of Catholic
Bishops of the United States. Again, it is worth quoting virtually
in its entirety:

The conflict in Lebanon is tragic. The plight of the nation and
its people cries out for understanding, compassion and concern
from the international community and from the Christian
Church in particular. The whole international community has
a stake in the fate and future of Lebanon because of what it has
represented in the modern history of the Middle East. The
Christian Church is particularly called on to show concern for
Lebanon because it has been the home of some of the oldest
and largest Christian communities in the Middle East.

To know the history of Lebanon is to be doubly distressed
at its present situation. Under difficult and dangerous
conditions, the Lebanese people have woven a delicate pattern
of political co-operation which has guaranteed an admirable and
remarkable freedom in the religious and cultural order. Few
would maintain that the system is without defects, but even
fewer can deny its substantial achievement in the conflict-ridden
history of the modern Middle East. Part of the present tragedy
in Lebanon is that this intricate fabric of religious, cultural and
political freedom is now at stake.

Those of us outside the daily conflict should not presume
too readily that we have grasped its complex nature. My purpose
in speaking is twofold: to express Christian concern for all parties

and to bring the issue before the Catholic community in the United States. Faced with an immensely complex situation, our first obligation is to seek understanding. In that spirit, I offer the following reflections.

[First], the present conflict is multi-dimensional: to isolate one element and to explain the total picture in the light of it is to miss the reality of the situation. At one level, it is a religious conflict involving members of the Christian and Muslim communities. In a society known worldwide for its religious tolerance, this dissolution of the fabric of peace is surely a great loss for all parties. The present strife has special significance for Christians since the importance of the Lebanese Christian community extends beyond the borders of that nation. In a sense the Christians of Lebanon have been a stabilizing and supportive force for other Christians in the Middle East; because of this, the preservation of religious freedom for all in Lebanon should be an objective for us outside and for those within the country. In a broader sense, the example of Christians and Muslims living together in the single society of Lebanon is unique testimony to religious liberty in the world; no effort should be spared in preserving the fabric of this unique society.

[Second,] while the religious factor is central to understanding the Lebanese conflict, it is not the only one. A second level of the conflict is socio-economic in nature. Social class divisions in Lebanon cut across existing religious differences: for a growing Muslim population, a key issue is the justice of the economic system. Observers of the situation vary in their assessment of the relative weight of the religious and economic issues, but no serious observer denies either of them.

Third, the religious and socio-economic divisions are set in the context of a political conflict. This involves fundamental questions about the very structure and shape of Lebanese society. The changing demographic composition and social complexion of Lebanon have placed serious strains on the social compact by which the society has been governed. There seems to be agreement that significant reform of the system is required, but substantial division exists about the kind of reform needed.

Finally, the unresolved political issues have now led to military conflict. This is now the most drastic aspect of the situation, but it is also a sign and a product of the deeper divisions in the social fabric.

Complex as these internal factors are, even they do not tell the whole story about the Lebanese situation. First, the internal conflict must be seen in the context of broader currents in the international system, since several outside forces are influencing the struggle. Second, it is necessary to understand Lebanon in light of the regional conflict which still prevails in the Middle East. For almost three decades Lebanon has remained precariously, but almost miraculously, at the very edge of the central conflict in the Middle East; though touched by it, Lebanon has not been subsumed within it. With the breakdown of civil order in Lebanon, it appears now to have been fully swept into the Middle East picture. It seems difficult to conceive now of a stable Lebanese settlement without the existence of a relatively stable regional peace.

Everyone recognizes the price of not achieving peace in the Middle East. The price of failing to achieve a lasting settlement in Lebanon should be equally clear to us; just as it is impossible to understand the conflict in Lebanon in isolation from other factors, so it is impossible to calculate the consequences of continued conflict solely in terms of the damage to Lebanon. For this reason the sustained attention and involvement of the international community, even perhaps an international peace-keeping force, is urgently required to protect the territorial integrity of the nation and to provide both emergency relief and reconstruction assistance.

The rationale behind such a response from those outside Lebanon is not limited to humanitarian concern, but should be based on an appreciation of the significance of Lebanon in the life of the Middle East politically, culturally, economically and religiously. It is the last reason which speaks directly to Christians today...

Our concern for Lebanon simply reinforces our interest in the broader problem of the Middle East. *An obvious link between Lebanon's internal strife and the wider Middle East problem is the Palestinian refugees in Lebanon.* There have been close links between Palestinians and the people of Lebanon. Recognizing the way in which the Palestinian problem is linked to the Lebanese conflict brings me back to the 1973 statement by the American bishops, 'Towards Peace in the Middle East'. In that statement we called for a comprehensive political settlement which would include:

> '*Recognition of the rights of the Palestinian Arabs, especially the refugees: this involves, in our view, inclusion of them as partners in any negotiations, acceptance of their right to a state and compensation for past losses to be paid not only by Israel but also by other members of the international community.*'

> *This recognition of the rights of the Palestinians should be accompanied on their part and by others in the international community by* 'recognition of Israel's right to exist as a sovereign state with secure boundaries'. Moreover, we continue to believe today, as we did in 1973, that UN resolution 242, as reaffirmed by UN resolution 338, provides the best basis for negotiation in the Middle East and should be maintained. These three elements still appear to me to be the basis for a just and peaceful settlement in the Middle East.

> There are signs that progress toward peace is being made in the Middle East. It continues to be true today, as it was in 1973, that substantial progress toward a just peace, in Lebanon and in the Middle East region, will require the significant and sustained involvement of major states in the international system and the international community as a whole. *It is also clear, I think, that no permanent peace can exist in the region unless the just claims of the Palestinian people are met.*

> The role of the United States is central to both of these points. I use the occasion of this statement to urge our government towards two actions: first, to set an example of disinterested and constructive diplomacy in the Middle East; *second, explicitly to take up the position that the Palestinians be included as partners in all negotiations to be undertaken on the solutions to the Middle East conflict.*[8]

As had been the case in the past, the two most active Western Catholic episcopates in moments of crisis in the Middle East were still those of the United States and France. However, whereas the American bishops' statement recognized the need to find a political solution to the 'just claims of the Palestinian people' as a necessary prelude to peace in Lebanon, and called upon its government to act towards this end, the French Church, traditionally close to the Lebanese Maronites, practically ignored the centrality of the Palestinian issue and called upon the faithful to show solidarity mainly with 'the Lebanese Church'. Examples of this attitude were to be found in an appeal issued on 27 March 1976 by Mons. R.

Etchegaray, president of the French Episcopal Conference:

> As Frenchmen and as Christians we have special ties with Lebanon. Many priests, monks and nuns from amongst us have dedicated their lives to it. Some have now even shed their blood. This is the time for an active demonstration of our friendship and our fraternity. I dare hope that all nations and all the inhabitants of Lebanon (including the Palestinian refugees), in search of a new and just balance, will rise above their own interests in order to re-establish... peace and unity. I associate my voice to that of Paul VI in recalling once more that 'Violence is no solution to the problems. In fact it aggravates them.' I ask all the Catholics of France to express their solidarity with the Church of Lebanon, which is profoundly martyred and whose very existence is threatened.[9]

In a letter sent to all parishes and those responsible for the communities in Paris, Cardinal François Marty, archbishop of Paris, said:

> In the face of these innumerable instances of excessive violence, it is no longer possible to limit ourselves to individual reactions. I call upon the Catholics of the Church of Paris to become aware of their solidarity with the whole population of Lebanon and the victims of this drama, particularly with the different Christian communities, [who are] 'profoundly martyred and whose very existence is threatened'.
>
> I ask you... insistently to invoke the faithful to pray next Sunday in communion with the Pope for peace and justice in Lebanon.
>
> ...We pray God with the [Maronite] Patriarch [Mons. Khoreiche] that his compatriots should rise above all considerations of confessionalism or of single groups, and collaborate fully in the reconstruction of the ruins and the rebuilding together of a renewed Lebanon.[10]

On 24 March 1976 Paul VI made the following appeal for peace in Lebanon, during a general audience in the Vatican:

> We cannot conceal our great distress which we must share with all of you this morning, inviting you to pray together with us.

The Catholic Church and the Question of Palestine

The situation in Lebanon, and particularly in Beirut, has once again become tragic. It is the scene of merciless combat, of the destruction of the vital points of the city, of the extermination of whole families. We feel this hardship in the depths of our heart since our affection for all the people of the Lebanon is so strong.

We make a pressing appeal to all who are involved in this terrible drama. We exhort all to put a truce into operation, to lay down the arms of fratricide, and this on all sides!

Violence is no solution to the problems. In fact it aggravates them. The people desire peace; they are tired of seeing the continuing massacres and destruction.

They are watching the very roots of all social life and of any possible co-operation between the various groups in Lebanon being destroyed.

We solemnly appeal to all parties to make every effort to arrive at an agreement as soon as possible, and to reach those solutions which that country and the entire world awaits.

If necessary, the friendly nations, without seeking their own interests, must help Lebanon to overcome these difficulties and must inspire sincere thoughts of peace in the various parties.[11]

The Lebanese-Palestinian issue was at the centre of the allocution that the Pope addressed to President Anwar Sadat, on the occasion of his visit — the first ever by an Egyptian president — to the Holy See, on 8 April 1976:

Your Excellency knows our profound concern with the problem of peace in the Middle East. *With deep concern for this generation and for generations yet to come, we extend our sincere encouragement to continue to seek the peaceful and just solution also to the problem of the Palestinian people, for whose dignity and rights we have repeatedly expressed humanitarian and friendly interest.* And the question of Jerusalem and of the Holy Places must be resolved with due regard for the millions of followers of the three great monotheistic religions, for whom these represent such supreme values.

We cannot forgo this opportunity to restate our anguish and preoccupation for the destiny of Lebanon. This conflict is also tragically situated within the framework of the problem of peace in the Middle East. In addition to the deplorable destruction of

154

human lives, this civil war does incalculable harm to fraternal co-existence, and may have very sad effects on Muslim-Christian relations in the entire region.[12]

In mid-April, following the unsuccessful missions carried out on behalf of the Pope by Cardinal Bertoli, Paul VI sent a pontifical delegation to Beirut, composed of Mons. Mario Brini, secretary of the Congregation for Oriental Churches, Fr Henry de Riedmatten, O.P., Mons. Francesco Monterisi of the State Secretariat, and Fr Marco Brogi. The delegation stayed in Lebanon from 16 to 25 April, made contact with the various religious communities and returned to Rome with a voluminous informative dossier. On 3 May, after having examined the documentation, the Pope addressed an allocution to the members of the delegation, centred exclusively on the question of aid to the population.

This was followed on 1 August by another appeal from the Pope on behalf of the Lebanese and of the Palestinians in Lebanon:

It is the Lebanese people that suffers, a people with great traditions, an industrious and open-minded people, who have in recent years built a modern nation in which the various communities, above all the Christians and the Muslims, collaborated freely and in harmony. To this suffering we must add that of the Palestinian refugee population, which for 30 years has been frustrated in its desire to have its own land, its own country.

...We hope that the leaders on all sides will continue... to work for a true and generous reconciliation. We turn to all those who are in a position to do so... to come to the aid of the defenceless population of children, of the injured, of exiles, of refugees and of prisoners.

We make an appeal to human common sense in order that, at least where there are groups trapped in camps without foodstuffs and assistance, neutral initiatives may bring the comfort of their humanitarian aid.[13]

Two weeks later, Paul VI evoked his past efforts for peace and the contacts he had established with all parties, including 'the representatives of the Palestinian populations, to whom... since the beginning, indeed for years, we have never denied our assistance and our aid...':

Rather than having recourse to denunciations or to public condemnations — even when it was Christians who were the victims of destruction and murder — we preferred to engage in discreet and constant action in favour of reconciliation and justice for all, without distinction.

Today, we suffer with all those who suffer from the recent, deplorable bloodshed and we fear for their future. And again today we wish to appeal for understanding, participation, and the avoidance of revenge and vengeance, for generous and courageous accords, which, after all the destruction wrought during a conflict that has lasted far too long, would permit us to look forward to a more serene future for all.[14]

11
Paul VI: The Final Years and an Overall Assessment

On 10 November 1977 the Holy See, for the first time since the occupation of the West Bank and the Gaza Strip in 1967, voiced its objections to the Israeli colonization of the Occupied Territories. The *Osservatore Romano*'s article of that date, headed 'Israeli Settlements on the West Bank of the Jordan', consisted almost entirely of a long and detailed compilation of the criticisms of Israel's colonization policies voiced in recent years by Western bodies other than the Church: the UN, Britain, the EEC and the US. The reader is referred to the original article for a short history of these settlements, together with the international criticism they aroused. Suffice it to say here that the Vatican paper left no doubt as to its own position on the subject:

> Since the beginning of last summer polemics have flared up again, with vast international repercussions, between Arabs and Israelis. This is in connection with the 'colonies', or settlements of Jewish population, that the government of Israel has decided or intends to create in the territories occupied during the war of June 1967, and particularly on the West Bank of the Jordan...
>
> ...It is clear to everyone that a massive Jewish presence in the Occupied Territories would make it impossible to return them to the Arabs. As regards the West Bank, the introduction of a Jewish population radically upsets the plans being made to set up a 'Palestinian homeland' there — whatever form this 'homeland' may take — in order to solve the Palestinian problem, which has now become the most complex and

fundamental difficulty in the whole tangled Middle East crisis...

As has been seen, criticisms of the Israeli decisions come under two headings. In the first place, there is the conviction that these decisions are contrary to UN resolutions and in particular to the 1949 Geneva Conventions...

The other reason is the fact that, objectively, the Israeli decisions appear as *faits accomplis*, which hinder the efforts being made towards progress in the Middle East. In a word, it is not possible to make headway with the negotiations while initiatives that prejudice its solution are going on...

In particular, there come to mind the words spoken by the Holy Father, in his address to the cardinals on 23 June 1974: 'On our side, we should not like to fail to encourage all those in a position of responsibility to make every possible effort... to search for a just and dignified way of solving the difficult and painful problem of the fate of the Palestinian populations.' On this subject, His Holiness's words on 22 December 1975 are more relevant than ever: 'Although we are conscious of the still very recent tragedies which led the Jewish people to seek protection in a sovereign state of its own — indeed, precisely because we are aware of this — we would like to ask the sons of this people to recognize the rights and legitimate aspirations of another people which has also suffered for a long time: the Palestinian people.'[1]

The article's appearance coincided with Sadat's announcement of his visit to Jerusalem. But the Pope's immediate reaction to the Egyptian president's trip seemed to oscillate between optimism and a scepticism expressed through a series of question marks:

The head of the Egyptian people is today in Israel, where he is warmly welcomed. Does this mean an end to the multiform war which has lasted for 30 years? Will peace flower in this strategic and painful region of the world? Is it possible to see the dawn of concord between populations which, beyond politics, are united by the sovereign cult of a single and unique living god? This is a great event; hope is reborn, for a real peace for all the peoples.[2]

Sadat's visit to Jerusalem came on 19 November 1977. A month later, during an address to the cardinals on 22 December 1977,

Paul VI still seemed uncertain of the outcome, but affirmed that if the initiative was to be crowned with success, Christianity's 'legitimate interests' would have to be taken into account:

> We are following developments in the [Middle East] situation with very special attention and interest. We do not wish to take sides amid the different and at times opposing opinions... but we cannot hide our hopefulness... that the initiatives now in progress, undertaken with a courage so daring as to appear rash, will succeed in setting in motion a process from which — thanks to the participation of all those concerned and through their goodwill and wisdom — there may at last emerge solutions corresponding to the criteria of justice, equity and political farsightedness, as well as those of human sensitivity. Only through these criteria can a balance be struck between demands, aspirations and interests that are so complex and often opposed.
>
> Again on this occasion, the Holy See has not failed to express its thoughts discreetly and confidently, especially on the points most clearly touching its mission of charity and its responsibility regarding the legitimate interest of the Christians. We now repeat our wish that the difficult longstanding question may be speedily directed towards an equitable settlement, and that all the people of an area so rich in the history of religion and civilization may at long last enjoy a just and lasting peace.

The last two paragraphs leave no doubt that the Vatican still saw solutions to the Palestinian question and to the longstanding problem of the status of Jerusalem as essential conditions for the success of Sadat's initiative. A US Catholic paper echoed the Pope's thoughts and convictions. On 11 December 1977 the *National Catholic Register* of California wrote, under the somewhat misleading title, 'Israel's Christian Minority':

> While many warlike gestures have made headlines as tall and long-lasting as has Mr Sadat's visit to Jerusalem, we cannot recall any gesture of peace that has so stirred the world's press and, we may infer, the world itself. Peace in the Middle East seemed impossible for three decades; for at least three years it has also seemed imperative. Now, with Mr Sadat's astonishing and decisive action, peace in the Middle East seems not only imperative but possible.

Unfortunately, the first fears of the Carter administration have proven fully justified: Mr Sadat's visit to Mr Begin in Jerusalem has been viewed in some Arab states as a base surrender and, despite its publicity, it has been interpreted as a stealthy first step toward bilateral peace between Israel and Egypt. What such an Egyptian-Israeli peace would mean for the rest of the Arab world is pretty clear from demography and geography: Egypt represents half of the world's Arab population, and borders on Israel. Without Egypt, war on Israel loses much of its menace.

Despite what Mr Sadat's overtures have prompted various journalists to assert, a satisfactory solution to the Palestinian problem remains essential to a lasting peace in the Middle East. The reason for this is simple: the Palestinian problem remains as a major cause of conflict in the Middle East. And despite the declared fears of various Arab leaders that Mr Sadat plans to abandon the Palestinians, his own studied actions in the past few weeks belie any such intention. He has repeatedly called the Palestinian question central to peace. He very significantly declined to put his signature to the communiqué issued at the end of his visit to Jerusalem, and the communiqué's failure to cite the Palestinian question probably accounts for his refusal.

Not only must a satisfactory solution to the Palestinian question be deemed essential to peace in the Middle East, and consequently essential to any formula for peace; it must be deemed essential to any formula for peace that will satisfy Christians. A Christian presence in the land of Christ and of the first Christians is as vitally important to Christians as a Jewish presence in the land of Abraham, our common father, is to Jews.

The point is this: a Christian presence in the Holy Land means the Palestinian presence in the Holy Land. Here the interests of Christians and the interests of world peace coincide, since peace seems impossible without guarantees to the rights of Palestinians living in the Holy Land, which is the land of their fathers long before them.

We quite understand that the presence of Palestinians within the Holy Land presents huge problems to the state of Israel. We most fervently hope that the state of Israel will not try to solve this problem by dismissing it, and the Palestinians.

History does not encourage optimism here. David Ben Gurion thought the Palestinian problem would just go away; he assured Israel that a new generation of Palestinians would forget the land their fathers and mothers had fled. Mr Begin himself, then commanding Jewish forces fighting for the establishment of a Jewish state in Palestine, justified terrorism against innocent populations on the grounds that it would scatter them and clear the way for a Jewish state. We can only hope that three decades of bitter experience has taught him better.

If Palestinians, born Christian and Muslim alike, are to be enabled to remain in the land holy to their religions as well as to Judaism, they must have real (not theoretical) access to the basics of life: work, shelter and education. Mainly for lack of reasonably easy access to these basic needs, Palestinians have been emigrating from the Holy Land by the thousands.

Exact numbers are very difficult to come by, partly because the redrawing of municipal lines by Israeli authorities has altered the terms of reference. But Pope Paul has often declared his concern at the prospect of a vanished Christian community in the Holy Land...

As for what Christians can do, we repeat what was said by Pope Paul: 'If this Christian community which originated in Palestine 2,000 years ago and is still there today is to ensure its continued survival... then the Christians of the whole world must be generous and help the Church in Jerusalem with the charity of their prayers, the warmth of their understanding and the tangible expression of their solidarity.'

By 'the tangible expression of their solidarity', Pope Paul means continued monetary help but also, as he implies with his next breath, outspoken demands by Christians that the Palestinians not be forgotten in any formula for peace. The 'just and prompt peace' the Pope hopes for can be found, he notes, 'in the equitable recognition of the rights and legitimate aspirations of all the people concerned'.

On 12 January 1978 Paul VI received in audience Israel's foreign minister, Moshe Dayan:

The conversation between the Holy Father and the minister — at which Archbishop Agostino Casaroli, secretary of the Council for Public Affairs of the Church State Secretariat, and Israeli Ambassador Zeev Shek were present — had as its principal theme the situation in the Middle East, with special reference to the initiatives now under way for the attainment of peace in the region.

His Holiness expressed his keen desire for a rapid and just solution of the crisis so as to put an end to the conflicts and sufferings of all the peoples of the Middle East, while respecting the rights of all and laying the foundations for a fruitful life together.

The Holy Father outlined the Holy See's point of view on the question of Jerusalem and the Holy Places, and pointed out that the solution proposed by the Holy See for Jeusalem should be understood as arising from the city's unique and sacred character and from the spiritual interests of millions of Catholics, as well as other believers of the three great monotheistic religions throughout the world, and of the respective communities residing in the Holy City.

For his part, the minister explained the Israeli position on the same questions and mentioned the efforts made by his government for the attainment of peace. He also pointed out what Israel had done to guarantee the protection of the Holy Places of all the religions and free access to them.

In conclusion, the Holy Father renewed his earnest hope for the reconciliation of the peoples of the Middle East and the Holy See's willingness to contribute, according to the possibilities open to it, to the establishment of peace.[3]

In his address on this occasion, Paul VI stressed three points: first, 'negotiations [which] may prove decisive for a just peace' must take place *'with the participation of all the interested parties'*, obviously including the Palestinians; second, the solutions reached should 'combine the *basic demands of both security and justice for all the peoples of the area* and lay the foundations for a peaceful future for those peoples'; and third:

We fervently hope for a solution that will not only satisfy the legitimate aspirations of those concerned, but also take into account the pre-eminently religious nature of the Holy City. We therefore trust that the proposal put forward several times by the Holy See, in view of the spiritual significance of Jerusalem, will be seen as a positive contribution to such a solution.[4]

Thus, three times in one short paragraph, Paul VI implicitly reiterated his distrust of any solution that did not clearly include a satisfactory settlement for the Palestinians. He also repeated the Holy See's stance on Jerusalem, rejecting the Israeli claim to unilateral sovereignty over the Holy City. On his return to Israel, Dayan admitted to the Israeli press that he had been disappointed by the Pope's insistence, all the more so because he had hoped to extract concessions from the Vatican on the question of Israeli sovereignty over Jerusalem in exchange for the liberation of Mons. Capucci.

Dayan did not consider the meeting satisfactory from Israel's point of view. He had hoped that an agreement with the Vatican over the question of Jerusalem would present Sadat (for whom this issue was particularly crucial in view of Egypt's future relations with the Muslim world, and especially with Saudi Arabia) with a *fait accompli*. But what did the proposal referred to by Paul VI consist of?

According to Vatican sources, the Pope never renounced the idea of a special statute for the Holy City and its surroundings. He considered the monopoly of a single state (representing a single religion) over Jerusalem as an unacceptable aberration for Christianity. Not even Israel's frequently proposed 'freedom of access' to the shrines could be taken seriously, particularly in view of the experience of the Israeli occupation since 1967. During these years, Israel had imposed architectural, demographic and cultural changes that had altered the very nature of the city. In innumerable statements, the Pope reiterated that there had to be effective guarantees, not only for the shrines sacred to the three religions, but also for the religious, civil and other fundamental rights of the various communities.

Faced, on the one hand, with Israel's opposition to any suggestion involving the United Nations and, on the other, with the impotence of the UN which had been incapable of enforcing its own resolutions on Palestine for the past 30 years, the Vatican suggested the mandating of a group of nations as guarantors of the extra-statal status of Jerusalem. France, Spain, Italy, Britain, Greece and the US, among others, were mentioned as guarantors on behalf of the various Christian communities, who would in turn be responsible before the Churches to which these communities were affiliated. Such an arrangement would eliminate Israeli jurisdiction over greater East Jerusalem, thus allowing Arab Palestinians of whatever religion to exercise their right to self-determination according to their political choice.

Although such a plan left many details to be worked out, Paul VI correctly considered it as a 'contribution to the establishment of peace'. For that very reason, it could not but be anathema to the state of Israel, whose ambition was the Judaization of Jerusalem.

On this point, therefore, the conversation between Dayan and the head of the Church could not but constitute a dialogue of the deaf. Israel had always seen the Sadat initiative as representing a 'separate peace' with the biggest and most important Arab state, while preserving its own freedom of manoeuvre in all other areas. Thus the Holy See's idea that here was an opportunity to settle the question of Jerusalem 'according to justice' was alien to Israel. The Begin government was to demonstrate this all too clearly two years later, when the Knesset passed a law declaring that Jerusalem was the unified, indivisible capital of Israel.

But for the moment, hopes were still running high at the Vatican. On 13 February 1978, almost exactly one month after Dayan's visit, Paul VI received the Egyptian president Anwar Sadat. Following expressions of cordial welcome and warm compliments on Sadat's 'intense work for peace', the Pontiff went on to point out:

> We are aware of the difficulty of attaining such a solution, which must necessarily comprise different elements: a prospect of justice and security must be reconstituted for all the peoples of the Middle East (and we are thinking here also of Lebanon, which has already paid a high price by reason of the unresolved situation); the legitimate aspirations of the Palestinian people must be satisfied; juridical and factual conditions must be ensured for Jerusalem such that the city ceases to be the cause of strife between the parties, and becomes — in accordance with its vocation — a religious centre of peace, where the local communities of the three great monotheistic religions can live together in peace and enjoy equality of rights, and where Jews, Christians and Muslims of the region and the entire world can meet and engage in fraternal dialogue.

The same issues were underlined in the joint communiqué:

> ...The Sovereign Pontiff renewed again the earnest hope that the problem of the Palestinians and also that of Lebanon should be brought to a just solution; he then recalled the well-known

position of the Holy See on the question of Jerusalem and the Holy Places.[5]

Paul VI's manifest concern that the Sadat initiative might create new problems for Lebanon was well-founded: on 13 March 1978 (exactly a month after Sadat's audience with the Pope) Israel launched the 'Litani operation', in which the Israeli army invaded part of southern Lebanon. A telegram from the Vatican's secretary of state Cardinal Villot to Mons. Alfredo Bruniera, the apostolic nuncio in Beirut, read as follows:

The Holy Father is deeply grieved at the huge number of victims caused by the indiscriminate Israeli bombing even of the defenceless population in refugee camps and Lebanese towns.

Your Excellency is charged to express, in the name of His Holiness, deepest sympathy to the authorities and to the families of the Lebanese and Palestinian victims, assuring them of his fervent prayers and of his consoling apostolic blessing.[6]

The Israeli war in southern Lebanon dragged on for months; houses were dynamited; villages and refugee camps were bombed; and there were massacres such as the one in the Lebanese village of Khyam, where scores of civilians, mostly women and children, were murdered in the mosque in which they had taken refuge by Israel's mercenaries of the Saad Haddad militia. The Holy See, meanwhile, pursued its diplomatic activities in view of the 'peace talks'. On 29 April Paul VI received King Hussein of Jordan. The Pontiff's allocution on this occasion leaves little doubt that the Vatican still saw the Hashemite king as a future partner to any settlement in Palestine:

Knowing Your Majesty's commitment to the search for a peace based on a well-balanced recognition of the legitimate demands of the various parties, we wish to declare to you our heartfelt desire that the leaders concerned may come decisively to grips with the crucial issues of the conflict, and through wisdom and goodwill find a speedy solution to them. In particular, we once again express the hope that a just end may be found for the sad situation of the Palestinians, and that Jerusalem, the Holy City... may become the 'pinnacle' of peace and a meeting-place for peoples from every part of the world...[7]

The audience granted to King Hussein was Paul VI's last public act concerning the Middle East. The Pope died four months later, as a new phase, characterized by yet more bloodshed and aggression, was to open in the region to which he had devoted much of his activity.

Paul VI's Contradictory Policies on Palestine

In summing up Paul VI's pontificate (1963-78) in relation to the question of Palestine, the following observations may be made:

1. Over the period as a whole, a *formal* continuity with the Vatican's traditional policy on Palestine was maintained. The Holy See remained almost the only Western state not to have accorded *de jure* recognition to the state of Israel and consequently not to have established formal relations with it. (Spain did not establish diplomatic relations with Israel until late 1986.)

2. However, the breach opened during the previous pontificate (John XXIII) in the Vatican's traditional stance that zionist statehood was to be rejected *as a matter of principle* was considerably widened under Pope Paul VI. The Church's refusal to legitimate the state of Israel became ever more visibly a *conditional* refusal. This change was determined by pressures both internal and external to the Church, as well as by new realities: i.e. the fact that after the 1967 war practically all the Church's interests in the Holy Land had come under Israeli rule. Recognition of Israel now became 'negotiable', which in turn implied the existence of some level of relations. Paul VI's policies also expressed a desire, on the part of the Vatican, to act as a mediator in the Middle East conflict. He hoped that this would help to achieve the basic conditions (a 'just peace') for the attainment of the Church's goals in the Holy Land: mainly, to save whatever could be saved of the Christian presence there. As a result, contacts were established on various levels between, on the one hand, peripheral and central Church bodies and Catholic milieux and, on the other, zionist circles, including Israeli government bodies.

3. In marked contrast with the past, and also with the type of relations entertained by the Holy See in cases where no diplomatic relations existed (i.e. the Soviet Union), a tone of deference was introduced in the case of relations with Israel. Moreover, during the 15 years of Pope Paul VI's pontificate, no less than three leading members of the Israeli government were received at the Vatican,

though in 'private' audiences.

4. The Vatican II statement on relations between the Church and the Jews (*Nostra Aetate*) was originally intended by Church liberals as a means of 'purifying' relations between Catholics and Jews and preventing religious prejudice, at least in codified forms, from leading to racial discrimination. Yet it ended up, against the will of its promoters, less as an instrument of inter-religious understanding than as a means of helping to legitimate zionist goals under the cover of theological dialogue. Ever more powerful zionist lobbies had developed in some Catholic environments, particularly in the traditionally influential French and American chapters of the Church, but also in the Vatican itself.

Until about the mid-1970s, this influence was often countered by pressure from Arab Christianity and Catholic circles sympathetic to the Palestinian cause. The Lebanese crisis and the growing divisions in the Arab world, however, brought about a constant decline in this activity, leaving the way open for Israeli pressure groups.

5. These developments did not, however, obfuscate the principles which guided Paul VI's policies on Palestine and constituted the basic conditions posed by the Holy See in its dealings with Israel and the Arab world. Notwithstanding the shifts in tone and the Vatican's evident effort to avoid 'irritating' Israel, these fundamental conditions remained: (a) a status for Jerusalem which would concretely and effectively guarantee the rights of the Church and of Christianity in the Holy Land so that an ongoing testimony of Christianity's continuity could be freely exercised; and (b) a 'just peace' in Palestine — 'just' being an internationally accepted code-word implying the need for a solution to the Palestinian question in accordance with the 'legitimate aspirations of the Palestinian people', in the first place the refugees' wish to return to their homeland. The two conditions were usually stated by the Pope in the same breath, as practically inseparable from one another, and as unattainable one without the other.

6. Israel's total rejection of both these conditions created, in theory, the basis for an alliance between the Arab world and the Vatican. Such an alliance never materialized, however, due on the one hand to Arab exclusivism and, on the other, to Jordanian claims over East Jerusalem.

7. As already stated, there is no doubt that Paul VI considered

the achievement of the 'legitimate rights and aspirations of the Palestinians' as an indispensable condition for peace based on justice in the region. A certain evolution had taken place in the terminology used by the Holy See: until 1973 the emphasis had been on the term 'refugees' or 'refugee populations', whereas from that year onwards the word *gente* (which in Italian may mean 'collectivity of people' or 'people' and also 'nation'), and then simply 'people' was employed. In all these cases, however, the Pope left no doubt that the Holy See continued to consider the Palestinian Arabs, whether Christian or Muslim, as 'the people of the Holy Land'. In this sense, the Pope's stance had always been far ahead of all other Western positions, including those of the European governments. In 1973 Paul VI preceded an Italian president by seven years when he pointed out to Golda Meir that the Jews who had suffered and then conquered a state of their own should have more understanding for the Palestinian people's similar aspirations.

At the same time, however, and notwithstanding the large number of Christians engaged in the Palestinian Resistance, the Vatican did not seem inclined to recognize the PLO as representing the Palestinians and their rights. There are many reasons for this, the first being that the Holy See, as a general policy, avoids giving formal recognition to liberation movements, especially those professing armed struggle, in whatever part of the world. This principle may perhaps be seen as the residual policy of an international Church which, until about a century ago, had itself been a colonial power, directly or indirectly. Alternatively, one can consider it as part of the conservative *realpolitik* which predominates in Vatican policies on all conflicts until the moment at which there is a demonstrable and unmistakable shift in the balance of power. In general terms, this principle could well be included in what progressive Catholics have defined as 'the lack of a prophetic streak' in Church policies. As far as the Palestinian question is concerned, however, it may be added that not only concerted zionist pressure, but also Arab ambiguity, have helped to put a brake on the establishment of contacts between the PLO and the Vatican. Paradoxically, the initial phase of the Lebanese civil war had been the occasion for a brief meeting in November 1975 between the Pope's special emissary, Cardinal Bertoli, and the PLO leader, Yasser Arafat. Further developments in Lebanon, however, blocked this process. The PLO's deep involvement in events in Lebanon, its alliance with the 'leftist' Lebanese National Movement (LNM), the subsequent effective division of Lebanon and the growth of PLO power there, accompanied by increasing hostility towards the latter on the part of the Maronite bloc, had a strong influence on the Vatican's attitude. During this phase, Vatican diplomats — undoubtedly also under pressure from Lebanese Maronite quarters — believed that any contacts between the Holy See and the PLO leadership might be interpreted as a legitimation of the armed Palestinian presence in Lebanon and its role there.

8. Paul VI was fully aware of the tragedy of the Lebanese conflict and of the consequent dangers for Christianity in the Middle East, and for Christian-Muslim relations in general. Although in his public speeches he seemed partially to accept the view that it was a confessional conflict, he made considerable efforts to encourage in every possible way the unity, integrity and pluralistic nature of Lebanon. If anything, the Lebanese tragedy confirmed the Pope's assessment of the centrality of a Palestinian solution to any Middle East settlement.

9. The question of Palestine, including Jerusalem, was a central theme of Paul VI's pontificate. In more than one way, and notwithstanding reservations in relation to the PLO, Giovanni Battista Montini had been, more than any previous Pontiff, the 'Pope of the Palestinians'. Through one of the many paradoxes which characterized his rule, his was also the pontificate during which, more than at any other time, zionist influence expanded in the Vatican to the point where any official condemnation of zionism was prohibited. In fact, by the end of Paul VI's pontificate the Holy See seemed poised at equal distance from zionist and Arab positions. It was waiting to see whether a new regional balance of power would open up fresh possibilities for its own demands in Palestine.

12
John Paul II
and the
Question of Palestine

Less than two months after his election as head of the Church, Pope John Paul II expressed a desire to visit the Holy Land. On 10 December 1978, before an audience of 70,000 people gathered in St Peter's for the recitation of the 'Angelus', he exclaimed:

Oh! How I wish I could go to the land of my Lord and Redeemer! How I wish I could find myself in those very streets in which the people of God used to walk at that time, climb to the top of Sinai, where the Ten Commandments were given to us! How I wish I could travel along all the roads between Jerusalem, Bethlehem and the Sea of Galilee! How I wish I could stop on the Mount of the Transfiguration, from which the massif of Lebanon appears...

This was and is my greatest desire, ever since the beginning of my pontificate. I am grateful for the requests and suggestions that have reached me in this connection. But, though regretfully, I must, at least for the present, forgo this pilgrimage, this act of faith, whose significance can be more deeply understood by the bishop of Rome, who is the successor of Peter.

Meanwhile, I beg you, beloved Brothers and Sisters, let us commend to the Lord, in our prayer, this part of the earth, so closely connected with the history of our salvation.

Let us pray for the Holy Land.

Let us pray for Lebanon, which has been sorely tried by war and destruction for many years.

Let us commend to the Lord the special mission entrusted

to Cardinal Paolo Bertoli, who has gone in these days to Lebanon.

Let us pray for peace in the Middle East.[1]

The question of the Middle East, and in particular of Palestine, was the first issue through which Karol Wojtyla — the first non-Italian to become Pope in 350 years, and the first Pope in decades not to have reached the papacy through a long training at the service of Vatican diplomacy — was to discover the conflict between his own will and the realities of the traditional, institutional foreign policy of the Holy See. Vatican sources confirm the disarray which spread through the State Secretariat at the arrival of the Polish Pope. A man liking power, a ruler by nature, a leader by instinct, with his own, rather medieval, vision of the Church and a somewhat old-fashioned taste for theatrical gestures, Pope John Paul II's entry into the Vatican was much like that of an elephant into a greenhouse. The idea of a pilgrimage to the birth-place of Christianity fitted well with his image of himself as a new religious emperor and of the Church as a spiritual kingdom to which are linked the various earthly national powers.

It cost the long-time, greatly experienced and caution-trained *monsignori* of Vatican diplomacy no little effort to dissuade the Pope from undertaking a trip which could well compromise the Church's position in an explosive area of the world at a particularly delicate moment: the Iranian revolution was aflame, southern Lebanon had been devastated by the Litani operation and the Camp David agreements had just been signed between Egypt and Israel. Moreover, the Pope's visit would be seen as supporting the Begin regime at a moment when the persecution of Christians in Jerusalem and elsewhere in the Holy Land seemed to be taking on new dimensions. A mere three weeks earlier, the *Osservatore Romano* of 19 November had quoted Mons. Beltritti, the veteran Latin patriarch of Jerusalem, on the emigration of Christians from the Holy Land:

Over the last 30 years 100,000 Christians have left the country. The present Christian population numbers 94,742 Catholics, 80,233 Orthodox and 7,200 Protestants. Over a third have emigrated. [According to Mons. Beltritti:] 'The Christians in the Holy Land must be guaranteed conditions which enable them to survive, because they are living on their land, in their homeland. They are not asking for privileges, only that their rights be respected... The new generations must not feel 'strangers' in the land in which they were born. The profession of faith must not be reduced to something merely private; it requires a space for expression through communion, in the institutions. The sanctuaries must be dynamic centres of evangelic testimony and of fervent ecclesiastic presence.'

John Paul II had obviously arrived at the summit of the Church without much idea of the complex problems of the Middle East. His idea of the state of Israel, moreover, must have been coloured by his life-long experience as a Polish nationalist who had fought fascism and nazism and had encountered anti-Jewish feeling not only among his people but also among his co-religionists. He must also have been influenced by his experience as an anti-communist militant for whom zionism represented, among Polish Jews, an antidote to communism.

But the Pope also demonstrated a considerable ability gradually to master the lacking information, a sensitivity to public opinion both inside and outside the Church and the intelligence to let himself be persuaded by events. Although the temptation to go to Jerusalem was to crop up again, as we shall see, he did not succumb.

In contrast with his Italian predecessors, the Polish Pope had had no previous contact with Third World realities. For better or for worse, European Jews were something 'familiar'. The Palestinians, on the other hand, were at best an abstraction. It is not surprising, therefore, that in his first allocution (quoted above) neither their name, nor the name of their homeland was mentioned, let along any hint at their drama. The first time that the Pope was to mention the Palestinians would be, moreover, in a negative context: that of Lebanon. Cardinal Bertoli, who had already accomplished similar missions under Paul VI, was sent to Lebanon on yet another mediation mission.

In a speech to the ambassadors accredited to the Holy See on New Year's Eve 1978, Pope John Paul II said:

It is the common good which inspires not only the social teachings of the Apostolic Seat but also the initiatives which it can take, in the domain which is its own. Such is the very topical case of Lebanon. In a country ravaged by hatred and destruction, with innumerable victims, what chance is there of renewing the relations and common life between Christians of various tendencies and Muslims, between Lebanese and Palestinians, other than through a loyal and generous effort which respects the identity and the vital demands of all... ? And if one looks at the picture of the entire Middle East, while certain statesmen tenaciously attempt to reach an agreement and others hesitate to commit themselves, who cannot see that the basic problem is not only military or territorial security, but also mutual confidence, the only factor which can help to harmonize the rights of all through a realistic division of advantages and sacrifices?

Although the context was a negative one, that of the Lebanese conflict, the text seemed to express yet again the Holy See's desire to preserve Lebanon's territorial and inter-communal unity. While Sadat could be identified as a statesman who 'tenaciously attempt[s] to reach an agreement', the Israeli leadership was clearly the one reluctant to think in terms other than 'military or territorial security'. But the Pope still had a long way to go in understanding the core problem of the region.

Between 28 December 1978 and 10 January 1979 the leadership of the Maronite Church of Lebanon, patriarchs, bishops and heads of religious orders, drew up a document intended as a sequel to Cardinal Bertoli's unsuccessful mission. The declaration opened with the usual ritual formula expressing the desire for unity between Lebanese of all religions and origins, and thanked the Pope and Cardinal Bertoli for their efforts in this sense. But it also warned that while the Lebanese Maronites 'wish to live in [a climate of] equal rights and duties', such equality must 'respect the characteristics which are specific to each spiritual family — and not conditioned by modifications or demographic changes'.

The Vatican never publicly commented on this document. There is reason to believe, however, that the local Church received the Holy See's support.[2]

On 25 March 1979 Pope John Paul II declared his blessing of the Egyptian-Israeli treaty which was to be signed the next day in Washington on the basis of the Camp David agreements:

We pray intensely that this event, which establishes peace between these two countries after so many years of war and tension, should give a decisive impulse to the entire region of the Middle East, in the respect of the rights of, and for the good of, all these populations, so that fraternity and concord may again reign in the Holy Land where Jesus was born and lived.[3]

Was this a purely rhetorical expression of solidarity with the US Camp David policy, a necessary tribute by Vatican diplomacy to the efforts of the Carter administration? It is well known that by that time the Vatican was sceptical as to Camp David's ability to bring real peace to the Middle East. One is inevitably reminded of Paul VI's reference to the Palestinian question as the key to the desired peace.

Early in his pontificate, John Paul II made changes in the Secretariat of State. The new secretary of state (officially: Prefect of the Council for the Public Affairs of the Church) was Mons. Agostino Casaroli, a man of vast experience and specializing in questions related to the Communist East. Under his authoritative leadership, Middle East affairs were now entrusted to Mons. Achille Silvestrini, a career diplomat with strong links to US foreign policy directives and particularly hostile to Third World liberation movements. The new mediator between the Middle East situation and the head of the Church was a far cry from the personalities who had personally dealt with the question of Palestine under Pius XII and Paul VI and had been critical of Israel.

On 23 April 1979 John Paul II granted a long private audience to the director-general of the Israeli Foreign Ministry, and agreed with him, in the words of a Vatican statement, 'to promote dialogue and more frequent contacts between the Holy See and Israel'. According to the *New York Times* of 24 April, the Israeli official, Yossef Chechanover:

briefed the Pontiff on the Egyptian-Israeli peace treaty and other developments in the Middle East. Human rights questions were also discussed, and it was understood — although it was not mentioned by Israeli and Vatican spokesmen — that the status of Jerusalem was also a topic. There was speculation that the papal audience may have marked a step toward the establishment of full diplomatic relations between the Vatican and Israel.

A high Israeli official who was asked about this interpretation remarked, 'A step, sure, but how many steps are necessary?'...

When the new Israeli ambassador to Italy, Moshe Alon,

started his assignment in Rome early this year, he was received in private audience by Pope John Paul II... Mr Alon and Meir Mendes, minister counsellor at the Israeli embassy in Rome, accompanied Mr Chechanover to the Vatican.

Mr Chechanover, who is close to Prime Minister Menachem Begin, presented Pope John Paul with a personal goodwill message from President Yitzhak Navon. The initiative was Israel's. The Vatican quickly concurred.

Other Vatican sources, perhaps in an effort to fend off Arab protests, maintained that the meeting had been less cordial than the article might lead one to believe. 'Mr Chechanover was told the whole truth, the way the Holy Father sees it,' a Vatican diplomat told an Arab ambassador, without going into details. It was also reported that the Pope had personally raised the question of human rights violations by Israel in the Occupied Territories. The message from President Navon, the sources said, contained a renewed invitation to John Paul II to visit Israel.

Prior to this meeting, on 12 March, the Pope had received in audience the president and representatives of the World Jewish Organization who had been meeting in Rome over the previous few days. To the Jewish leaders, all of whom in reality represented zionist groups, John Paul II spoke in terms of Christian-Jewish dialogue, in other words, in religious terms. Two fleeting references, however, had political implications. The first was related to the theme of human rights. In mentioning 'the dedicated and effective work of my predecessor Pius XII on behalf of the Jewish people' during the Second World War, the Pope underlined his determination to repudiate 'in principle and in practice all violations of human rights wherever they may occur throughout the world'. Immediately afterwards, he added:

> Following also in particular in the footsteps of Paul VI, I intend to foster spiritual dialogue and do all that is in my power for the peace of that land which is holy for you as it is for us, in the hope that the city of Jerusalem will be effectively guaranteed as a centre of harmony for the followers of the three great monotheistic religions of Judaism, Islam and Christianity, for whom the city is a revered place of devotion. [4]

The latter affirmation would seem to indicate that Pope John Paul II had taken on, and was determined to pursue, Paul VI's stance on Jerusalem, rejecting exclusive Israeli sovereignty over the Holy City. The Israelis, however, seized on the fact that the Pope's allocution had omitted to mention the term 'special statute' and the international nature of the guarantees. This Israeli interpretation has been firmly rejected by senior Vatican officials. When questioned by the author, a senior ecclesiastic responded with an impatient dismissal of all speculation. He wryly observed that only international guarantees can be effective, and that legislation by a single state that can be unilaterally and arbitrarily modified cannot possibly be regarded as such. Like other ecclesiastics and diplomats, he pointed to the fact that Israel did not even have a constitution on the basis of which legislation could be challenged by the judiciary. This thesis of the Holy See would be fully confirmed just over a year later, when the Knesset passed a law declaring that Jerusalem was the unified capital of Israel, a step which led to a considerable increase in tension between Israel and the Vatican.

The Pope's statement regarding 'that land which is holy for you as it is for us' was hardly designed to please Israel's leaders; even less welcome was the reference to Pius XII, whose stance has been reviewed at length in previous chapters. The zionist lobbies in the Church environment, especially in France, had for years attempted to establish the principle of a 'special, unique and privileged link between the Jewish people and the Promised Land', a 'mysterious' link which gives the Jews exclusive rights in Palestine. By mentioning the relationship between the Jews and Palestine on the one hand, and Christianity (which does not identify faith with a particular land) and the Holy Land on the other, and by giving them equal importance, the Pope seemed to reject this thesis.

Finally, there was the matter of the Pope's reference to the defence of human rights everywhere 'throughout the world'. If, as the Israeli interpretation would have it, the Pontiff's statement was intended to cover the rights of the Jewish communities in the communist countries, it could hardly be said to omit Israeli violations of human rights in the Palestinian Occupied Territories. On this issue, however, the Pope might have been expected to be more explicit and specific. The fact that he was not, was due to a precise political desire 'to avoid irritating the Israelis' — as would be admitted several months later to a Palestinian emissary during a discussion in the Secretariat of State relating to the cancelled visit to the Pope of Bethlehem's Christian mayor, Elias Frej.

Mayor Frej, the most moderate Palestinian leader in the West Bank, was granted an audience with the Pope through the apostolic delegate in Jerusalem in June 1979. Upon his arrival in Rome he discovered, however, that the appointment had been cancelled, with various excuses related to the Pontiff's timetable. The episode caused no little bitterness among Palestinian Christians. What credibility, they asked, could be ascribed to the Holy See's declared stance in favour of Christians in the Holy Land if even a visit to the Pope by a moderate Christian Palestinian dignitary and the mayor of a 'Holy Place' like Bethlehem could not take place due to fears of Israeli pressure? When the question was raised in an article reviewing the Vatican's attitudes at that time, the editor of *Middle East International*, which had published it, received a letter of denial from the administrator of the Pontifical Mission for Palestine:

> As an example of such pressures alleged to be made by the Israelis upon the Vatican, it is stated that an audience for Mayor Elias Frej of Bethlehem with the Pope was cancelled at the last moment by the Vatican. That I know to be entirely untrue. Mayor Frej asked for an audience through the usual channels... but unfortunately the Pope had only just returned from an emotionally and physically tiring journey to Poland and was resting in his summer residence in Castelgandolfo.[5]

This should be compared with the related note in a memorandum by Fr Ibrahim Ayad regarding his meeting with Mons. Monterisi at the Vatican's Secretariat of State (Middle East section):

> Concerning the fact that the Holy Father did not receive the mayor of Bethlehem in private audience, in spite of the fact that he had received Moshe Dayan and other Israeli dignitaries, we were told by Mons. Monterisi that... they [the Vatican] preferred not to publicize the Holy See's position but to follow the events with discretion. In fact, the Holy Father fears that the press or mass media [speaking of Frej's visit] could damage the undercover work that the Holy See has undertaken for an equitable and just settlement for the Palestinians.[6]

On 2 October 1979, during the course of an allocution to the UN

General Assembly in New York, John Paul II declared that he was ready 'to appreciate according to its real value every concrete move or attempt to establish peace in the Middle East', but that the initiatives underway (i.e. Camp David) could not be considered other than as 'a first stepping-stone towards a general and global peace... which must include a just solution to the Palestinian problem'. He likewise linked such a settlement to the 'territorial integrity of Lebanon' and to a 'special statute for Jerusalem'. *Le Monde* commented:

> It cannot really be said that John Paul II was audacious when, before the UN General Assembly, he pleaded for 'a just solution to the Palestinian problem'. One could even say that his formulation lagged behind that expressed by Paul VI, who in December 1975 appealed for the recognition of 'the legitimate rights and aspirations of the Palestinian people'... Nor did the Pope pronounce himself in regard to the juridical forms that the 'just solution'... should take.
>
> ...John Paul II did not, on the other hand, mention the PLO, with which the Vatican does not have relations, while he addressed an assembly whose great majority recognizes the *fedayeen* organization as the only legitimate representative of the Palestinian people and has accorded it observer status.
>
> It is nevertheless significant [first] that the Middle East constituted the only political subject on which the Pope spoke in a detailed manner in his allocution, [second] that he did not explicitly approve the Israeli-Egyptian treaty, and [third] that he insisted on the necessity of a 'global settlement'. Peace, for him, passes without doubt through the evacuation of the Occupied Territories. Exactly two years ago, the *Osservatore Romano* published a severe requisition regarding the Jewish settlements in the West Bank and Gaza which, the Vatican said, 'would turn upside down the plans underway for the constitution of a Palestinian homeland'. In short, the Holy See's attitude does not differ from that of Washington in regard to this problem...
>
> In summary, the ideas of John Paul II concerning the conflict in the Middle East are characterized by such caution as to risk if not the irritation at least the indifference of the peoples of the region. These peoples, in their distress, are waiting more than ever before for bold, daring initiatives.[7]

Two months later, the head of the Catholic Church went to
Turkey. By this time, the broad outlines of the Pope's religious-
political design had emerged quite clearly. His objective was that
of 'ecumenism' — or inter-Church alliance — as a barrier against
communism. The ideas prevailing in the Vatican in the 1950s
concerning a Catholic-Muslim front for 'the defence of peace and
freedom' were taken up again. It was to this end that an effort was
made to calm the growing tension between the 'Christian' West
and the 'Muslim' East. Within this framework some reference to
the Palestinian question was inevitable. In Ankara, John Paul II
received the PLO representative together with the other
ambassadors. 'I am interested in your cause,' he told him, 'and for
this reason I spoke of it at the UN.'[8]

By the spring of 1980, the Palestinians and the supporters of
their cause in the Middle East and elsewhere had ever more reason
for concern in regard to the Holy See's policies in Palestine. At
Easter, John Paul II conceded an audience to King Hassan of
Morocco, in his capacity as president of the 'Jerusalem
Commission' of the Islamic Conference. In the one-hour
conversation, the Pope apparently never mentioned the
Palestinians, nor was there the slightest reference to the question
of Palestine in the published texts of the allocutions of both the
Holy Father and the King. As for Jerusalem,[9] the formula chosen
by the Holy See was by far the most complicated, enigmatic and
ambiguous yet used by the Church:

> It is necessary to find a new impulse, a new approach, which
> will permit not a further division, but... with the help of God,
> a solution: perhaps original, but immediate, definite, guaranteed
> and respectful of the rights of all.[10]

With increasing unease, Arab diplomats in Rome were asking
whether such a 'solution' was already being concocted in
Washington between Carter, Sadat and Begin, with the blessing
of the Holy See.

Meanwhile in Israel, in January 1980, there was a wave of attacks
on Christian institutions in Jerusalem, perpetrated by followers of
Rabbi Meir Kahane's Kach movement. According to the *Jerusalem
Post* of 23 January 1980:

> Despite promises to step up police patrols near Christian sites...

police have been unable to prevent dozens of incidents of window-breaking, slogan-smearing, and even physical attacks on Christian clergymen in the city.

...Incidents included the smashing of the stained glass windows at the Dormition Abbey, after mailed and telephone threats were received at the Mt Zion Monastery. At the Baptist Church, which is linked to the Southern Baptist Convention of America, twice since late December windows have been broken and a door smashed. At least ten times vandals have sprayed slogans on the white walls of the Russian Compound, and the secretary of the Russian Orthodox Church in Israel has received several letters threatening him and his six-year-old son.

Other incidents are even more severe. A week before Christmas a youth wearing a skullcap burst into the Christian Information Office at Jaffa Gate and began destroying the Christmas display at the office. In the market, priests have been spat at and cursed by young religious Jews.

In a recent letter to [Jerusalem Mayor Teddy] Kollek, David Jaeger, liaison secretary of the United Christian Council in Israel, complained of the 'mounting anxiety within the Christian community... caused by recently stepped-up activities of anti-Christian fanatics'.

...City officials thus link the alleged Kach actions with anti-mission actions by violent extremist Jews... who may be responsible for spraying the walls of the Bible Society shops with swastikas and slogans, [and] calling the shop-owners 'pigs and nazis'... Similar slogans and swastikas have been painted on secular schools in the city, as well as St Joseph's Monastery...

Both [Mayor] Kollek and the city council this week sent urgent letters asking Premier Menachem Begin publicly to deplore the vandalism... So far Begin has not replied.

Begin never responded to this request. Moreover, not one of the Jerusalem rabbis or of the Jerusalem-based chief rabbis of Israel agreed to any public condemnation of the attacks on Christians.

On 2 February 1980 *The Times* of London reported a statement by Yossi Dayan, spokesman for the Kach organization: 'The Christians have no place in Jerusalem, which is the Jewish capital.' The paper commented:

The impression is persistent and pervasive within the Christian community that the Israeli civil authorities have failed to exhaust all the possibilities open to them to curb such manifestations.

In the same month, the *Christian Information Centre Bulletin* of Jerusalem (no. 253) published an article by Fr Médebielle of the Latin Patriarchate of Jerusalem, under the heading, 'The Recent Wave of Violent Attacks by Fanatic Jewish Elements against Christian Persons and Institutions in Jerusalem and the Holy Land Raises again the Question of an Internationally Guaranteed Special Statute for Jerusalem'. In March the Holy See received another report from Jerusalem which stated that the Christian minority there, which had fallen from some 45,000 in 1948 to about 10,000 in 1980, was 'counting on the Pope of Human Rights for a word of encouragement, of solidarity, of hope, and for the assurance that they have not been abandoned to their fate'.

None of these events or appeals elicited any public reaction on the part of the supreme authorities of the Church. Not only did the Pope avoid any mention of them in his numerous allocutions and addresses throughout these months. The Vatican's official press organs — the *Osservatore Romano* and Vatican Radio — carefully refrained from reporting on them. On 2 June 1980 there were terrorist attacks by Israeli extremists on three Palestinian mayors in the occupied West Bank, in which the mayors of Nablus and (Christian) Ramallah were mutilated. A few hours after the attacks, Begin publicly addressed from the Knesset podium an invitation to Pope John Paul II to visit 'the Holy Land'. Once again, there was no response from the Vatican, either to the attacks on the Palestinian mayors or to Begin's invitation.

When questioned by us in regard to Begin's invitation, extended 'in response to the wish informally expressed the previous day by Karol Wojtyla, during a meeting with leaders of the French Jewish community in Paris' (according to the Italian state radio news bulletin of 2 June), an official Vatican spokesman declined to comment. According to a senior Vatican official interviewed by us, 'The only possible reaction for the Holy See was silence, seeing the offensive and highly provocative nature of Begin's invitation in the context of the events.' Interpretations of this silence varied, however. On 14 June the Rome daily *Paese Sera* carried an article by a prominent Catholic intellectual, Raniero La Valle, which reflected the unease felt by European Catholics in the face of the Pope's far from clear intentions. In an article entitled 'The Pope Must Not Go

To Israel', La Valle, former editor-in-chief of the foremost Italian Catholic paper *L'Avvenire d'Italia*, wrote:

> We appreciate the Pope's recent trips. But there is one trip, which he was invited to undertake by Begin at the very moment in which bombs tore to pieces the two Palestinian mayors of Nablus and Ramallah, which he ought not to make: the trip to the Holy Land and Jerusalem. There are very serious reasons against the Pope's undertaking such a trip, if indeed in his acts, especially in his symbolic public acts, he wishes to express not a personal, isolated 'leadership' but the conscience of the entire Church. The Pope is not Sadat. His motivations must be different, just as the nature and intensity of his relationship with the people that he represents, and with the whole history of humankind, must be different.
>
> The first reason concerns the Church in the strictest sense. For a Pope to go to Jerusalem does not mean a visit to a church, or to a multitude of believers. The number of Christians in Jerusalem has fallen in recent years from 45,000 in 1948 to 10,000, while 60,000 Jews have installed themselves in the Arab quarters of the city. To go to Jerusalem means, essentially, for a Pope, to bring the Church to a confrontation with its roots and with its origins, to compare it with Christ's Sepulchre, to verify the gap between the promise made at its foundation and the way it is today. This cannot be an itinerary of triumphs, it must be one of confession and penitence. [When] Paul VI went, he confessed the weakness of his Church. 'So many times have we been unfaithful in our faith,' he said on the empty Sepulchre. The Church that he took with him to Jerusalem was a Church that, in the unique historical moment represented by the Ecumenical Council, was intent on initiating a profound conversion... That conversion has not yet been achieved...
>
> And there is another reason. One must go to Jerusalem in order to proclaim peace. Of course, it is always possible to do this through words. But never as much as today would such words be in striking contrast with a reality of hostility, of violence and of blood which has its centre, even its cause, precisely in Jerusalem. The intensification of the Israeli repression in the Occupied Territories that now also hits directly the leaders of the Arab population, with deportations of mayors (Halhul, Hebron) and terrorist attacks on other mayors (Nablus, Ramallah), is one

aspect of this reality. But even beyond this, a perverse plan is at present being outlined for the Occupied Territories: a plan which could previously have been seen as [sponsored by] extremist groups alone but which now, with the failure of the illusions of Camp David, is clearly becoming the official policy of the Israeli government. [It is] a plan designed to lead to a massive new exodus of the Arab Palestinian population from its land and from its homes, to fill new refugee camps in Lebanon and elsewhere; a plan that aims to empty the territories conquered in 1967 of the unwanted Arab presence... These are not just speculative designs but precise and explicit intentions.

For example, Hannan Porat, leader of Gush Emunim, has declared, 'Clashes between Arabs and Jews can no longer be avoided: by proving that Jews and Arabs cannot co-exist, this will bring about the expulsion of all the Arabs.'

On 5 May General Aharon Yariv said that there are plans 'to exploit a war situation in order to expel 700,000 or 800,000 Arabs from the Occupied Territories'. Last 26 December [1979], during Begin's visit to Kiryat Arba, Chief Rabbi Goren... commented: what a pity that the Arab population of Hebron did not escape and go away beyond the Jordan river in 1967.

It is obvious that this line followed by Israel... precludes all possibility of peace in the Middle East... But what have the Pope and his Church to do with it? The Pope could speak of law and peace but his very presence there would sound like the recognition of a 'unified' Jerusalem as the capital of Israel (according to the Knesset vote of 30 July), and above all as approval of a plan that aims, in the name of a 'Greater Israel', deliberately to cause renewed suffering for a whole people, to produce a new wandering mass of hundreds of thousands of refugees. The 'Pope of Human Rights' must never let himself be involved in this plan nor let himself be used for this purpose.

There is by now a mass of evidence that such a plan is in the offing. In the first place, there are the Israeli settlements, now established not only in relatively unpopulated areas but even in the midst of towns with large Arab populations such as Hebron and throughout the entire occupied lands... Second, [there is] the expropriation of Arab lands, and the expulsion and intimidation of their owners, among other things through the use of defoliants as in four villages in the Hebron area... Third, the increasing repression (arrests, curfews, censorship, destruction of houses, attacks on persons and property, and so on) aims at convincing the Palestinians that for them there is no future, that on that land it will be impossible for them to go on living.

What makes this plan even more serious is the fact that, in order to carry it out, a climate of confrontation has to be created and the general tension in the Middle East must become more acute. If this can be done, the extremist leaders who are sustained and protected by the government believe, a chain reaction will be produced which will lead to the departure of the inhabitants.

On 21 June 1980 the Pontiff received US President Jimmy Carter in Rome. The terms used by John Paul II in his address to the American president were, once more, a far cry from those formulated in the past by Paul VI: 'I would renew my earnest plea that just attention be given to the issues affecting Lebanon and to the whole Palestinian problem.'[11]

The 'legitimate rights and aspirations of the Palestinian people' were not invoked. Nor was their right to a state of their own. The human rights situation in the Occupied Territories was once more not mentioned. Perhaps the most negative new element in the Pope's policy, as it emerged at this stage, was that the question of the people of Palestine and their destiny, and that of Jerusalem, no longer seemed to be organically linked. For the new Pope, these issues were not a kind of 'package', as they had been for his predecessors Pius XII and Paul VI. A slight shift was also emerging over the question of Jerusalem itself. As the Begin government placed the bill establishing Jerusalem as Israel's unified capital on the Knesset agenda, the *Osservatore Romano* of 30 June–1 July 1980 recalled the Holy See's traditional stance, according to which 'any unilateral act tending to modify the status of the Holy City would be very serious'. In other words, this position was clearly opposed to the act of annexation. The article continued, however:

The Holy See considers the safeguarding of the sacred and universal character of Jerusalem to be of such primary importance as to require any power that comes to exercise sovereignty over the Holy City to assume the obligation, before the three religious confessions spread throughout the world, to protect not only the special character of the city but also the rights connected with the Holy Places and the religious communities concerned on the basis of an appropriate international body.

It would seem, from this paragraph, that the Catholic Church was for the first time openly ready to accept the 'sovereignty of a power' (i.e. of Israel) over Jerusalem, although making such acceptance conditional on the establishment of an 'appropriate international body', which, however, would be have to be subordinated to the 'sovereignty' of the ruling power.

The *Osservatore Romano* editorial deserves to be reprinted almost in full, both in order to compare it to previous Vatican pronouncements on the issue, and because of the contradiction it contained, which seemed to characterize Pope John Paul II's attitude on all aspects of the question of Palestine:

In his speech to the president of the United States of America, Mr Jimmy Carter, on Saturday 21 June 1980, the Holy Father spoke of Jerusalem in these terms: '*The question of Jerusalem, which during these very days has attracted world attention in a special way, is pivotal to a just peace in those parts of the world*, since this Holy City embodies interests and aspirations that are shared by different peoples in different ways. It is my hope that a common monotheistic tradition of faith will help to promote harmony among all those who call upon God.'

In His Holiness's words we find references to permanent historical features (the 'common monotheistic tradition of faith'), to present facts (the 'interests and aspirations that are shared by different peoples') and to a 'hope' for Jerusalem (that 'harmony among all those who call upon God' may be promoted in Jerusalem, in the Middle East and throughout the world).

History and Contemporary Reality

Throughout the centuries Jerusalem has been endowed with deep religious significance and spiritual value for Christians, Jews and Muslims.

The Holy City is the object of fervent love and has exercised a constant appeal for the Jewish people ever since David chose it as his capital and Solomon built the Temple there. Much of the history of Judaism took place within it, and the thoughts of the Jews were directed towards it down the centuries, even when scattered in the 'diaspora' of the past and of the present.

There is no ignoring either the deep attachment of the Muslims to Jerusalem 'the Holy', as they call it. This attachment was already explicit in the life and thought of the Founder of

Islam. It has been reinforced by an almost unbroken Islamic presence in Jerusalem since AD 638 and it is attested by outstanding monuments such as al-Aqsa Mosque and the Mosque of Omar.

There is no need to point out that Jerusalem also belongs spiritually to all Christians. The voice of Christ was heard there many times. The great events of Redemption — the passion, death and resurrection of the Lord — took place there. It was there that the first Christian community sprang up, and there has been, even if at times with great difficulty, a continuous ecclesiastic presence ever since. Numerous shrines indicate the places connected with Christ's life and, ever since the beginnings of Christianity, there has been a constant flow of pilgrims to them…

At present all three communities, Christian, Jewish and Muslim, are part of the Holy City's population and are closely linked with its life and sacred character.

Each community is the 'guardian' of its shrines and Holy Places. Jerusalem has a whole network of organizations, reception centres for pilgrims, educational and research institutes and welfare bodies. These organizations have great importance for the community they belong to and also for the followers of the same religion throughout the world.

In short, the history and contemporary reality of Jerusalem present a unique case of a city that is in itself deeply united by nature but is at the same time characterized by a closely intertwined religious plurality. Preservation of the treasures of the significance of Jerusalem requires that this plurality be recognized and safeguarded in a stable, concrete manner, and therefore publicly and juridically, so as to ensure for all three religions a level of parity, without any of them feeling subordinate with regard to the others.

The International Community
The three religious communities of Jerusalem, the Christian, the Jewish and the Muslim, are the primary subjects interested in the preservation of the sacred character of the city and they should be partners in deciding their own future. *No less than the monuments and Holy Places, the situation of these communities cannot fail to be a matter of concern for all.* As regards the presence of the Christians, everyone is aware of the importance, both in the past and to this

day, not only of the Catholic community with its various rites, but also of the Greek Orthodox, the Armenian and the other Eastern communities, not forgetting the Anglican groups and others springing from the Reformation.

In short, the Jerusalem question cannot be reduced to mere 'free access for all to the Holy Places'. Concretely it is also required: (1) that the overall character of Jerusalem as a sacred heritage shared by all three monotheistic religions be guaranteed by appropriate measures; (2) that religious freedom in all its aspects be safeguarded for them; (3) that the complex of rights acquired by the various communities over the shrines and the centres for spiritual study and welfare be protected; (4) that the continuance and development of religious, educational and social activity by each community be ensured; (5) that this be actuated with equality of treatment for all three religions; (6) that this be achieved through an 'appropriate juridical safeguard' that does not derive from the will of only one of the interested parties.

This 'juridical safeguard' corresponds, in substance, to the 'special statute' that the Holy See desires for Jerusalem: 'This Holy City embodies interests and aspirations that are shared by different peoples.' The very universality of the three monotheistic religions, which constitute the faith of many hundreds of millions of believers in every continent, calls for a responsibility that goes well beyond the limits of the states of the region. The significance and value of Jerusalem are such as to surpass the interests of any single state or bilateral agreements between one state and others.

Furthermore, the international community has already dealt with the Jerusalem question; for instance, UNESCO very recently made an important intervention with the aim of safeguarding the artistic and religious riches represented by Jerusalem as a whole, as the 'common heritage of humanity'.

The United Nations Organization and Jerusalem

As early as its second session, the General Assembly of the United Nations approved on 29 November 1947 a resolution on Palestine of which the third part was devoted to Jerusalem. The resolution was confirmed in the next two sessions, on 11 December 1948 and 9 December 1949, while on 4 April 1950 the Trusteeship Council approved a detailed 'special statute' for the city on the basis of the Assembly's decisions. The solution proposed by the United Nations envisaged the setting up of a *corpus separatum* for 'Jerusalem and the surrounding area', administered by the Trusteeship Council of the United Nations.

This 'territorial internationalization' of Jerusalem was not of course put into effect, because in the 1948 conflict the Arab side occupied the eastern zone of the city and the Israeli side the western.

The position of the United Nations does not appear, at least as yet, to have been formally revoked. The General Assembly, as well as the Security Council, has repeatedly, beginning with the resolution of 4 July 1967, insisted on the invalidity of any measure to change the status of the city.

The Holy See considers the safeguarding of the sacred and universal character of Jerusalem to be of such primary importance as to require any power that comes to exercise sovereignty over the Holy City to assume the obligation, before the three religious confessions spread throughout the world, to protect not only the special character of the city but also the rights connected with the Holy Places and the religious communities concerned on the basis of an appropriate international body.

What Hope for Jerusalem?

In his address to President Carter, the Holy Father referred to the fact that the question of Jerusalem 'during these very days has attracted world attention in a special way'.

The positions of the two sides on the question of sovereignty over Jerusalem are known to be very far apart; *any unilateral act tending to modify the status of the Holy City would be very serious.* The Holy Father's hope is that the representatives of the nations will keep in mind the 'common monotheistic tradition of faith' and succeed in finding, in the historical and present-day reality of Jerusalem, reasons for softening the bitterness of confrontation and for promoting 'harmony among all those who call upon God'. The aim will be to ensure that Jerusalem is no longer an object of contention but a place of encounter and brotherhood between believers of the three religions and a pledge of friendship between the peoples...

Israel ignored the Holy See's warning not to take unilateral action to change the status of Jerusalem, however. The far-reaching concession on the part of the Vatican — a conditional recognition of Israel's sovereignty over the Holy City — was also dismissed. John

Paul II's 'opening up' towards Israel was of no consequence to the Begin government, which saw the city as (to use Begin's own words), 'holy to the Jews, in the first place and above all'.

On 6 July *La Documentation Catholique* published a 'Common Declaration' by three Christian leaders — the Rev. R. Kreider, secretary of the Co-ordination Committee of the United Christian Council in Israel, Fr Ignazio Mancini, O.F.M., director of the Christian Information Centre in Jerusalem, and Fr Bargil Pixner, O.S.B., representing the Dormition Abbey Community — on the worsening of anti-Christian violence in Jerusalem. The declaration stated:

> There is a persistent and predominating impression within the Christian community that the civil authorities have not yet taken all the means at their disposal to repress the fanatical anti-Christian manifestations. We hear quite often within the Christian community that the authors of such acts enjoy relative impunity. A Christian spokesman has already drawn attention to this fact, both publicly and in informal talks with the representatives of the government.
>
> ...Some of the organizations involved in the systematic humiliation of the Christian Churches have been active in the country for a generation. But the latest incidents have shown the emergence of a new and by far more dangerous element. It seems, in fact, that at least in regard to some of these, the responsibility lies with an organization known for its racist tendencies and its cult of violence, more than for its religious zeal...
>
> One cannot fail to mention in this context the brutal assassination, at the end of last year, of the monk who served as a guardian of the sanctuary of the Greek Orthodox Patriarchate known as the 'Wells of Jacob', in Nablus. We must stress that the lack of official information on the results of the inquiry into this crime... cannot but feed the rumours and extremely harmful speculations, which in turn damage all confidence and the relations between the communities. This declaration would not be complete without recalling the necessary plan, desired by the Churches as well as by the international community, of a special, internationally guaranteed statute concerning the rights and freedoms of the three great monotheistic religions in Jerusalem and throughout the Holy Land.

On 30 July 1980 the Knesset passed the bill declaring Jerusalem the unified capital of Israel. During the following weeks John Paul II received, first, King Hussein of Jordan, then Egyptian vice-president Hosni Mubarak, and finally, on 19 September, a special emissary from Yasser Arafat with a message from the Palestinian leader. The press underlined the importance of this direct contact, the first since the meeting between Arafat and Cardinal Bertoli in 1976 at St Francis Monastery in Beirut (when the objective had been to discuss the Lebanese situation). *Il Giorno* of 19 September, however, went on to say:

> The latest developments concerning the issue of Jerusalem, with Israel's intransigence over the question of the Holy City, have probably facilitated the concession of an audience, on the part of the Holy See, also to the Palestinian component [of the Arab world].

According to Arafat's emissary, Afif Saffieh:

> The Vatican charged me to transmit to Arafat its categoric condemnation of the illegal annexation of Jerusalem decided upon by the Israeli parliament... The Pope said to me, 'Palestine, the Palestinians and Jerusalem are among my principal preoccupations.'[12]

But Arab weakness had little to offer the Vatican in terms of bargaining power against Israel's string of *faits accomplis*. And, on the other hand, the situation in Lebanon seemed to be degenerating into a spiral of violence which, over the next two years, would become uncontrollable. The Vatican's various attempts to exercise a moderating influence over all sides in the conflict would result in failure. The Holy See kept up its contacts with Israel, however, and in February 1981 Begin's foreign minister, Itzhak Shamir, was scheduled to be received in audience by John Paul II.

Israel's proclamation of Jerusalem as the unified capital nevertheless led to increasing tension in its relations with the Vatican. An Israeli attack on Lebanon was now in the air. Begin repeatedly asserted an alleged Israeli role in the 'protection of the Christians in Lebanon' as the major objective of a planned invasion of Lebanon which would also bring about the destruction of the PLO and the exit of the Syrian Arab Deterrent Force. On the pretext of a delay in Shamir's arrival in Rome and of subsequent complications due to the Sabbath, the audience was then cancelled at the last minute. Soon afterwards, Israel launched large-scale military operations in southern Lebanon. West Beirut itself was several times subjected to aerial bombardment in 1981.

The July bombings were followed by a US-mediated cease-fire. During this period a new audience with the Pope was fixed for Israel's foreign minister on 7 January 1982. This time, Shamir carefully refrained from announcing that there would be any discussion of Lebanon, and made no attempt to present Israel as the 'protector' of the Christians there. However, Shamir's statement prior to the audience that his government renewed its invitation to the Pope to make a pilgrimage to the Holy Land, and that during the audience 'the situation in Poland would also be discussed', was considered as highly provocative by Vatican circles. Vatican commentators of all shades of opinion were unanimous in stating that the Holy See had, quite exceptionally, gone out of its way to present the 30-minute audience, 'granted to Shamir at his request', as a 'flop'. The Vatican spokesman made no secret of the fact that Shamir was asked to avoid raising the question of the Pope's 'pilgrimage to the Holy Land'. 'Much as His Holiness would cherish the idea of holding prayers in the Holy Places, it is unthinkable that he could do so as long as Jerusalem remains an occupied and illegally annexed city,' one highly placed Vatican source said. Shamir, the same source added, had also been informed in detail of the Vatican's attitude on the annexation of the Golan. 'The Holy Father condemned the Israeli government in no uncertain terms as an international law-breaker for its unacceptable violations of all international codes of law and behaviour,' Under-Secretary of State Mons. Silvestrini told Arab ambassadors after the audience.[13]

Comments in the Italian press reflected identical attitudes. 'Shamir's Attempt to Invite Pope to Jerusalem Fails', 'Initiative Defined in Vatican as Provocative and Inopportune', 'Pope and Shamir: Polemical Meeting regarding Palestinians', 'The Pope Invites Israel to Negotiate with the Palestinians' and 'Basic Divergences Remain after Shamir-Wojtyla Talks' were some of the significant headlines. Other points mentioned as crucial divergences were:

1. For the Vatican, Camp David was not a sufficient framework

for negotiations. The latter 'should involve all the interested parties' (and the Palestinians, Shamir was told, are certainly no less of an interested party than anyone else). In contrast with Begin's 'autonomy' formula, the Vatican insisted that the Palestinian problem be negotiated and solved globally, with, as a result, 'a just and dutiful commitment for the Palestinians, whether they live in the Holy Land or as refugees in the surrounding countries'.

2. There must be 'full respect of all the rights of the Palestinians in the Occupied Territories of the West Bank and Gaza', i.e. including their political and national rights. The Pope and Secretary of State Cardinal Casaroli revealed a detailed knowledge of Israeli violations of human and civil rights and of the general repression in the Occupied Territories.

3. The Holy See made no secret of its knowledge that Israel had been active in Lebanon 'to maintain a state of tension and insecurity in that country', with terrorist attacks in Beirut and elsewhere. John Paul II demanded that the cease-fire in Lebanon 'should be extended and consolidated with commitment and in a spirit of moderation'.[14]

Israel's military actions and political stance since 1980 had thus led to a certain shift in favour of the Palestinians in the Pope's policy. John Paul II had initially given the impression of leaning towards Israel. The fact that he was an 'outsider' to traditional Church policy on Palestine, and that he initially lacked the 'feel' for the issue, caused, in the first three and a half years of his pontificate, a marked regression from the positions acquired under Paul VI and conforming, in their broad outline, to the UN General Assembly resolutions on Palestine. These positions had not yet been fully regained by the spring of 1982, although on 4 April John Paul II for the first time referred to the Palestinians as 'a people', thereby placing them on virtually the same level as the Israelis. He urged 'both peoples to conquer their relentless antagonism and [each] to accept the existence and the reality of the other', with a view to 'a just solution which would permit both to live in peace, dignity and freedom'.[15]

Afterword: 1982–1987

From early 1982 issues relating to the Middle East, and more specifically to Lebanon and the Palestine question, loomed larger in Vatican concerns than they had in previous years. In the course of 1982 there was a marked shift in the way Pope John Paul II formulated his attitude to the Palestinians. In an Angelus message on 4 April, he referred for the first time to the Palestinians as a 'people' rather than as refugees (see page 193) and appeared to place them on an equal footing with the Israelis:

> For decades that land [Palestine] has seen two peoples opposed in an irreducible antagonism. Each of them has a history, tradition and experience of its own, that seem to make settlement difficult...

He continued with a rhetorical question:

> Even after so many disappointments, is it unreal to hope that one day these two peoples, each accepting the existence and reality of the other, might find a way of dialogue that will have them reach a just solution in which both can live in peace, in their own dignity and freedom, mutually giving each other the pledge of tolerance and reconciliation?

Although this message tacitly acknowledged Israel's right to exist, it constituted a new departure to present the Palestinians in this light. The Pope also alluded, unusually, to the 'painful events' in the

Occupied Territories — referring to the uprising of March–April 1982 in which some 20 Palestinians were killed and many others injured. He described the Palestinians in the territories as 'a population that is yearning for a situation in which their legitimate aspirations can be recognized and affirmed'.[1]

The same line on the Occupied Territories had been taken in February 1982 by Mons. Mario Brini, secretary of the Sacred Congregation for the Eastern Churches. On a pontifical mission to Jordan, Mons. Brini described the work of the Holy See for a just solution to the Palestine problem and its 'intense activity, on the educational, social and humanitarian level, to encourage Palestinians to remain on their native soil and maintain their identity'.[2]

Another significant indication of the shift in Vatican thinking was the audience granted in March to the head of the PLO's political department, Farouk Qaddoumi, by the Pope's secretary of state, Cardinal Agostino Casaroli. According to the US Catholic paper the *National Catholic Reporter*, there was no communiqué after the meeting, but Qaddoumi had the task of converting the Vatican to the view that the PLO was essentially a political movement which had taken up arms only out of necessity. He was also trying to persuade the Pope to accept that the Palestinians are a people and that they need a homeland.[3]

While this visit clearly did not convince the Vatican that it should go as far as to recognize the PLO, it may have contributed to the shift in emphasis evident in the 4 April Angelus message. The *National Catholic Reporter* suggested that the Pope had also been influenced by the urging of the Melchite patriarch, Maximos V Hakim, based in Damascus, that he should recognize the Palestinians as a people with a right to a homeland.

The other major factor in the Vatican's changing perspective on both the Palestinians and the Israelis was the Israeli invasion of Lebanon in June 1982. In the months which followed — and particularly during the Israeli siege of West Beirut — the Pope made still more explicit reference to the Palestinians as a people with rights of their own. On 27 June he asked for prayers 'for the Palestinian people, that an end be put to their sufferings, and their rights be recognized, as it is just that it be so for all the peoples of the region'.[4] In an address in St Peters two days later he said:

Let us offer our prayers that Lebanon may be able to find peace again, rise again from the ruins, reorganize its unity and be changed from the battlefield that it is today into an active and peaceful factor of balance in the Middle East... Another people is suffering on Lebanese soil: the Palestinian people, no less dear to me than the others. Let us pray that they may see their legitimate aspirations recognized — first of which is to be able to have a homeland of its own — and that they may live in tranquillity with all the peoples of the region.[5]

During the invasion, the Pope issued frequent calls for prayers for 'suffering Lebanon' and expressed concern for the impact of the invasion on world peace, something he raised at a meeting with President Reagan as early as 7 June, though Reagan did not respond beyond a brief acknowledgement of the Pope's observation. At the end of June, the Pope announced that he would be prepared to visit 'the martyred land of Lebanon', or to take 'any other initiative to aid that people'.[6] It is possible that he was advised against such a course, because the next day he said that it was not possible to undertake this journey as he had hoped. The Vatican's statements did not explicitly name the Israelis as aggressors or refer directly to them in the numerous statements issued by the Holy See between June and September 1982. But on 26 June the Pope took the unusual step of addressing a message in English to President Navon of Israel. It was delivered via the Israeli embassy in Rome, and asked the president to ensure strict enforcement of the cease-fire, adding (presumably in reference to the Palestinians): 'It is supremely important that the people overcome in battle be guaranteed honourable treatment.'[7] The Pope also reiterated his call for recognition of the 'just aspirations' of the peoples involved.

Other Catholic sources were more outspoken about Israel's role in Lebanon. In the US, the liberal *National Catholic Reporter*, in an editorial headlined 'Israel the Oppressor', was not only fiercely critical of Israel's role in Lebanon and its treatment of the Palestinians, but also castigated its role in supporting dictatorships in Latin and Central America, arguing that its policies in both spheres demonstrated severe moral flaws.[8] At an official level, the National Conference of Catholic Bishops in the US demanded an Israeli withdrawal from Lebanon, as well as an immediate cease-fire, stressing the integrity of Lebanon, as well as 'the resolution of the larger issues in the Middle East: Israel's security, the achievement of a homeland for the Palestinians and the end of the virtual state of war in the region'.[9]

It was only in the aftermath of the invasion, however, that the Vatican came into head-on conflict with the Israelis. In September, soon after the withdrawal of the PLO from Beirut, the Holy See took its strongest step: to invite PLO Chairman Yasser Arafat to attend an audience with the Pope. Although the Vatican did not seek to publicize the visit widely in advance, it was soon blazoned in headlines in the international press and provoked the sharpest ever verbal clash between the Vatican and the Israeli government. On 12 September, prior to the meeting, a statement was issued through the Israeli Foreign Ministry in a tone of violent accusation. It read:

> The same Church that did not say a word about the massacre of Jews for six years in Europe, and did not say much about the killing of Christians in Lebanon for seven years, is willing to meet the man who perpetrated the crime in Lebanon and is bent on the destruction of Israel which is the completion of the work done by the nazis in Germany. If the Pope is going to meet Arafat, it shows something about the moral standards [of the Church].[10]

The vituperative tone of these remarks (assumed by some in the Israeli press to have been issued on the direct orders of Prime Minister Menachem Begin) drew an unprecedentedly sharp response from the Vatican. The statement, the Holy See's communiqué observed:

> contains words which, more than surprising, are almost unbelievable. They would lead one to suppose that the point has been reached of forgetting — even if in an emotional context which, objectively, has very little justification — all that the Pope, the Holy See, the Catholic Church... in various countries have done... to protect and save thousands and thousands of Jews, before and during the Second World War... One does not wish to boast about this; but it is necessary to recall it to those who have forgotten, because one cannot allow to pass without answer such an outrage to the truth, couched in language so lacking in respect for the person of a Pope, when one cannot pretend to be ignorant of what he has said on numerous occasions, and especially during his visit to Auschwitz, to condemn and execrate the genocide carried out by the nazis against the Jewish people (and not merely against them).[11]

According to *The Times*, the Vatican statement may have been inspired by the Pope himself, particularly the remarks about the Church's record during the Second World War.[12] In this acrimonious exchange, the two major areas of contention between Israel and the Vatican overlap: the question of Palestine and the question of the Church's attitude to anti-semitism.

On 15 September, the day on which the meeting between the Pope and Arafat took place, the Israeli Foreign Ministry issued a further accusatory statement, almost as strongly worded as the previous one. It expressed 'shock' and 'disappointment' that the visit had gone ahead, and continued:

> It shall now be recorded in the national memory of the state of Israel and of the Jewish people that the spiritual leader of millions of believers around the world did not recoil from meeting with the head of an organization that has written into its constitution as a central aim the annihilation of the Jewish state...[13]

Although the visit drew protests from Jewish and zionist sources and from some Catholics sympathetic to Israel, others sought to set the visit in context. The *National Catholic Reporter* considered the violent Israeli reaction to the meeting as unwise, and remarked that 'the argument that Arafat should be cold-shouldered because he is a "terrorist" is not accepted by the Vatican any longer. Receiving people does not imply approval of them or diplomatic recognition.'[14] International sympathy for Israel in this case was generally lessened by the fact that the invasion of Lebanon, with its scenes of destruction and brutality, had left Israel's international standing at an unprecedentedly low ebb. From the Palestinian point of view, this meeting, for which Qaddoumi's visit earlier in the year had laid the ground-work, was viewed as a considerable diplomatic coup, and a much-needed boost to morale after the traumas of the invasion and the evacuation of the PLO from Beirut in August. A PLO official in Rome described the audience as 'a turning-point in the PLO's favour'.[15] Arafat himself characterized the audience, which took place while he was in Rome to address the Interparliamentary Union, as 'a very warm, very important and historic meeting'.[16]

No official communiqué was issued after the audience, and the only indication of the Vatican's position can be gleaned from the Pope's address to his general audience later in the day. He repeated his earlier characterization of the Palestinians and the Israelis as two people in conflict:

> The Pope, the Catholic Church, look with sympathy and consideration on both these peoples, heirs and guardians of different religious, historical and cultural traditions, but both of them rich in values equally to be respected.[17]

While this statement had clearly moved some way from the position taken by the Pope earlier in his pontificate, it was still far from constituting recognition of the PLO, as Arafat might ideally have wished. It also underlined the Pope's insistence on mutual recognition by Israel and the Palestinians. Yet there is no doubt that the combination of diplomatic initiatives and the impact of the invasion of Lebanon had put Israel very much on the defensive *vis-à-vis* the Vatican.

Within days of the Arafat audience came the news, first, of the assassination of Lebanese president-elect Bashir Gemayel, and then of the massacres of Palestinians in the refugee camps of Sabra and Chatila by Maronite militiamen under the eyes of the occupying Israeli forces. The Pope's response to this event did not level direct accusations at those implicated in the killings. He said, 'There are no words adequate to condemn such crimes which are repugnant to the human and Christian conscience.'[18]

If the Vatican's attitude to the Palestinians generally became more positive in the light of the Israeli actions in Lebanon, there was a good deal less clarity in its attitude to the warring factions in Lebanon, and in particular to the role of the Maronites. The Vatican's traditionally close relations with the Maronite Church meant that there was no outspoken criticism on the issue of the massacres, or any other actions of the Maronite political groups. When the Pope met President Amin Gemayel in late September 1982, he made no reference to the Sabra and Chatila massacres. He simply expressed his confidence that the Lebanese government:

> will be prepared, while being engaged in the work of rebuilding the country, to contribute actively to the definitive solution of the crisis in the Middle East and to the settlement of the problem of the Palestinian people.[19]

There was little in his subsequent meetings with Maronite leaders,

both political and religious, to indicate his views on the role of the
Palestinians in Lebanon itself, or to indicate that he favoured any
fundamental restructuring of the power relations between the
various communities in Lebanon.

As far as the Palestinians in Lebanon were concerned, the
following years of intermittent fighting and constantly shifting
alliances elicited no new pronouncements of significance from the
Vatican. During the inter-Palestinian fighting in Tripoli in 1983,
Arafat appealed to the Pope for solidarity. In response, the Vatican
said it feared the outbreak of war 'on a vast scale' in the Middle East
and urged the Palestinians to end their 'fratricidal struggle'. The
PLO representative in Rome interpreted this as an important and
'positive' message. On the whole, however, the dispersion of the
PLO and the disarray in its ranks over the next few years have not
favoured any further diplomatic initiatives of importance on either
side.

Nevertheless, the Vatican has generally continued to put forward
the line on the Palestinians formulated by Pope John Paul II during
1982. For example, in September 1983 a delegation from the Holy
See had observer status at the International Conference on the
Question of Palestine held in Geneva. Fr Raymond Roch,
delivering the Holy See's address to the conference, referred back to
a number of the Pope's pronouncements made over the course of
the previous two years. The address rejected recourse to 'arms and
violence of all kinds, to terrorism and reprisals' but added, 'The
most urgent problem is not only to stop the obvious abuses by
condemning them; rights must be restored so that these abuses will
cease.' He reiterated the Pope's words after his meeting with Arafat
in September 1982, calling for the recognition of the rights of both
peoples: 'Among these rights, one that is primordial and cannot be
set aside is that of existence and security on its own territory while
safeguarding the proper identity of each one.' In this version, the
stress on security and identity seems to favour the Israeli position
above that of the Palestinians. However, Roch added an explicitly
critical statement on the situation in the Occupied Territories,
though it fell short of a demand for Palestinian political rights:

The inhabitants of the Occupied Territories are subject to harsh
and highly regrettable constraints. Many times the United
Nations, and in particular the Security Council, have condemned
measures which tended to be repeated, such as expropriation of

land, not to mention political, psychological and administrative pressure. Such measures oppress the people and, in the long run, force them to leave their place of residence. It is high time that this exodus be ended which spares neither the Muslim nor the Christian communities, and that the intellectual, cultural and religious development of these communities no longer be delayed or prevented.[20]

Though critical of the Israelis, this statement does not go so far as to imply that they should withdraw from the territories; it simply asks for the establishment of the Palestinians' civil rights. At this level, the Vatican was undoubtedly being made increasingly aware of the effects of Israeli policy in the territories through the Pontifical Mission, and particularly through its role in administering Bethlehem University. Since the early 1980s this university, like the other universities in the territories, has suffered closures, raids by the army, attempts to control the terms on which foreign staff can work there, and numerous administrative restrictions, as well as frequent arrests and detentions of students.

In general, however, the Vatican's concerns on the question of Palestine reverted from specific issues, such as the situation in the Occupied Territories and Lebanon, to the broader ground of the question of diplomatic recognition of Israel and the internationalization of Jerusalem. After the events of 1982-83 Vatican relations with Israel have generally remained uneasy and the Vatican has occasionally spoken out over particular instances of Israeli aggression. After the Israeli bombing raid on the PLO headquarters in Tunis in 1985, for example, the *Osservatore Romano* published the following statement:

Without wishing to enter into the question of the legitimacy of actions of reprisals — something the Vatican had condemned in the past — it seems to us necessary and urgent to ask ourselves what value and credibility the declared intentions to negotiate towards a resolution of the Mideast problem have, when everything seems to continue in the logic of provocations, threats and reprisals. One cannot affirm a desire to support the prospect of negotiations and then in fact lash out in merciless ways like the bombing raid into Tunisia...[21]

In both the 1970s and early 1980s the whole question of Jewish-

Catholic relations had, as described earlier in the present book, centred not merely on theological issues, such as the question of the responsibility of the Jews in the death of Christ, but also on two key political questions: first, the attitude of the Catholic Church to the holocaust and to anti-semitism in general and, second, the question of recognition of the state of Israel. Zionists, and also Catholics sympathetic to Israel, had put pressure on the Vatican to recognize Israel, and after 1982 this pressure was revived on a number of occasions. In the debates and polemics associated with this issue there were increasingly explicit links made between the demand for the Vatican's diplomatic acceptance of Israel and for its condemnation of anti-semitism.

In June 1983, for example, Sir Immanuel Jakobovits, the chief rabbi of Great Britain, urged the Vatican formally to recognize Israel. Speaking at the annual meeting of the Council of Christians and Jews, of which he was president, he said that 'the new form of anti-semitism was linked with anti-zionism, and Christians and others who wished to resist it must come to terms with Israel'. The chief rabbi apparently also addressed a personal plea to the Pope to this effect.[22]

Despite the fact that the Pope asserted on several occasions that relations between Jews and Christians had 'radically improved' — for example, when speaking to a delegation from the American-Jewish Committee in 1985[23] — the accusations that the Vatican had not stood out against anti-semitism in Europe during the nazi era continued to resurface in the context of its relations with Israel and zionism.

In June 1985 the Vatican published 'Notes on the Correct Way to Present the Jews and Judaism in Preaching and Catechesis in the Roman Catholic Church'. This was a further gloss on *Nostra Aetate* and other subsequent Vatican pronouncements on Jewish-Catholic relations (see chapters 5 and 9). It reiterated that the charge of deicide, which Catholics had formerly levelled against Jews, was untenable. But it was the section on 'Judaism and Christianity in History' that was the focus of Jewish criticism. The reference to the holocaust — 'Catechesis should... help in understanding the meaning for the Jews of the extermination during the years 1939-45 and its consequences — was described by Rabbi Jakobovits as 'painfully casual'.[24]

However, it was the passage on the association of the Jews with the state of Israel which caused the most furore:

Christians are invited to understand this religious attachment which finds its roots in biblical traditions, without however making their own any particular religious interpretation of this relationship (cf. Declaration of the US Conference of Catholic Bishops, 20 November 1975).

The existence of the state of Israel and its political options should be envisaged not in a perspective which is in itself religious, but in their reference to the common principles of international law.[25]

This convoluted statement asked Catholics to distance the question of the acceptance of the Jews and Judaism as part of a monotheistic tradition from the question of Israel's existence as a political state. For many Jews, particularly zionists, this formulation was unacceptable. Thus the impasse over Israel remained, with continued demands from Jewish sources that the questions of anti-semitism and acceptance of the zionist project should be linked. Sidney Brichto, director of the British Union of Liberal and Progressive Synagogues, put the argument as follows in a letter to *The Times* on 12 April 1986:

For all Jews, non-zionists included, recognition of Israel by the Roman Catholic Church would be to confirm full acceptance of the right of the Jewish people to entertain its own messianic hopes alongside those of Christianity.

He further argued that:

the Vatican's recognition of the state of Israel would prove once and for all that the Holy See had ceased to consider the Jews as a rejected race and would remove the remaining seeds of anti-semitism in Catholic theology. Until the Vatican takes this bold step, all declarations of tolerance will be mere words.

If the question of diplomatic recognition of Israel continued to be an issue in the wider Catholic-Jewish context, the other major issue, the question of the status of Jerusalem, continued to affect Vatican-Israeli relations, already soured by the events of 1982. In April 1984 Pope John Paul II returned to the theme of the need for an internationally guaranteed status for Jerusalem 'so that one side or the other cannot place it under discrimination'. This message came in a Maundy Thursday apostolic letter to 'the bishops, clergy, religious and faithful of the whole Church in Jerusalem'. The Pope also linked the status of Jerusalem to the Palestine question:

> I am convinced that the religious identity of Jerusalem, and in particular the common monotheistic tradition, can provide a way to promoting a coming together among all those who feel the Holy City to be their own. [This, he added:] is fundamental for a just peace in the region of the Middle East, as are the safeguarding of Lebanon and a just solution for the Palestinian people.

He repeated this statement later in the year to the new ambassador of Egypt when he presented his credentials.[26]

The Israeli government reacted with predictable hostility to the Pope's Easter message. According to a Foreign Ministry statement, Israel's position remained unchanged. Jerusalem was the capital of the Jewish nation alone, had been so for generations and would remain the Jewish capital 'for ever'.[27] The audience granted to Prime Minister Shimon Peres in February 1985 — the first Israeli prime minister to meet the Pope since Golda Meir — only served to confirm the impasse over Jerusalem. Peres said in a statement after the audience:

> I said clearly that our government will continue to respect the religious rights, needs and expectations of all peoples. Politically, Jerusalem will remain the united capital of Israel. [He continued:] It was clear in our discussion that we have to distinguish between the spiritual and religious part of Jerusalem, and the political part.[28]

Meanwhile, in Jerusalem itself, religious tensions have been heightened over the past few years by the increasingly militant and violent activities of right-wing Jewish religious groups in the city. Though most of their hostility and aggression has been directed towards the Muslim Palestinian community, they have also attacked Christian institutions which they see as evangelizing and conducting missionary activities. Catholic institutions have not been immune from these attacks. Although the activities of these groups are not officially condoned by the Israeli city or state authorities, their members have generally been treated with extraordinary leniency on the occasions when they have been prosecuted for such attacks.

The questions of recognition of Israel and of the status of Jerusalem were brought sharply into focus in early 1987 in what can only be described as a diplomatic fiasco for the Catholic Church. In January 1987 the Vatican suffered considerable embarrassment over the visit to Jerusalem of Cardinal John O'Connor of New York. According to the *Jerusalem Post*, O'Connor had been invited by Prime Minister Shimon Peres to visit Israel to hear the 'Israeli side' of the Middle East conflict.[29] He had apparently also been encouraged to make the visit by the Jewish community in New York. He eventually went to the Middle East, however, in his capacity as president of the CNEWA, the sister agency of the Pontifical Mission to the Middle East, which concerns itself mainly with humanitarian aid to the Palestinians.

After a stop in Amman, Cardinal O'Connor went on to Jerusalem, where he had arranged meetings with President Herzog and senior Israeli officials, in contravention of the Vatican policy that official meetings with Israelis in Jerusalem are barred because they would constitute recognition of Jerusalem as the Israeli capital. Consequently, the apostolic delegate (the Vatican's representative in Jerusalem) informed the Israeli Foreign Ministry that Cardinal O'Connor would not be able to attend these meetings and would curtail his visit to Israel. In the event, the Cardinal did meet Herzog on 4 January, in his residence rather than his office. As a result of this comedy of errors, the Vatican's position on Jerusalem had been somewhat compromised, and Cardinal O'Connor returned to the US to the wrath of the Jewish community, which objected both to the Vatican's attitude to the visit and to statements made by O'Connor himself. He had expressed his concern for the Palestinians under Israeli rule and the need for a Palestinian homeland, and had allegedly remarked that the holocaust was a 'gift' by the Jewish people to the world. This allegation, and the Vatican's intervention in the Cardinal's schedule, led to further accusations of anti-semitism. An editorial in the *Washington Post* on 13 January accused the Vatican of being 'an institution whose past is stained with anti-semitism'.[30] After the Cardinal had met with Jewish groups, they issued a joint statement which represented a considerable watering-down of the Vatican's position on the Palestinian-Israeli conflict. They expressed agreement on 'Israel's right to secure and recognized boundaries and the importance of addressing the Palestinian problem and the plight of the refugees'.[31]

The position of the Vatican on the question of Palestine has varied according to the attitudes and experience of particular Popes. It has also been affected by wider political considerations within the Catholic Church and by its relationships with other states and religious groups. Yet, throughout the period since the 1950s, the Vatican has continued to press a set of minimum demands as a prerequisite for the recognition of the state of Israel: some kind of international status for Jerusalem; and recognition of the 'rights' of the Palestinians — in the earlier years as 'refugees', more recently as a 'people'. Although the meaning of these terms has not been unambiguous, the Vatican has never considered them to have been met, and thus the impasse over the question of Palestine continues.

Sarah Graham-Brown
London, May 1987

Notes

Throughout the notes, the following abbreviations have been used:

AAS Acta Apostolicae Sedis (Rome)
DC Documentation Catholique (Paris)
OR Osservatore Romano (Rome)

Chapter 1

1. *Civiltà Cattolica*, 1 May 1897.

2. Pope Pius X to Theodor Herzl, 24 Jan. 1904, *The Diaries of Theodor Herzl* (New York, 1956).

3. The French response — given on 9 February 1918 — was that 'agreement is complete between the French and British governments concerning a Jewish establishment in Palestine'. The Italian pronouncement — given on 9 May 1918 by Foreign Minister Baron Sonnino — was more reticent. It said, 'The government of His Majesty confirms the previous declarations... i.e. that it is prepared to act with pleasure to facilitate the establishment in Palestine of a national Jewish centre, under the understanding that no prejudice will derive through it to the juridical and *political* status of the already existing religious communities and to the civil and political rights that the Jews already enjoy in other countries' (J.M.N. Jeffries, *Palestine — The Reality* (London, 1939) emphasis ours).

4. Nahum Sokolov, *History of Zionism* (London, 1919).

5. Christopher Sykes, *Crossroads to Israel* (New York, 1968).

6. Gibbons' letter was published in the American diocesan press on 24 November 1918. His acceptance of the ZOA invitation to produce a pro-zionist statement led to a vigorous protest by Mons. Barlassina, the Latin patriarch of Jerusalem, and subsequent recriminations from the Vatican (*Molad 27*, 1971).

7. Ernest Oldmeadow, *Francis Cardinal Bourne*, vol. II (London, 1944).

8. *AAS*, 10 March 1919.

9. John Marlow, *The Seat of Pilate* (London, 1959).

10. *Catholic Historical Review*, 7 April 1921; *Ave Maria*, 21 May 1921.

11. *AAS*, 18 June 1921.

12. *New York Times*, 16 June 1922; Quincy Wright, *Mandates Under the League* (Chicago, 1930).

13. Paul L. Hanna, *British Policy in Palestine* (American Council for Public Affairs, Washington DC, 1941).

14. Esther Yolles Feldblum, *The American Catholic Press and the Jewish State 1917–1959* (New York, 1977).

15. *US Statutes at Large*, vol. 42, part 1 (US GPO, Washington DC, 1923). The resolution was introduced in the Senate by the then chairman of the Senate Foreign Relations Committee, Henry Cabot Lodge. Almost 40 years later, President Kennedy was to appoint Cabot Lodge as the White House special envoy to the Vatican.

16. See, for example: *Tablet*, 31 Aug. 1929; *Tidings*, 3 Sept. 1929; *New World*, 13 Sept 1929. Mons. Barlassina's clear anti-zionist views are also confirmed in Chaim Weizmann's autobiography, *Trial and Error* (New York, 1949).

17. *Commonweal*, 4 Sept. 1929. The zionist Revisionist Party was the political and ideological matrix from which the terrorist organizations of Irgun and the Stern Gang developed, later to become the Herut Party, headed by Menachem Begin.

18. *Tablet*, 7 Sept. 1929.

19. Quoted in *America*, 31 July 1937.

20. Vatican memorandum to British government against Peel Commission recommendations.

21. August 1938.

22. A.G. Cicognani to Myron Taylor, 22 June 1943, National Archives 867, N, 01/6-2443.

23. *Congressional Record*, 19 Dec. 1945.

24. *Commonweal*, 17 May 1946 and 12 Dec. 1947.

25. *Pilot* and *Tablet*, 1 Dec. 1945.

26. Robert I. Gannon, *The Cardinal Spellman Story* (New York, 1962). Cardinal Spellman fully supported McMahon's action in favour of Palestine.

27. *Commonweal*, 27 Feb. 1948.

28. *Tablet*, 13 March 1948.

29. Deir Yassin was a Palestinian village in the Jerusalem area. At 4.30 am on 10 April 1948 'a combined force of Irgun and Stern, 132 strong, descended on the sleeping village. By noon they had slaughtered two-thirds of the inhabitants.' (David Hirst, *The Gun and the Olive Branch*, London, 1977).

30. *Commonweal*, 7 May 1948. Fr Anthony Bruya filed his reports through the NCNS. Supported by Mons. Assemani, he tirelessly pleaded the cause of Palestine and was highly effective in keeping up a flow of information from the Palestinian side to the Catholic press.

31. *AAS*, 10 May 1948.

32. Walid Khalidi, *From Haven to Conquest* (Institute of Palestine Studies,

Beirut, 1971). The Dalet Plan was the 'master-plan for the seizure of most or all of Palestine' by the zionists. See Hirst, *Gun and Olive Branch*, pages 138-9.

33. Charlotte Klein, 'Theological Dimensions of the State of Israel: a Christian Perspective', address to a seminar of Judeo-Christian studies, 28 Oct. 1970.

Chapter 2

1. *America*, 22 Dec. 1917. Typical of such expectations was a *New York Times* report of 18 Jan. 1918 which quoted Mons. Arthur Barnes, Catholic rector of Oxford University, as predicting that England would declare Pope Benedict XV the protector of the Holy Places in Palestine.

2. *America*, 14 Dec. 1929.

3. Myron Taylor, 138, HSTL, Taylor Papers; Ennio di Nolfo, *Vaticano e Stati Uniti 1939–1952* (Milan, 1978).

Chapter 3

1. Copy of the original document by courtesy of Fr Ayad of the Latin Patriarchate of Jerusalem. Large excerpts were filed by the NCNS on 7 June 1948. Note that the emphasis added here, and at all the quotations throughout the present book, is the author's.

2. The appeal was signed by Archbishop Theodoritoz, representative of the Armenian Orthodox Patriarchate; Rev. Hazakial El Antouny, representative of the Coptic Patriarchate; Rev. Boulos S. Gelphy for the Syrian Orthodox Patriarchate; Rev. Ibrahim Ayad for the Latin Patriarchate; Mons. Michel Assaf, the Greek Catholic archbishop; Fr Bonaventura Akiki, O.F.M., in the name of the Latin patriarchs of the Holy Land; and Mons. Jacques Ghiragossian, patriarchal vicar of the Armenian Catholic Church.

3. NCNS, 7 June 1948. Among other newspapers that reported it were: *Michigan Catholic*, 3 June 1948; *Tablet*, 5 June 1948; *Commonweal*, 23 July 1948.

4. *America*, 29 May 1948.

5. From a copy of the original document, widely published among others through the syndicated diocesan service *Our Sunday Visitor* of 29 August 1948.

6. Constantine Rackaseskas, *The Internationalization of Jerusalem* (Washington DC, 1957).

7. *AAS*, 2 June 1948.

8. *AAS*, 26 Oct. 1948; *Tablet*, 30 Oct. 1948.

9. *AAS*, 15 April 1949; *Tablet*, 23 April 1949.

Chapter 4

1. Moshe Sharett, *Yoman Ishi* (Tel Aviv, 1978) (in Hebrew): entry of 10 Nov. 1953.

2. Ibid.
3. Ibid., 12 Nov. 1953.
4. Ibid., 26 Oct. 1955. The bishop of Milan mentioned was Mons. G.B. Montini, formerly Vatican substitute secretary of state under Cardinal Tardini, and later to become Pope Paul VI.

Chapter 5
1. *OR*, 10 June 1962.
2. Letter of 9 March 1980 from Mons. Loris Capovilla to the author. The passages from the *Pacem in Terris* he refers to subsequently are nos. 34, 36, 43, 99, 100, 103 and 104.
3. From the time of Pope John XXIII's pontificate, representatives of the Israeli embassy were invited to attend official Vatican ceremonies for diplomats.
4. Esther Yolles Feldblum, *The American Catholic Press and the Jewish State 1917–1959* (New York, 1977).
5. Arthur Gilbert, *The Vatican Council and the Jews* (Cleveland and New York, 1968); Floyd Anderson (ed.), *Council Daybook, Vatican II*, session 3 (NCWC, Washington DC, 1965).
6. Feldblum, *American Catholic Press*.
7. Raniero La Valle, *Il Concilio nelle nostre mani* (Marcelliana, Brescia, 1967).
8. Ibid.

Chapter 6
1. *OR*, 5 June 1967.
2. Ibid.
3. *DC*, 2 July 1967.
4. *OR*, 9 June 1967.
5. Ibid., 12-13 June 1967.
6. Ibid., 11 June 1967.
7. When questioned by the press on this definition, the Vatican spokesman Mons. Fausto Vallainc replied on 9 June that: 'the internationalization of Jerusalem should be applied permanently to the status of the Holy City, in times of war and peace alike, while the additional concept of "Open City" should apply to times of war and emergency' (*OR*, 10 June 1967). This concept was expressed by Paul VI for the first time during his allocution to the general audience of 7 June 1967:

It is of capital importance... that Jerusalem be declared an Open City.... In the name of Christianity which trembles for its fate, and also in the name of all civilized humanity, we address this earnest appeal to the rulers of the belligerent governments and nations and to the heads of the armies fighting each other: that Jerusalem be spared a state of war, that it remain the Holy City, a shelter for the non-combatants and the wounded, a symbol of hope and peace. [*OR*, 8 June 1967]

8. *OR*, 27 June 1967.

9. *DC*, 2 July 1967.

10. The UN forces commander, a Norwegian called General Odd Bull, reported in November 1967, i.e. six months after the alleged end of the war, that Israeli troops were still engaged in forcefully driving out the Palestinian population across the Jordan river.

11. Copy of letter in English distributed to the press accredited to the Vatican. French original in *DC*, Sept. 1967.

12. *OR*, 28 July 1967.

13. *DC*, Sept. 1967.

14. *OR*, 6 July 1967.

15. Ibid., 23 Dec. 1967.

16. Ibid., 27 Dec. 1967.

17. Ibid., 30 Dec. 1968.

18. *Le Monde*, 8 Jan. 1969; *La Croix*, 9 Jan. 1969.

19. *OR*, 1-2 Sept. 1969.

20. *La Semaine Religieuse d'Alger*, 11 Sept. 1969; *DC*, Dec. 1969.

21. *OR*, 29-30 Sept. 1969.

22. The audience conceded by the head of the Church to an Israeli foreign minister nevertheless constitutes one more example of the political success scored by Israel through its policies of the use of force and of the creation of *faits accomplis*. The Vatican has shown that it is no less subject to this logic than the secular powers.

23. *OR*, 23 Dec. 1969.

24. Ibid., 2 Jan. 1970.

25. In November 1967 a unanimous resolution of the UN Security Council (resolution 242) had proposed a 'bargain' by which Israel would return the territories occupied in the June 1967 war in exchange for recognition by the Arab governments, the bargain to be sealed by a peace treaty whose provisions would be guaranteed by the international community. Israel refers to the English text, which speaks of withdrawal from 'territories', whereas the French text reads 'les territoires' (the territories).

Chapter 7

1. *OR*, 24 Sept. 1970.

2. Ibid., 28 Sept. 1970.

3. Ibid., 16 March 1971.

4. In October 1969 the US government had put forward a series of peace proposals, personally sponsored by the US secretary of state William Rogers: Israel was to withdraw from the territories occupied in 1967; the Arab 'refugees' were to be given the choice between returning to Israel and receiving compensation; and Jordan was to be given equal status with Israel in Jerusalem. (The future political status of Jerusalem was not specified.)

5. *OR*, 25 June 1971.

6. *La Semaine Religieuse d'Alger*, 29 July 1971.

7. *DC*, 21 Nov. 1971; *OR*, 25 Nov. 1971 (English edn).

8. *DC*, 21 Nov. 1971.

9. Ibid.; *OR*, 2 Dec. 1971.

10. *OR*, 6 Jan. 1972.

11. On 30 May 1972 three members of the Japanese Red Army opened fire in the arrival lounge at Tel Aviv airport: 26 people were killed and 72 wounded. The Popular Front for the Liberation of Palestine (PFLP) later claimed responsibility.

12. At the 1972 Munich Olympic Games eight Palestinians belonging to 'Black September' entered the Israeli pavilion, killed two Israeli athletes and took nine others hostage, demanding the release of 200 political prisoners in Israel and safe passage out of Germany. In the subsequent shoot-out between the Palestinians and German marksmen at a military airport, all the remaining athletes and five of the Palestinians were killed.

13. *OR*, 7 Sept. 1972; *DC*, 1 Oct. 1972.

14. *La Semaine Religieuse d'Alger*, 15 June 1972; *DC*, 6-20 Aug. 1972. The declaration was signed by: Cardinal Léon-Etienne Duval, archbishop of Algiers; Bertrand Lacaste, bishop of Oran; Paul Pinier, ex-bishop of Constantine; Gaston-Marie Jacquier, auxiliary bishop of Constantine; Jean-Marie Raimbaud, bishop of Laghout; and Jean Scotto, bishop of Constantine.

Chapter 8

1. *Sunday Times*, 15 June 1969.

2. *La Croix*, 23 Jan. 1973.

3. Ibid.

4. *OR*, 15 Oct. 1973. The final sentence quoted here seems to suggest that Paul VI was fully aware of the US design underlying the 1973 war. This design (which bore the name and political trademark of Henry Kissinger) was subsequently to lead to a 'new equilibrium' which, through the 'disengagement agreements' and the consequent war in Lebanon, brought about the Camp David accords.

5. Ironically, on the very same day that the statement was issued, the Israeli government deported several leading Palestinian figures from the West Bank to Jordan. Among them was Hanna Naseer, president of Bir Zeit University.

6. *DC*, 20 Jan. 1974.

7. *OR*, 27 Dec. 1973.

8. Ibid., 20-21 March 1974.

9. The complete documentation containing the attitudes and pronouncements of Paul VI leaves no doubt that he considered the Palestinians as the 'people of the Holy Land', and therefore judged their 'rights and aspirations' as 'legitimate'. In this instance too, however, the Holy See

engaged in Byzantine verbal games intended to fend off Israeli pressure. The Vatican adopted a similar tactic during the Second World War, when in its pleas to the nazi authorities to save the Jews, the latter were defined as 'non-aryans'.

10. *L'Avvenire*, 8 Feb. 1974.

11. *La Croix*, 13 April 1974.

12. *OR*, 11 Dec. 1974. This Vatican declaration was vociferously attacked by the chief rabbi of France, Jacob Kaplan, in a letter addressed to the Vatican's secretary of state, Cardinal Jean Villot, on 20 December 1974. Kaplan accused the Vatican of:

complicity with alleged killers of children and innocent civilians! ...It seems that the Vatican deplores the condemnation of the prelate, not his conduct. This impression is reinforced by the sentence in the statement according to which the Vatican would not pronounce itself on the incriminating facts. Thus it leaves some doubt as to the guilt of Mons. Capucci and consequently it creates suspicion as to whether the charge is well-founded... This is extremely grave as the reader will forever be left with this doubt in his mind at Israel's expense. You cannot ignore the reality of the criminal acts committed by Mons. Capucci. One has the right to ask if the arms and grenades introduced by the prelate before his arrest may not have been used by the terrorists guilt of a hateful recent attack on a cinema in Tel Aviv... That the Vatican should judge it its duty to throw a veil over the role of this bishop — a carrier of death — is its affair, but that it should do so in favour of those who have provided arms to killers in Israel cannot leave French Jews indifferent, since they consider themselves the brothers of those Israelis who are daily exposed to terrorist attacks. How can all this be reconciled with the spirit and the letter of the declaration on the Jews of the Second Vatican Council, which recommends the establishment of better relations between Christians and Jews? [*DC*, 16 March 1975]

Cardinal Villot replied to this threatening letter on 27 January 1975, calmly reaffirming, although in friendly tones, the essential points of the Vatican's statement, and expressing the hope that 'the painful episode will not have unfortunate repercussions on the improvement of relations between Jews and Christians, as desired by Vatican II'. (Ibid.)

Chapter 9

1. *New York Times*, 26 May 1971.

2. John M. Oesterreicher, *The Rediscovery of Judaism* (Seton Hall University, New Jersey, 1971).

3. *Midstream*, Oct. 1972.

4. Esther Yolles Feldblum, *The American Catholic Press and the Jewish State 1917-1959* (New York, 1977).

5. *Catholic Review* (Baltimore), 12 Dec. 1969.

6. See also page 124.

7. *OR*, 6 May 1971.

8. Origins NC Documentary Service, 22 Nov. 1973.

9. 1978 resolutions (*OR*, 15 Jan. 1979).

10. The MECC includes all the Christian Churches in the Middle East except for the Catholic Church, which nevertheless maintains relations with it and often participates in its initiatives. Prominent Catholics in the Middle East, such as Fr Carbon, have asked that the Catholic Church become a full member of the MECC.

11. *DC*, 5 July 1970.

12. Ibid.

13. See pages 119-20.

14. *DC*, 1 July 1973.

15. Ibid.

16. Ibid.

17. Ibid.

18. Ibid.

19. Ibid.

20. *La Croix*, 16 June 1973.

21. *DC*, 1 July 1973.

22. The document was signed by Stephanos I, cardinal patriarch of Alexandria, on behalf of the 'Assembly of the Catholic Hierarchy of Egypt'.

23. *OR*, 3 Jan. 1974.

24. *DC*, 16 March 1975. In the article quoted, Rabbi Yais warned both the Jews and the Catholic Church that any real dialogue between Christianity and Judaism is in any case impossible because Christianity's true goal is to convert the Jews.

25. Ibid.

26. *La Croix*, 7 Jan. 1975.

27. *OR*, 27 Nov. 1975.

28. *DC*, 7 Dec. 1975.

29. Ibid.

30. See also pages 158-60.

31. In March 1980 we interviewed Mons. Pietro Rossano, secretary of the Commission for Relations with the Muslims, at his Rome office. We were, perhaps understandably, surprised to learn that Mons. Rossano considered: 1. that 'the Palestinian problem is of no interest at all to, and in, the Arab world'. According to Mons. Rossano, who claimed to have travelled widely in the Arab world, 'no one has ever raised the question of Palestine' with him; 2. that 'the Palestinian Arabs living in occupied Palestine are much better off under Israeli rule, because their standard of living has increased considerably'. Mons. Rossano also volunteered the information that he maintained constant contacts with zionists.

32. *OR*, 26 Feb. 1976.

33. The two omitted paragraphs were published separately in *OR* (9–10 Feb. 1976) in an editorial on the Tripoli seminar by the paper's political editor, Don Virgilio Levi.

Chapter 10

1. *DC*, 20 Oct. 1974.
2. Ibid., 7–21 Sept. 1975.
3. *OR*, 22–23 Sept. 1975.
4. *DC*, 7 Dec. 1975.
5. *OR*, 11 Nov. 1975. On the occasion of this visit to Lebanon, Cardinal Bertoli met briefly with PLO leader Yasser Arafat to discuss the Palestinian stance on the Lebanese civil war.
6. *DC*, 6 June 1976.
7. *OR*, 23 Dec. 1975.
8. Ibid., 26 Feb. 1976.
9. *DC*, 18 April 1976.
10. Ibid.
11. *OR*, 25 March 1976.
12. Ibid., 9 April 1976.
13. Ibid., 2–3 Aug. 1976.
14. Ibid., 17–18 Aug. 1976.

Chapter 11

1. *OR*, 10 Nov. 1977.
2. Ibid., 21 Nov. 1977.
3. Ibid., 13 Jan. 1978.
4. Ibid.
5. Ibid., 14 Feb. 1978.
6. Ibid., 14 March 1978.
7. Ibid., 30 April 1978.

Chapter 12

1. *OR*, 11 Dec. 1978.
2. *DC*, 18 March 1979.
3. *OR*, 26 March 1979.
4. Ibid., 13 March 1979.
5. Letter from Carol Hunnybun to Michael Adams of 20 May 1980.
6. Report of 3 March 1980, courtesy Fr Ayad.
7. *Le Monde*, 4 Oct. 1979.
8. *La Repubblica*, 2–3 Dec. 1979.
9. See declaration on persecution of Christians in Jerusalem in *DC*, 6 July 1980.
10. *Middle East International*, 11 April 1980.
11. *OR*, 22 June 1980.
12. Ibid., 30 June – 1 July 1980.

13. Information collected by the author.
14. *Il Corriere della Sera, Il Giorno, Il Messaggero, Paese Sera, l'Unità, La Stampa,* 6–8 Jan. 1982.
15. *OR*, 5 April 1982.

Afterword
1. *OR*, 19 April 1982.
2. Ibid., 8 Feb. 1982.
3. *National Catholic Reporter*, 24 Sept. 1982.
4. *OR*, 5 July 1982.
5. Ibid.
6. *The Times*, 29 June 1982.
7. Ibid., 10 July 1982.
8. *National Catholic Reporter*, 18 June 1982.
9. *OR*, 28 June 1982.
10. *Jerusalem Post*, 14 Sept. 1982.
11. *OR*, 20 Sept. 1982.
12. *The Times*, 14 Sept. 1982.
13. *Jerusalem Post*, 16 Sept. 1982.
14. *National Catholic Reporter*, 24 Sept. 1982.
15. *Jerusalem Post*, 16 Sept. 1982.
16. *The Times*, 17 Sept. 1982.
17. *OR*, 20 Sept. 1982.
18. Ibid., 27 Sept. 1982.
19. Ibid., 13 Dec. 1982.
20. Ibid., 10 Oct. 1983.
21. Ibid., 14 Oct. 1985.
22. *The Times*, 24 June 1983.
23. *OR*, 4 March 1985.
24. *The Times*, 29 June 1985.
25. *OR*, 1 July 1985.
26. Ibid., 29 Oct. 1984.
27. *The Times*, 21 April 1984.
28. Ibid., 20 Feb. 1985.
29. *Jerusalem Post*, 3 Jan. 1987.
30. *The Times*, 14 Jan. 1987.
31. *Jerusalem Post*, 31 Jan. 1987.

Index

Abdallah, King (Jordan) 49
Académie Française 126
Alessandrini, Prof. Federico 106, 107, 113, 126
Algeria 54-6, 98, 103, 125, 132
Algiers 76, 98
Allenby, General Edmund Henry 12
Alon, Moshe 175-6
America *see* Central America; Latin America; United States of America
America 18, 28, 36, 54
American Bishops Conference *see* National Conference of Catholic Bishops of the United States
American Bishops Secretariat for Promoting Christian Unity 119
American Catholic Quarterly Review 13
American-Jewish Committee 63, 203
Amman 206
Anawati, Fr G.C. 52
Angelus message (John Paul II) 195, 196
Anglican Church 83, 121, 188 *see also* Protestantism
Ankara 180
anti-semitism
    attitude of Church to 199, 203

Church accused of 26, 124, 206
    condemned by Church bodies 65, 122, 128-9
    and John Paul II 173
    and zionism 131, 204
Antonius, George 30
Antwerp 127
Apostolic Delegation (Jerusalem) 33
al-Aqsa Mosque (Jerusalem) 86-8, 187
Arab Awakening, The (Antonius) 30
Arab Confederation 30
Arafat, Yasser 168, 191, 198, 199, 200, 201
Armenian Churches 146, 188
Armistice Committee 35
Assaf, Mons. Michel 34
Assemani, Mons. Abraham 22
Assumptionist Fathers (Jerusalem) 33
Athenagoras, Patriarch 68
Athens airport, Palestinian attack on 85-6
Auschwitz 198
Auspicia Quaedam (Pius XII) 24-5, 31, 33, 40
Australia 45
Ave Maria 54
L'Avvenire d'Italia 55, 183